Anatoly Lunacharsky

On
LITERATURE
and ART

Progress Publishers   Moscow

А. В. ЛУНАЧАРСКИЙ

О ЛИТЕРАТУРЕ И ИСКУССТВЕ

Оригинальное издание

На английском языке

First Printing 1965

TRANSLATED FROM THE RUSSIAN
DESIGNED BY Y. GANUSHKIN
COMPILED BY CAND. (Phil. Sc.) A. LEBEDEV

CONTENTS

FROM THE COMPILER

THE Soviet Republic's first People's Commissar of Education, a trusted friend of Lenin, one of the new society's most eminent ideologists, a scientist, journalist, and outstanding public speaker, a dazzlingly erudite person—such was Anatoly Vasilyevich Lunacharsky (1873-1933).

Lunacharsky's passionate, at times impulsive, character embodied a number of significant evolutionary features of a whole generation of the Russian intelligentsia—a generation, whose aspirations to help the people in its struggle for freedom and material prosperity remained a spiritual compass which, through all the storms and tempests of history, through all the twists and turns of their own characteristic individualism, led them to an awareness of their position in life. At that time—throughout the epoch of the proletarian revolution—only Marxism was able to provide such an understanding of history and such a realisation of one's place and part in it. Lenin, with his works and personal influence, played a most important part in ridding Lunacharsky of his ideological errors and misconceptions. Lunacharsky rightly said of himself and his generation: "No matter how much slag and mistakes there are in what we have done, we are proud of our role in history and face the judgement of future generations without fear, without a shadow of doubt as to their verdict."

The last outstanding critic of Russian pre-revolutionary culture, and the first brilliant critic of socialist culture, Lunacharsky lived at a time when the art of the old Russian society was already history and the art of a new world was being born. As a critic, Lunacharsky seemed to link these two cultural worlds. Both the line of aesthetical continuity and the break with accepted aesthetical tradition passed through Lunacharsky's "critical heart". This heart retained all that the world's greatest artists had given; but it also harboured dreams of the unprecedented beauty of the art of the future.

Lunacharsky left behind a truly tremendous heritage. The sphere of the creative interests of this "exceptionally gifted personality", as Lenin put it, was extraordinarily versatile. Lunacharsky wrote about fifteen hundred articles on various questions of classical and contemporary literature, painting, music and sculpture. He wrote series of lectures on the history of Russian and West European literature, works on literary and aesthetical problems, papers on the most important problems of art and politics, brilliant essays dedicated to almost every celebrated artist the world has known. Lunacharsky's collected works, which appeared literally one after another in the twenties and thirties and were a significant factor in the cultural life of the young society, were filled with his recorded lectures, impromptu speeches noted down by newspaper reporters and introductions to new editions.

It is impossible not to consider the almost complete disregard of Lunacharsky's literary heritage during the period of the Stalin personality cult as a large gap in contemporary culture. Only in the last decade have books, dedicated to Lunacharsky's life and work, and editions of his articles begun to appear; an eight-volume edition of his collected works is in preparation at the moment.

The present edition, which includes only a fraction of his critical articles, can claim to present no more than the most general idea of Lunacharsky's critical heritage, of the nature of his critical gifts and of the breadth of his cultural interests. These articles have been chosen not only for the significance for contemporary art of the personalities discussed in them, but also for the way in which the critic's own personality is revealed. The book consists of three parts, in which Lunacharsky is shown as theoretician and ideologist, as a critic of Russian art and as a critic of foreign art. Dates of the writing of the articles are given, but when not available, dates of first publication are provided.

Many of Lunacharsky's significant, large-scale theoretical works, including *Lenin and Literary Scholarship* and courses of lectures on Russian and foreign art, have not been included here owing to lack of space; neither have his early critical speeches been included. The compiler has never considered abbreviating any of the articles published here, or publishing extracts from these articles. This is not merely because Lunacharsky's articles represent in themselves a unique manifestation of art: the "spirit of the times" becomes organically revealed in Lunacharsky's works, and very often some fleeting remark about some fact or other of the social life of those years turns out to be an essential detail which recreates in our minds the epoch which gave us Lunacharsky's talent.

I

THESES ON THE PROBLEMS
OF MARXIST CRITICISM

CHERNYSHEVSKY'S ETHICS
AND AESTHETICS:
A CONTEMPORARY
EVALUATION

THESES ON THE PROBLEMS
OF MARXIST CRITICISM

OUR literature is passing through one of the decisive moments in its development. A new life is being built in the country, and literature is learning more and more to reflect this life in its as yet undefined and unstable forms; evidently, too, it can pass to a problem of a still higher order—to the political and, in particular, the moral influence on the very process of construction.

Although our country represents a contrast of individual classes much less than any other, it is still, nonetheless, impossible to consider it entirely classless. Without dwelling on the inevitability of the difference in tendencies between peasant and proletarian literature, it is clear that there are elements in the country which have retained their old attitudes; elements which have either not reconciled themselves with the dictatorship of the proletariat, or which are unable to adapt themselves even to the most basic tendencies of the building of socialism by the proletariat.

The conflict between the old and the new continues. The influence of Europe, of the past, of the remnants of the old ruling class, of the new bourgeoisie which is to a certain extent flourishing under the New Economic Policy—all these are making themselves felt. They are revealed not only in the prevailing moods of individual groups and people, but also in admixtures of every kind. It should be remembered that apart from the direct and deliberately hostile bourgeois currents, there is yet another element which is perhaps more dangerous and which is at any rate harder to defeat—the everyday petty-bourgeois element. This has wormed its way deeply

into the everyday attitudes of the proletariat itself,
of many Communists even. This explains why the
class struggle, in the shape of a struggle for the
building of a new way of life which bears the
imprint of the socialist aspirations of the proletariat,
is not only not abating, but, while retaining its
former strength, is acquiring ever more subtle and
profound forms. It is these circumstances which
make the weapons of art—particularly literature—
extremely important at the present time. They cause,
however, proletarian and kindred literature to
appear, side by side with hostile literary emanations,
and by this I mean not only the consciously and
specifically hostile elements, but also the unconsciously hostile elements—hostile in their passivity, pessimism, individualism, prejudices and distortions,
etc.

II

With the significant role that literature has to play
under such conditions, Marxist criticism bears a very
considerable responsibility. Together with literature
it is called upon to partake with intensity and energy
in the process of the establishment of the new man
and the new way of life.

III

Marxist criticism is distinguished from all other
types of literature first of all by the fact that it
cannot but be of a sociological nature—in the spirit,
of course, of the scientific sociology of Marx and
Lenin.
Sometimes a distinction is made between the tasks
of a literary critic and those of a literary historian;

the distinction is based not so much on an analysis of the past and present, as on, for the literary historian, an objective analysis of the origins of the work, its place in the social fabric and its influence on social life; whereas for the literary critic, it is based on an evaluation of the work from the point of view of its purely formal or social merits and faults.

For the Marxist critic such a distinction loses nearly all its validity. Although criticism in the strict sense of the word must of necessity be a part of a Marxist's critical work, sociological analysis must be an even more essential fundamental element.

IV

How does the Marxist critic carry out this sociological analysis? Marxism looks upon social life as an organic whole in which the separate parts depend one upon the other; and here the decisive role is played by the most natural and material economic relationships, above all, the forms of labour. In a general analysis of an epoch, for example, the Marxist critic must strive to give a complete picture of the entire social development of that epoch. When one single writer or work is being discussed, there is no essential need for an analysis of the basic economic conditions, for here the ever-valid principle, which may be called Plekhanov's principle, comes especially into its own. It states that artistic works depend upon the forms of production in a given society only to an extremely insignificant extent. They depend on them only through such intermediate links as the class structure of society and the class psychology which has formed as a result of class interests. A work of literature will always reflect, whether consciously or unconsciously, the psychology of the class which the writer represents. Either this or, as often happens, it reflects a mixture of elements in which the influence of various classes on the writer is revealed, and this must be subjected to a close analysis.

V

The ties in every work of literature with the psychology of this or that class or of large groups of a broad social nature are determined chiefly by its content. Literature—the art of the word, the art which is closest to thought—is distinguished from other forms of art by the significance of the content as compared with its form. It is especially evident in literature that it is the artistic content—the flow of thoughts and emotions in the form of images or connected with images—which is the decisive element of the work as a whole. The content strives of itself towards a definite form. It can be said that there is only one optimal form which corresponds to the content. To a greater or lesser extent the writer can find those modes of expression of his thoughts and feelings which reveal them with the greatest clarity and which make the strongest impression on the readers for whom the work is intended.

And so the Marxist critic takes first of all as the object of his analysis the *content* of the work, the *social essence* which it embodies. He determines its connection with these or those social groups and the influence which the force of expression of the work has on social life; only then does he turn to the form, and above all he shows the way in which the form corresponds to the basic aims of the work, that is, to serve the ends of maximum expressiveness and impact.

It is impossible, however, to ignore the specialised task of the analysis of literary *forms,* and the Marxist critic must not turn a blind eye to this. The form of a given work is in fact determined not merely by its content but also by other elements. The psychological thought processes and conversations of a given class, its "style" of living, the general level of the material culture of a given society, the influence of its neighbours, the inertia of the past or the striving for renovation, which can manifest itself in all of life's aspects—all this can affect the form, can act as a subsidiary factor defining it. Often form is linked not just with a single work, but with a whole "school", a whole epoch. It can even be a force which harms or contradicts the content. Sometimes it can become divorced from the content and acquire an isolated, elusive nature. This happens when works of literature are the expression of class tendencies which are devoid of content, which fear real life and which try to hide from this life behind a screen of verbal gymnastics of a high-flown, pompous or, on the contrary, facetious and frivolous nature. All such elements must of necessity be a part of a Marxist's analysis. As the reader can see, these formal elements, which arise from a direct formula—in every masterpiece the form is determined wholly by the content, and every literary work aspires to become a masterpiece—are by no means divorced from social life. They, in turn, should be socially interpreted.

We have hitherto confined our attention mainly to the sphere of Marxist criticism as a function of literary scholarship. The Marxist critic appears here as a scientific sociologist, who is specifically applying the methods of Marxist analysis to a special field—literature. The founder of Marxist criticism, Plekhanov, strongly underlined that this is the real role a Marxist is called upon to play. He maintained that the Marxist is distinguished from the "enlightener", for example, by the fact that the "enlightener" assigns to literature specific aims and specific demands; whereas the "enlightener" judges it from the point of view of specific ideals, the Marxist elucidates the natural causes of the appearance of this or that work.

When Plekhanov rightly opposed the objective and scientific Marxist method of criticism to the old subjectivism, to the capricious approach of the aesthete and the gourmet, he did yeoman's service in establishing the true paths for future Marxist criticism to follow.

It must not in any way be thought, however, that it is a characteristic of the proletariat merely to determine and analyse external data. Marxism is not simply a sociological doctrine, but an active programme of building. Such building is unthinkable without an objective evaluation of the facts. If a Marxist cannot objectively sense the ties between the phenomena which surround him, then he is finished as a Marxist. But from a genuine, all-round Marxist we demand still more—a definite influence on this environment.

The Marxist critic is not some literary astronomer explaining the inevitable laws of motion of literary bodies, from the large to the very small. He is more than this: he is a fighter and a builder. In this sense the *factor of evaluation* must be regarded as one of the most important and loftiest features of contemporary Marxist criticism.

What must be the *criteria* on which the *evaluation* of a work of literature should be based? Let us first of all approach this from the point of view of content. Here, generally, everything is clear. Here the basic criterion is the same as that of proletarian ethics: everything that aids the development and victory of the proletariat is good; everything that harms it is evil.

The Marxist critic must try to find the fundamental social trend in a given work; he must find out where it is heading, whether this process is arbitrary or not. And he must base his evaluation on this fundamental, social and dynamic idea.

Even in the field of the evaluation of the social *content* of a work, however, everything is far from being simple. The Marxist critic needs to be very skilful and extremely sensitive. By this is meant not only specific Marxist training but also specific talent, without which there can be no criticism. In the case of a really great artistic work, there are too many aspects to be weighed, and it is too difficult in this instance to use any kind of thermometer or scales. What is needed here is what is called social sensitivity, otherwise mistakes are inevitable. The Marxist critic must not prize only those works which are devoted to topical problems. Without denying the special importance of burning questions, it is completely impossible to ignore the tremendous significance of issues which at first sight appear too general and remote, but which, in fact, after looking at them more closely, do exert an influence on social life.

Here is the same phenomenon as in science. To demand that science give itself up entirely to practical tasks is a profound error. It is a well-known fact that the most abstract of scientific problems can,

when solved, sometimes turn out to be the most fruitful.

And yet, it is just when a writer or a poet turns to the solution of general tasks, striving towards—if he is a proletarian—a proletarian re-evaluation of the fundamentals of culture, that a critic can easily become confused. Firstly, in such cases we do not as yet have any true criteria; secondly, hypotheses may be of value here—the most daring hypotheses— for we are concerned not with a final solution to the problems, but with posing the problems and analysing them. To a certain extent, however, all this refers likewise to literary works of purely topical interest. The artist, who illustrates in his works the ideas of our programme which have already been fully developed, is a bad artist. The artist is valuable when he turns up virgin soil, when he intuitively breaks into a sphere which logic and statistics would find hard to penetrate. To judge whether an artist is right, whether he has correctly combined the truth and the basic aspirations of communism, is by no means easy; here, too, perhaps, the correct judgement can be worked out only in the conflict of opinions between critics and readers. All this does not make the critic's work any less important or necessary.

An extremely important factor in the evaluation of the social content of literary works is the second judgement of a work, which, at first analysis, seemed to belong to a range of phenomena which were alien, sometimes hostile to us. It is indeed very important to know the attitudes of one's foes, to make use of eyewitness accounts coming from a background different from ours. They can often lead us to profound conclusions, and, in any case, can greatly enrich the treasure-store of our knowledge of life's phenomena. The Marxist critic, who has stated that such and such a writer or work is, for example, a

purely petty-bourgeois phenomenon, must never dismiss this work or writer with a wave of his hand. A great deal of benefit can be extracted from it. For this reason, a second evaluation from the point of view not of the origin and tendentiousness of a given work, but of its potential use in our constructive effort, is the direct task of a Marxist critic.

I should like to qualify this. Alien and hostile elements in the sphere of literature even if they are of some benefit in the above-mentioned sense can of course be extremely harmful and poisonous and be dangerous manifestations of counter-revolutionary propaganda. It goes without saying that this is the cue for the appearance not of Marxist criticism but of Marxist censorship.

IX

The task of the Marxist critic becomes, perhaps, even more complicated, when he turns from evaluation of content to evaluation of form.

This is an extremely important task, and Plekhanov emphasised its importance. What then, is the general criterion for evaluation here? The form must correspond to the content as closely as possible, giving it maximum expressiveness and assuring the strongest possible impact on the readers for whom the work is intended.

Above all, the most important formal criterion, which Plekhanov also advocated, should be mentioned here; that is that literature is the art of images and every invasion of naked ideas or propaganda is always detrimental to the given work. It is self-evident that this criterion of Plekhanov's is not an absolute. There are excellent works by, for instance, Saltykov-Shchedrin, Uspensky and Furmanov, which clearly sin against this criterion, and this means that hybrid literary works combining belles-lettres with publicist thought can exist in their own right. By and large, these should be cautioned against. Of course, publicistic literature which is brilliant in form is an excellent type of propaganda and literature in the broadest sense of the word, but on the contrary, artistic belles-lettres loaded with purely publicistic elements will leave the reader cold, no matter how brilliant the argument. In this sense, the critic has every right to speak about the inadequacy of the artistic digestion of the content by the author if this content, instead of flowing freely in images of brilliant molten metal in the work, sticks out of this stream in large, cold lumps.

The second particular criterion, which is a natural outgrowth of the whole, as defined above, concerns the originality of the form. In what should this originality consist? Precisely in this: the formal body of a given work should merge into one indivisible whole with its idea, with its content. A genuine work of art should, of course, be new in content. If the content is not new, the work has little value. This is obvious. An artist should express something that has not been expressed before. Reproduction is not art (some painters find this difficult to understand) but only a craft, albeit sometimes very fine. From this point of view, new content in every new work demands new form.

With what can we contrast this genuine originality of form? In the first place, there is the stereotyped form which prevents a new idea being really incorporated into the work. A writer can be enthralled by previously used forms, and although his content is new, it is poured into old wineskins. Inadequacies of this kind cannot fail to be noticed. In the second place, the form may simply be weak, i.e., with a new, interesting conception, the artist may not possess the formal resources in the sense of language—a wealth of vocabulary, construction of the phrase, of the entire story, chapter, novel, play, etc.; and in the sense of rhythm and other forms of poetry. All this must be pointed out by the Marxist critic. A genuine Marxist critic—an integral type, so to say, of such a critic—must be a teacher, especially of the young writer or beginner.

Finally, the third major sin against the above-mentioned particular rule for the originality of form, is the "organisation" of form, where the emptiness of content is camouflaged by formal inventions and ornamentation. Writers infected by the formalists, those typical representatives of bourgeois decadence, have been known to try to adorn and embellish their honest and weighty content with various trickery, thereby ruining their work.

One must also approach the third criterion of a formal nature—the *universality* of the work—with caution. Tolstoi spoke out strongly for this. We who are extremely interested in the creation of a literature which would be addressed to the masses, and would appeal to them as to the great creators of life, are also interested in this universality. All forms of reticence, of isolation, all forms intended for a small circle of specialised aesthetes, every artistic convention and refinement should be rejected by Marxist criticism. Marxist criticism not only can, but must indicate the inner merits of such works in the past and present, at the same time condemning the frame of mind of the artist who tried with such formal methods to cut himself off from reality.

But as mentioned above, the criterion of universality must be treated with great care. In our press, in our propagandist literature we are going from the very complicated journals and papers, which demand considerable intelligence from the reader, to the most elementary popular level; similarly, we cannot bring all our literature down to the level of the as yet uncultured peasant masses or even of the workers. This would be a very serious mistake.

Glorious is the writer who can express a complex and valuable social idea with such powerful artistic simplicity that he reaches the hearts of millions. Glorious is also the writer who can reach the hearts of these millions with a comparatively simple, elementary content; and the Marxist critic should highly value such a writer. The Marxist critic's special attention and wise assistance are needed here. But of course, one should not deny the value of works which are not sufficiently intelligible for *every* literate person, which are addressed to the upper stratum of the proletariat, to the sophisticated party members, to the reader who has attained a considerable level of culture. Life presents many burning problems to this part of the population which plays an immensely important role in the construction of socialism; and of course these problems should not be left without an artistic answer simply because they have not yet faced the vast masses or because they cannot yet be worked out in universal form. It should, however, be noted that we have gone too far the other way, our writers concentrating their attention on an easier task—writing for a cultured circle of readers at a time when, I repeat, literature for the good of the workers and peasants, provided it is talented and successful literature, must be especially valued.

X

As has already been said, the Marxist critic is also to a significant degree a teacher. It is pointless to criticise unless the criticism results in some kind of progress. And what must this progress be? Firstly, the Marxist critic must be a teacher in his attitude towards the writer. It is quite possible that angry voices will be raised at this, saying that no one gave the critic the right to consider himself superior to the writer, and so on. When the question is properly phrased, such objections become completely invalid. Firstly, once it has been said that the Marxist critic must be the writer's teacher, the conclusion must be drawn from this that he must be an extremely resolute Marxist, an erudite person of irreproachable taste. It will be said that we have no such critics or only a very few. In the first case our opponents will be wrong; in the second they will be closer to the truth. But there is only one conclusion to be drawn from this: it is necessary to learn. There will be no lack of good will and talent in our great country, but there is a lot of hard learning to be done. Secondly, of course, the critic not only teaches the writer without in any way considering himself superior, but he also learns a great deal from the writer. The best critic is the one who can look on the writer with admiration and enthusiasm, and who, at any rate, is well disposed towards him. The Marxist critic can and must be a teacher to the writer in two ways: firstly, he must point out to young writers—and generally to writers capable of making a large number of formal mistakes—the faults in their work. It used to be widely held that we need no Belinskys, for our writers no longer need guidance. This may have been true before the revolution, but it becomes simply laughable after the revolution, when the masses are giving birth to hundreds and thousands of new writers. A firm, guiding criticism, Belinskys of every calibre, including the conscientious workman with a good knowledge of his literary trade—all these are absolutely essential.

The Marxist critic must, on the other hand, be a teacher to the writer in the social sense. Not only

is the non-proletarian writer very often merely a
child in his social attitudes, committing the crudest
of errors as a result of his primitive ideas about
the laws of social life and his failure to understand
the fundamentals of the epoch, etc., but this also
happens only too often with a Marxist, proletarian
writer. This is said not as an insult to the writer,
but partly almost in his praise. Writers are sensitive
beings, immediately receptive to all the influences
of reality. In most cases writers possess neither
special gifts nor special interest in abstract and
scientific thinking; it is for this reason, of course,
that they sometimes impatiently refuse any offer
of help from the publicist-critic. But this can often
be explained by the pedantic way in which such
help is offered. Yet it is, in fact, precisely as a
result of the co-operation between the important
writers and the most gifted literary critics that
truly great literature has always arisen and will
continue to arise.

XI

The Marxist critic, in trying to teach the writer
usefully, must also teach the reader. Yes, the reader
must be taught to read. The critic as a commen-
tator, as the person who warns of poison which
may taste sweet, as the person who cracks a hard
shell to reveal the pearl inside, as the person who
dots all the *i*'s, who makes generalisations on the
basis of artistic material—this is the guide who is
essential now, at a time when so many valuable
but as yet inexperienced readers have appeared.
This is his relation to our past and to world literature, this is how he must be related to contemporary literature. We once again emphasise, therefore,
the exceptional demands which the epoch is
making on the Marxist critic. We have no desire

to intimidate anyone with our theses. The Marxist critic can begin modestly, he can even start off by making mistakes, but he must remember that he will have to climb a long, steep staircase before he reaches the first landing, and even then he must look upon himself only as an apprentice. It is impossible, however, not to count on the gigantic upsurge of general culture and talented literature; it is impossible not to believe that the present—not entirely satisfactory—state of Marxist criticism will very soon improve.

XII

I should like, as a corollary, to touch on two more questions. Firstly, Marxist critics are often accused of what almost amounts to informing. It is indeed quite dangerous now to say about a writer that he entertains "unconscious" or even "semi-conscious", counter-revolutionary ideas. And in those cases when a writer is considered an alien element, a petty-bourgeois element, or a fellow traveller standing way to the Right, or when one of our writers is accused of some deviation or other, then the whole affair seems somewhat dubious. Is it really, people ask, a critic's business to say whether this or that writer is politically suspect, is politically unsound or has political failings? We must hasten to vehemently refute such protests. The critic who uses such a method to settle his personal accounts or deliberately to slander someone, is a villain; and such villainy, sooner or later, always comes to light. It is a heedless and careless critic who, without thinking or weighing the matter, hurls such accusations. But the man who distorts the very essence of Marxist criticism because he is afraid to declare aloud the results of his objective social analysis, must be labelled as careless and politically passive.

Not that the Marxist critic must shout: "Be watchful!" This is not an appeal to state organs; this is objective evaluation of some work or other for our construction. It is for the writer himself to draw conclusions, to correct his line. We are in the sphere of a struggle of ideas. Not a single conscientious and honest Communist can deny the nature of this *struggle* in the question of present-day literature and its evaluation.

XIII

And finally, this question: are sharp and bitter polemics to be allowed?

Generally speaking, sharp polemics are useful in that they keep the reader interested. Polemical articles, especially where both sides are wrong, all other things being equal, have more influence on the public and are better understood. In addition, the martial spirit of the Marxist critic as a revolutionary leads him to express his thoughts sharply, but at the same time it should be mentioned that to camouflage the weakness of his arguments with polemical brilliance is one of the critic's great sins. Generally when there are not many arguments but a multitude of various scathing remarks, comparisons, mocking exclamations, and sly questions, then the impression may be gay but not at all serious. Criticism must be applicable to criticism itself, for Marxist criticism is at the same time scientific and artistic work. Anger is not the best guide in criticism and often means that the critic is wrong.

Admittedly, sometimes biting sarcasm and tirades are torn out of the critic's heart. Always a more or less discerning ear of another critic or reader can from the very beginning distinguish between natural anger and mere malice. In our constructive effort there must be as little malice as possible. It must not be mixed with class hatred. Class hatred strikes with intent, but like a cloud over the earth it is above personal malice. By and large, the Marxist critic, without falling into cheerful indulgence, which would be very wrong on his part, must be a priori benevolent. His supreme joy must be in finding the positive and revealing it to the reader in all its splendour. Assistance must be another of his aims—to channel and to warn—and only rarely should it be necessary to attempt to undo the villain with the piercing arrow of laughter or contempt or with overwhelming criticism, which can easily annihilate any puffed-up nonentity.

1928

CHERNYSHEVSKY'S ETHICS AND AESTHETICS:
A CONTEMPORARY EVALUATION

THE connection between Chernyshevsky's aesthetical and ethical doctrine and his personality, is usually traced by both his friends and his foes; but this is done incorrectly, I think, because generally Chernyshevsky's portrait is not painted with sufficient clarity. From his correspondence, memoirs, diary and all the abundant material we have at our disposal, it is perhaps not difficult to extract his characteristics as a person; but, as yet, such material has been used extremely meagrely.

The prevailing image of Chernyshevsky is one of a man with unusually firm convictions, an exceedingly strong intellect, a wide education, a courageous nature and an extremely serious personality; one of the outstanding men of his time certainly, but all the same a man with a prosaic frame of mind, a nihilist, "a bilious man", as Herzen called him. The expression which Turgenev used of him when talking to him: "You, Nikolai Gavrilovich, are simply a snake, whereas Dobrolyubov is a cobra," shows that even Turgenev considered him a very wise, wily and cunning person. Be that as it may, for anyone with a second-hand or even superficial knowledge of Chernyshevsky, he appears as a somewhat dry person, to whom any idealism is quite alien.

We very often used to confuse theoretical and philosophical idealism with practical idealism; perhaps we still do. The well-known poet Tretyakov, for example, proclaimed only recently that it was necessary to declare war on pathos and to place one's stake on to the practical; and we are indeed frequently inclined to consider Chernyshevsky a practical person, without pathos, a man who reacted to the aesthetic as ironically as Bazarov reacted to pretty phrases—in short, an essentially practical, rational nature.

It is from this that people conclude his lack of talent as a writer of fiction. They say that *What Is to Be Done?* is without doubt a great work of its kind, which caused a tremendous stir and was, for its time, a lodestar for many; but if judged from a strictly artistic viewpoint, it lacks a certain fantasy and lyricism—precisely those elements which would be lacking in someone who, although very learned and respected, on his own terms great even, is all the same a prosaic person. It seems that he should have been given the same advice which Apollo gave to Socrates, a person with an overintellectual and rational nature, not long before his death: Apollo advised Socrates to take up music, this softening, harmonising element with its blend of intuition and romanticism which was evidently completely missing in Chernyshevsky. Those people who set their sights on the practical without doubt revel in this "realism" of Chernyshevsky, and must be extremely impressed by such a dry image of him.

It may be considered that this dryness of heart, this overwhelming "intellectuality" prompted Chernyshevsky to the thought that in fact only egoism existed; that a person had only a rational choice, from an egoistic viewpoint, as to how he should behave; and that there was not, and could not be, any form of ethics other than the ethics of rational egoism. Dry and rationalistic, Chernyshevsky sees nothing of that imponderable quality, the unconscious—everything slips by unnoticed. It is easy to come to the conclusion that the author of such a theory, Chernyshevsky, was himself too rationalistic a person, someone who possessed an exclusively intellectual nature.

What is the main idea of Chernyshevsky's treatise *The Aesthetic Relationship of Art to Reality*? It is a refutation of all things aesthetic which goes so far that even Pisarev felt that Chernyshevsky, by treating such subtle phenomena as art and aesthetics so roughly, had managed to stifle them—for the good of everyone, in Pisarev's opinion. It is true that Plekhanov set out to show that nothing of the sort happened, that Chernyshevsky's treatise was a serious and exhaustive scientific work. But the very posing of the question—the suspicion that art is somehow impractical, the attempts to prove that reality as such is far higher than any dream or any kind of artistic creation—all this, of course, forced the liberals surrounding Chernyshevsky to look on him as an anti-aesthetic monster, an extremely practical and dry type of person.

It is Plekhanov who has painted the most brilliant picture of Chernyshevsky, of all the facets of his unusually rich personality. Volumes 5 and 6 of Plekhanov's works are the most brilliant volumes dedicated to Chernyshevsky. But even Plekhanov's main thesis—I would even say his basic line of approach in his interpretation of Chernyshevsky—is one something akin to portraying Chernyshevsky as a dry person, a nihilist, a Bazarov.

Chernyshevsky, the "educator", the enlightener of the eighteenth-century type—this is Plekhanov's main thesis in his portrayal. The enlighteners of the eighteenth century were, as is well known, intellectuals par excellence, people for whom the rational approach remained supreme, people who were quite unable to appreciate the instinctive and the subconscious; instead of approaching phenomena from a historical, or, as Marx said, a dialectical viewpoint, they put their questions from a logical, common-sense position, from the demands of the intellect.

On what does Plekhanov base such accusations against Chernyshevsky? Mainly, of course (and here Plekhanov is absolutely right) he bases them on Chernyshevsky's world outlook, on the basic features of his philosophy, above all his social philosophy. Plekhanov indeed establishes that Chernyshevsky was a staunch and unswerving materialist, a follower of Feuerbach, and that, like many such men, he ceased to be a materialist as soon as he set about solving social problems. His image of the world and of man was a materialistic one; only matter with its characteristics and evolution was, as it were, recognised by him. And yet, as Plekhanov said, he considered that the world was controlled by opinions. That is, once you have understood the laws that govern Nature and man, you can impose your rational will onto this world. This was also the approach of the outstanding figures of the French revolution; once you have understood that Nature is the natural aggregate of force and matter, then you should not only become properly acquainted with it, but also bring the existing order of things before the court of reason, rejecting everything which reason finds worthless trash, and keeping everything which it finds advantageous for the people. The whole problem lies in cognition, judgement and the realisation of a rational plan. Such a concept of the way society develops, and the consequential means for its transformation to be found in the realisation of a rationally established plan, whose strength is its convincingness, its rationality—this of course is an idealistic approach.

The pre-Marxist materialists, therefore, fall into idealism when they attempt to tackle social problems. Since they approach sociological, historical, economic and political problems from this idealistic standpoint, they are rationalists and enlighteners, people who consider that ideas are the driving force behind the process of historical development. It is from this that the exaggerated idea about the significance of the ideologists inevitably arises.

A clever, educated and critical man is the bearer of an idea. An idea is a force which transforms the world. It follows then that it is precisely this rational person who transforms the world and guides the course of events. The most important factor in this rational being is his intellect. Everything else—feelings, etc.—fade into the background.

In his definition of Chernyshevsky as an enlightener, Plekhanov does not himself say that he is an intellectualist. He does not completely side with those people who paint a portrait of a dry person, whose life was governed entirely by his brain and his convictions (many of these people, I may add, respect Chernyshevsky). But since the accusation that Chernyshevsky overrated the importance of ideas and exaggerated the importance of intellectuals and their intellects was supported, before and after Plekhanov, by criticisms along the lines of this narrow image of Chernyshevsky, then it can be said that Plekhanov enabled such a portrayal to be consolidated.

I want to restore the image of the real Chernyshevsky, as an overwhelmingly emotional person with a sensual nature: one could call him a man of the heart. He was a richly endowed and passionate man, fervently in love with life and with the real processes of a personal, even an intimate existence. It is precisely this image of Chernyshevsky which I want to recreate, since in fact his ethics and aesthetics spring neither from his intellectuality nor from his one-sidedness, but from his powerful impassioned feelings and his many-sidedness, from his realism which can only be interpreted as a love for life, as a manifestation of Chernyshevsky's colossal vital strength. If I can succeed in recreating these qualities, then Chernyshevsky's portrait will look very different, and he will, perhaps, have to be evaluated anew.

The first volume of Chernyshevsky's literary heritage was published recently. His diary, which covers his years as a young man, is one of the main sections of this volume. The best section of this wonderful diary, which is capable of inspiring into all those who read it a tremendous love for the man, is the last part which Chernyshevsky himself calls: "The Diary of My Relations with the Girl Who Is Now My Happiness". All the conversations which he had with his bride are noted down here with extraordinary detail. When we read through the following two pages from his diary, we are listening to Chernyshevsky himself at an important moment of his life, and we are at once able to appreciate the pace at which he lived and the music which was inherent in him as an individual. It is all very distant from the portrait the liberal landowners painted of him; a portrait which they were able to spread unhindered, by taking advantage of his modesty and his dislike of taking himself into consideration, a portrait which was to be repeated later by Volynsky and other idealists, at a time when people were beginning to debunk Chernyshevsky and to be disillusioned with him.

The method used is very interesting; it is interesting to see the excitement and the precision with which this 26-year-old high school teacher, preparing himself for revolutionary and literary activity, notes down his conversations with his wife-to-be.

"Having had some tea, we sat down—she by the window, and I on the other side of the table—the long side, so that there was a corner of the table between us. It was 5:30. I glanced at her for a moment or two, and she didn't take her eyes off me.

" 'I haven't the right to say what I am about to
say, but I'll say it all the same, even though you
may laugh at me: you want to get married because
relations at home are strained.'

" 'Yes, it's true. When I was young, I was happy
and didn't want anything; but now when I can see
how I am looked upon at home, my life has become
miserable. And if I am gay, the gaiety is forced
rather than genuine.'

" 'It is quite impossible for me to answer you as
I should.' (I continue at 11 p.m. Tomorrow I must
go to Stephany to have my chest examined.)

" 'Tell me, have you any suitors?'

" 'Yes, two.'

" 'But are they bad people? What about Lindgren?'
(I pronounced the name in such a way as if to
say: Of these two you certainly wouldn't consider
him.)

" 'No.' (In a tone which said: How could I?)

" 'What about Yakovlev? He's not a bad chap, is
he?'

" 'It's for that reason that I cannot marry him.
He's an old acquaintance of Papa's. On our way to
Kiev we went to Kharkov (to see an uncle or some
other relation—I can't remember whom she
mentioned). There one of the landlords—fairly rich
ones, 150 serfs, but an old man—asked me for my
hand and I told him that I couldn't do anything
without Papa's consent, and that even with his
consent I still wouldn't marry him. How can one
take a decision that will ruin one's youth?'

" 'Listen to what I have to say in all sincerity. I
cannot live here, in Saratov, because I shall never
earn as much money as I require. There is no future
for me here. I shall have to go to St. Petersburg.
But that's not the half of it. I cannot marry here,
because I shall never be able to achieve independence and set up a home and family, as I would

like to. My mother, it is true, loves me very much and she will love my wife even more.'

"(Continued 21st February, 7 a.m., before I set off to Stephany.)

" 'As things are at home, I certainly couldn't settle down there. For this reason I'm a stranger at home; I remain outside all family affairs, and all I do there is joke with Mama. I don't even really know what is going on at home. I must therefore go to St. Petersburg. When I'm there I shall have to be extremely busy and work hard to get my affairs in order. On my arrival there I shall have *nothing*: how can I possibly arrive married? It would be mean and despicable of me to join my life with someone else's, especially since I am not sure how long life and freedom will be granted to me. My way of thinking is such that I can expect the police to come any day to take me away to St. Petersburg and put me in prison, God knows for how long. I'm saying things in class, and doing things here that can end in penal servitude.'

" 'Yes, so I've heard.'

" 'And I can't change my way of thinking; perhaps I'll cool down in time, but I doubt it.'

" 'Why? Do you really think you can't change?'

" 'I cannot rid myself of my way of thinking because it is part of my nature, which has become embittered and dissatisfied with everything around me. Now I don't know whether I'll ever cool down in this respect. Up till now, anyway, such a tendency has only been increasing, becoming more and more acute and playing a greater and greater role in my life. And so I expect the police to appear any minute, just as a devout monk awaits the Day of Judgement. Apart from this, there is going to be an uprising shortly, in which I shall certainly take part.'

"This seemed such a strange and improbable idea to her that she very nearly burst out laughing.

" 'What do you mean? How?'

" 'Have you given this any thought at all?'

" 'No.'

" 'It is inevitable. The people's dissatisfaction with the government, taxes, bureaucrats and landowners is increasing. Just one spark is needed to set the whole thing alight. The number of people from the educated circle who are against the present order of things is also increasing; the spark which will start the fire is also ready. Just one thing is uncertain—when will it start? Within ten years, perhaps, but I think it will be earlier. And if it starts, I shan't be able to hold myself back, despite my cowardice, I shall take part in it.'

" 'And Kostomarov, too?'

" 'I don't think so—he is too high-flown and poetic a character; carnage and filth will frighten him off. I am not afraid of filth, or of drunken peasants wielding bludgeons, or of carnage.'

" 'Neither am I.' (My God, if only she realised the significance of what she is saying!)

" 'But what will be the result of all this? Penal servitude or the gallows. So you see how impossible it is for me to link anyone else's life with my own.' (From her expression it could be seen that she was finding such talk boring.) 'You see—you are already bored by all these discussions—but they will go on for years because there is nothing else I can talk about. It is enough that Mama's fate is linked with mine—and she will never survive such happenings. And what will happen to the wife of such a man? Let me give you an example. You remember the name Iskander?'

" 'Yes.'

" 'He was a very rich person who married for love the girl with whom he was brought up. After some time, the police came and took him away and he spent a year in prison. His wife was pregnant (please excuse such details), and because she was so frightened, she gave birth to a son who was deaf and dumb. Her health was permanently shattered. Finally he was released and allowed to leave Russia. The excuse for this was that his wife was ill (in fact she did need to take the waters) and that his son needed treatment. He settled somewhere in the Sardinian Empire. Suddenly, Louis-Napoleon, now the Emperor Napoleon, wishing to render Nicholas I a service, seized him and sent him back to Russia. His wife, who was living somewhere in Ostend or Dieppe, heard about this and fell down dead. This is what happens to girls who marry such people. I am not saying that I am equal to Iskander—in intellect, for example—but my way of thinking is just as uncompromising as his and I must expect a similar fate.' "*

This is the young Chernyshevsky's self-portrait. He yearns to marry her, as he writes elsewhere: "If I let this opportunity slip, I shall have no personal life, no personal happiness, and yet it is for a personal life and a family that I have been created. . .", and so on. Despite this passionate desire for personal happiness, he is able to say: I am afraid neither of blood nor of prison, and I cannot possibly withdraw from the revolution.

Already this has very little in common with the usual image of him as a dry person.

It is his inner strength which is without doubt the vital source of his aesthetical ideas. In his work on aesthetics he defines his approach to the subject in this way:

"What is in fact beauty? . . . The feeling which beauty evokes in us is a radiant joy, such as we feel in the presence of someone who is dear to us.

---

* N. G. Chernyshevsky, *Literaturnoye Naslediye, (Literary Heritage)*, Vol. I, Gosizdat, 1928, pp. 556-57,

We *love* beauty selflessly; we delight in it and it fills us with joy, just as a loved one does. Hence beauty possesses something which is near and dear to our hearts. But this 'something' must be something which is all-embracing, something capable of incorporating the most varied forms, something of an exceedingly general nature, for beauty appears to us in the most varied forms, each quite unlike the other.

"The phenomenon which is dearest to man in general is *life*: first and foremost, man loves the life he would most like to lead; after this he loves just any kind of life because it is better to live than not to live. By its very nature, his whole being is terrified at the thought of death, of non-existence, and he therefore loves life. And it seems that the definition: 'Beauty is life'—that is, the person in whom we can see life such as it should be, as we understand it, is beautiful; the object in which life is manifested, or which reminds us of life is beautiful—this definition, it seems, is able to explain satisfactorily all those occasions when the emotion of beauty is evoked in us."*

As you can see these are indeed poetical lines. Notice from where he draws his analogies—from the sphere of life, of the heart, of love and sex, but in the loftiest possible meaning of the word. So that he can say that life is more precious to him than anything; that above all he wants this life to develop harmoniously and reach its full maturity; that where life is developing harmoniously, there both beauty and radiant joy are to be found—to express all this he says: It is just like meeting a loved one. Such passages completely change the usual picture of Chernyshevsky as an ascetic *razno-*

---

* N. G. Chernyshevsky, *Collected Works,* Vol. II, Goslitizdat, Moscow, 1949, pp. 9-10.

*chinets.** What strikes us in Chernyshevsky is an insatiable thirst for life, an acceptance of the most real and genuine life.

Chernyshevsky's letters to Nekrasov have recently been published. There is one page in this correspondence which is indeed remarkable. Even I, who love Chernyshevsky and who have studied him since my youth, found it unexpected.

Nekrasov had written Chernyshevsky a complaining letter. We do not know its contents, but it is clear from the reply that he had written that he had grown tired of life, that everything bored him and that he was wondering whether death was not in fact better. And these are the lyrical lines which Chernyshevsky wrote in reply:

"Please do not think that in my evaluation I am being carried away by your tendency—a good tendency cannot make up for a weak talent. I know this as well as anyone—besides I am by no means an out and out supporter of this attitude; I only seem one because I am a person of extreme opinions, which I sometimes have to defend before people without any opinions whatever. But I myself know from experience that convictions are not everything in life; the heart has its needs, too, and the life of the heart means for each of us real grief or real joy. This, too, I know from experience better than anyone. It is only when our hearts are resting from grief or joy that convictions can occupy our minds. I would even say that, for me, my own affairs are more important than problems of world importance; people do not shoot themselves, or drown themselves, or become drunkards because of world

---

* The *raznochintsy*—(literally, men of various social estates) were educated members of Russian society drawn from the small townsfolk, the clergy, the merchant classes and the peasantry, as distinct from those drawn from the nobility.—*Ed.*

problems. This has been my own experience, and I know that the poetry of the heart has its rights as well as the poetry of the mind, and I find the first more attractive than the second. This explains, for example, why I am more impressed by your plays that are free from any tendency than your plays with a tendency. *When from the confusing gloom..., Long since spurned by you..., I was at your graveside..., Oh fatal, useless passion...,* and so forth, positively make me weep—something which no tendency can do. If I have been frank about myself, it is to let you know that I personally by no means regard poetry merely from a political standpoint. On the contrary, politics forces its way into my heart—a heart which does not live by politics at all, or at least which has no desire to live by politics."*

What does this mean? Is it perhaps retraction on Chernyshevsky's part? Have we perhaps touched on the weak point of his heart? Have we perhaps been taking him for a heroic revolutionary, whereas all the time in fact he wanted to leave politics entirely alone? No, Chernyshevsky's criticism here is, in fact, a correct and rational one.

What was the essence of Chernyshevsky's politics, to which his whole life was devoted? It was the abolition of serfdom, autocracy, the bourgeois system, and so on. Why did he desire the abolition of these things so passionately? Because it would enable him to live the real life of the heart, to live a cultured existence with its wealth of experiences. The aim of political struggle is the establishment of a happy human existence. Without such an aim, what would be the point of politics? It is necessity

---

* *Chernyshevsky's Correspondence with Nekrasov, Dobrolyubov and A. S. Zelyony*, Moskovsky Rabochy, Moscow-Leningrad, 1925, p. 28.

which makes us occupy ourselves with politics. If each one of us thought only of his own personal welfare and thereby diminished the energy which each put into the general struggle, we would be defeated. But this does not mean that a genuine revolutionary is one who is passionately enamoured of politics—just as a chess player or card player is passionately attached to his game—and must consider it the aim of the whole world. Of course not. A revolutionary's political activity is expedient, and serves to lead mankind out of the colossal ocean of evil towards happiness, prosperity and a rational existence. Therefore Chernyshevsky had the right to say what we have learned from this letter, which shows what a passionate thirst for happiness he had and what a rich and healthy personality he possessed. It becomes clear that his rules of conduct stemmed precisely from this vital force.

Chernyshevsky writes, incidentally: "I myself know from my own experience that one can sometimes become a drunkard as a result of life's calamities." Did something of this sort in fact happen to him? Yes it did, and it is to be found in these very letters to Nekrasov. It is quite remarkable to see such a tender trait in such a strong character. This is what he writes in another letter:

"Lessing and I have not enough time to compile 'Foreign News'—that is, there would be enough time, if only I were calm, but if only you knew what I have lived through these last six weeks, you would be amazed that I can write anything at all just now. I shall merely say this: the longer I live, the more I grow convinced that, although people are full of irrationalities and stupidities, there is nonetheless more good in them than evil. To allay your fears I will tell you that these unpleasantnesses did not arise out of literature, and concern no one but myself. I have become more than ever convinced that all present institutions are stupid and harmful, however wonderful they might appear: love, friendship, enmity—if this is not complete nonsense, then it leads to complete nonsense. Yet man is, all the same, a good and noble creature, it is impossible not to respect and love people, or many people anyway."*

What kind of experiences had these been, from which he had formed the impression that everything was stupid and absurd, but which had in the end strengthened still further his belief in man? Here are some extremely intimate lines which again show Chernyshevsky in an unusually tender light:

"You will perhaps remember that I love my wife and that the birth of her first child was accompanied by many difficulties, including loss of milk, etc. The doctors said that this could happen again if she gave birth to a second child, and would perhaps result in death. So I decided to be content with just one offspring, but it turned out that, for my sins and against my will, another child was on the way. You can imagine what torments of doubt I was in, that this affair would end happily. September was the last month in which I managed to retain any calm; but, from October onwards, depression and anxiety of mind completely confused my thoughts. Four months passed like this; I wrote what I could, but it was very little—and for weeks on end I could not put two words together; I became drunk twice, something that I am not in the habit of doing at all. Only in the last few days when everything has turned out well, and my wife is already starting to walk, have I become like a person again. Both mind and soul were in a ghastly state. It is good that this stupid affair is over."**

_____

* *Chernyshevsky's Correspondence*, p. 35.
** *Ibid.*, p. 42.

Here is your "egoist", your "prosaic person"; his passionate nature drives him into the arms of his young and beautiful wife. He knows that their intimacy can kill her, and when it appears that perhaps he has killed her, he goes completely out of his mind; he loses his grip on everything; and the thought that he himself has killed this person so dear to him, has sacrificed her to his own passion, takes prevalence over all else. But when he recovers from this shock, he is reminded of many words which were said here, many heartfelt emotions; and he says: "What a wonderful being man is!"

I should like to show you, too, his personal attitude to poetry. We shall see later, when I am analysing his aesthetical views, that, to Plekhanov, Chernyshevsky's attitude to poetry is an intellectual one, that he judges it according to the degree of moralising which it contains. But we have already seen that this is not so; we have seen that he reacted warmly to lyrical works depicting human emotions. (This does not mean, on the other hand, that he passed by, let us say, Nekrasov's lyrics, inasmuch as they were of a social nature, with indifference; on the contrary, such lyrics moved him tremendously.) This is how Chernyshevsky, cornered like some wild beast, his reason fading from complete inactivity, wrote to Pypin from the icy wastes of Siberia, when he heard that Nekrasov was dying:

"If, when you get my letter, Nekrasov still breathes, tell him that I love him warmly as a person, that I thank him for his kind attitude towards me, and that I embrace him; tell him that I am convinced his fame will never die, that Russia's love for him, the most noble and the greatest genius of all her poets, will be everlasting. I am weeping for him. . . ."*

* *Chernyshevsky's Correspondence*, p. 13.

43

Nekrasov still breathed, and Chernyshevsky's words, read out by Pypin, brought him great joy and deeply stirred him.

As you can see—this also came from the heart.

Here is Krasnov, Chernyshevsky's secretary, telling how Chernyshevsky used to read Nekrasov in Siberia:

"Nikolai Gavrilovich asked me to listen to *A Knight for an Hour*. His slightly drawn-out, rhythmical manner of reading, with its logical stresses, made a tremendous impression on me; completely absorbed, I did not notice Nikolai Gavrilovich's voice becoming more and more resonant. *The ascent to the belfry* he read as if he himself were living through it. In a hoarse, broken voice he began to read the last verse, the poet's self-adjuration when thinking of his mother. Suddenly Nikolai Gavrilovich could contain himself no longer, and burst out sobbing, continuing to read the poem. I had not the heart to stop him, for I was also moved. Olga Sokratovna interrupted this scene so charged with emotion, saying:

" 'It is harmful for you.'

" 'All right, dear, all right', and a short while later we set to work."

It appears that poetry inspired in Chernyshevsky anything but the "cold observations of the mind", or calculations based purely on the amount of new knowledge contained in the work. Nikolai Gavrilovich was the most gentle and responsive of readers, in whose rich and noble soul the call of poetry resounded with immense fervour. That is why it is difficult to believe that he stuffed his aesthetics, his theory of art, with that dry intellectualism, of which not only the idealists, like Volynsky, but also, to a significant degree, Plekhanov accuse him. We shall speak about these accusations in more detail later on.

You know that Chernyshevsky was extremely well disposed towards Dobrolyubov, and that the two were very fond of each other. To conclude this part of my lecture, I shall quote two more extracts. The first—from Cheshikhin-Vetrinsky's book—characterises the way in which people reacted to Chernyshevsky. The second is what Chernyshevsky said about Dobrolyubov, which one can apply fully to Chernyshevsky himself and which we, the friends and disciples of Chernyshevsky, can use to reply to anyone, who dares, yet again to accuse him of intellectual dryness, nihilism, egoism, etc. This is what Cheshikhin-Vetrinsky writes:

"Two basic features run through Chernyshevsky's early years and afterwards throughout his life; the student's attention is involuntarily arrested by these two characteristics.

"First, he has by nature an unusually gentle and compassionate heart which captivates all that surrounds him.

"In his childhood he was an 'angel in the flesh'; as an adolescent, he was surrounded by the adoration of children whom he would win with his games. His fellow students simply worshipped him, not only because of the outstanding quality of his student genius, but also because of the charm of his character and gentle nature. As a young man, he was seen as someone 'who was made, above all else, to be believed, someone to whom one could confide anything'. Young people attached themselves to him 'like dogs', as one of them confessed; and his high school pupils will remember their teacher with tears in their eyes for the rest of their lives. The young man Lobodovsky and the poet Nekrasov, disillusioned and suffering bitter grief, compared him with Christ."*

* V. E. Cheshikhin-Vetrinsky, *N. G. Chernyshevsky, 1828-1889*, Kolos, Petrograd, 1923, p. 103.

This was, in those days, the highest possible praise.

"Those who met him in later years will also remember him with adoration—long after his death, one of them will say, remembering their forced separation: the wound has not yet healed."*

" 'He who has known him will never forget; he will suffer a torment of grief,'—one of his friends in exile (Shaganov) quoted these lines of Nekrasov about him.

"But more remarkable is the effect of this nature on simple people—this ability must have developed in him in his early years, for, generally speaking, it is only rarely that the ability for sociable intimacy grows with the years. A striking story is told by Mr. Nikolayev, who witnessed the quietening effect of Chernyshevsky's words on an angry and excited mob of Poles, uneducated and extremely reactionary men, who had ganged up in a prison against the socialists, their fellow inmates. He saw them weep as 'Pan Chernyshevsky' came to the end of his simple, but direct and heartfelt speech."**

This can be added to what I have already said; it fully characterises this person who was wholly exceptional in the direct appeal of his nature.

This charm originated in his powerful vital force and the extraordinary sympathy which he extended to everything—except, of course, that which was evil and hindered life's development.

Chernyshevsky ended his article on the death of Dobrolyubov with the following words:

"You have called, dear sirs, our friend a soulless and heartless man. I now have the honour of addressing you in my own name and the name of everyone who reads these pages, you yourselves

---

* V. E. Cheshikhin-Vetrinsky, *op. cit.*
** *Ibid.*

included, and you will repeat to yourselves what I am about to tell you—I now have the honour of calling you dull-witted simpletons. I challenge you to appear, you worthless dullards, to support your former opinions, I challenge you.... You're afraid to! I can see you retreating."*

We could repeat the same words to every liberal, aesthete or idealist who says: "Ah yes, Chernyshevsky—the *raznochinets,* the first seminary democrat, of whom Tolstoi wrote, 'he smells of bedbugs'; surely this man is completely devoid of any poetry, an impossibly dry pedant in whom there is nothing that speaks to the heart, some kind of a Bazarov in a seminarist's frock."

Chernyshevsky's materialism is also drawn from his unusually passionate and strong nature. We live now in a different atmosphere; many concepts have been completely replaced, but not long ago the general idea of the materialist and the idealist was exactly that as portrayed in a picture by Makovsky called *The Materialist and the Idealist,* which is in the Tretyakov Art Gallery. The materialist is portrayed as a fat cook with an unusually large belly (so that it is immediately obvious that this is a materialist—he lives for his belly); he has a thick neck and is shortsighted, with spectacles on his nose (an allegory of course); on his face there is an expression of sceptical self-sufficiency. He is listening irritably and with obvious disapproval to what the foppish-looking idealist has to say to him. The latter is a slim man who could fly through the air with the ease of a feather; his clothes are ragged and worn, his neck is such that one could strangle him with only two fingers; his hair is in disarray (mental preoccupation prevents him from combing it); he has a faraway look in his eyes and the pink

---

* *Chernyshevsky's Correspondence,* p. 59.

diffuse glow on his face betrays a dream. Maybe an idealist so depicted is not to your liking, but at least he is better than that overweight cook. This view that the materialist is a rather stupid man whose horizons are more or less limited, who values only the material, and that the idealist is a flighty individual who lives in other worlds, who is full of brilliant and intangible images and wondrous music—this image is repeated again and again and has come to have a certain force in the conflict of the two philosophies. In fact, the idealist is fluid, and his *Weltanschauung* is idealistic and liquid— nebulous even.

The idealist does not like reality and cannot come to terms with it.

There are times, it is true, when reality is detestable, when it becomes a kind of stone face which sees through pitiless eyes. To come to terms with such a life is to come to terms with the pettiness of life.

Militant materialists, on the other hand, accept and love reality, and look upon it as the raw material for their struggles and creative activity. The idealist cannot see this creative factor—and this arises not simply from the essential shallowness of his nature, not because Ivan Ivanovich has a stronger character and is able as a result to become a materialist, whereas Pyotr Petrovich has a weak stomach and flabby muscles, and consequently trembles at the sight of reality. Not because of this at all. No, the reason for this lies much deeper: classes, groups and individuals who find themselves outcasts from life, who are unable to come to terms with life because they have received nothing from it but unpleasantness—even though outwardly they have attained the highest run of the social ladder, their nerves and stomach are in shreds, and they are completely cut off from life, quite incapable of en-

A. V. Lunacharsky, 1920-22

joying it—these classes, groups and individuals have cast themselves off from the shores of reality and headed for an imaginary world, a fluid and nebulous dream world which begins, for them, to take the place of life. This they may well find wonderful. We give them up for dead—what are they to us? Let them poison themselves however they like. And yet they are creating a philosophy, a pseudo-science and a form of art which is generally a negation of life. Our contemporary, the literary and fine arts scholar Eichenbaum, for example, said these remarkable words: "What makes you think that art is linked with life? Perhaps it is linked rather with death." To Eichenbaum it appears that death has a greater poetic quality than life, because he is evidently a fluid person, lacking stability and a firm basis to his life; it is because of this that he likes everything of a soothing, lulling nature, everything which is alien to the utilitarian, everything which is of itself beautiful.

Chernyshevsky understood that formalism asserts that it is only form which has value in art, that art is illusory, to be valued precisely for its illusory nature.

But Chernyshevsky himself was not like this. It can be said that a materialist, such as Chernyshevsky, is someone who is passionately, with every cell and fibre of his being, in love with Nature, with reality, with life. Yet this does not mean that he accepted life unconditionally. On the contrary, it was because he loved life and its development, loved all that was positive in life, that he saw that life in nature, and particularly in society, was set in abnormal conditions. It was a result of his love for life that his hatred for anything that retarded its growth increased, and he accepted a struggle and all the suffering that went with it, because he could glimpse victory ahead. Victory was the transformation of reality itself purged of every impurity, of everything that was absurd, monstrous, laughable or vice-ridden.

As has already been pointed out, Chernyshevsky was constantly drawing the analogy between love for life and sexual love; but this does not mean that he was something in the nature of a Freudian. The meaning of the analogy is as follows: the love of someone for the body of another person, the desire for possession and for fruition—all these feelings are linked in a fundamental way with the very richness of life, with its real strength; it is this joy of life, so characteristic of the representatives of the new, rising classes, which leads to that courageous philosophy, based on the idea of labour, of the victorious fighter, which forms a materialist. And I repeat: we consider it *a priori* unlikely—and this I shall try to show convincingly—that there was not a radiant quality in Chernyshevsky's *Weltanschauung*, that it contained nothing that might be called beauty or poetry. As we come closer to Cherynshevsky, we shall realise that his was a life that reached its full flowering, that Chernyshevsky was one of the most wonderfully versatile and mature people, who has ever lived. And his whole outlook, and indeed his whole life, is stamped with the imprint of strength, beauty and poetry.

We know that Chernyshevsky was a *raznochinets*, a seminarist, the son of a priest. Why was it that the landowners of the time, people of a manor house type of culture (including the more liberal landowners like Turgenev), were inclined towards dreams and daydreams, and why did reality appear so coarse to them? It was, of course, because they were quite divorced from hard work, from the struggle for existence. This is why the landowner in his manor house was only half-alive. Artificial would find so much filth. In their moral principles they are as hard as steel, whereas we are shattered people.' "*

What must Chernyshevsky, a great person and seminarist, a representative of the first wave of democratic movement close to the people, what must he have said when he approached the problem of aesthetics? He must have said that a genuine, healthy person loved reality, loved nature, loved man, loved life. The genteel aesthetes—both those who philosophised and those who practised—and the artists filled life with all sorts of rubbish, with aesthetic trash, painted, discordant and stylised; they maintained, moreover, that all this was the reflection of ideas, a divine radiance shining down into our dim world; that it was geniuses who were the bearers of these magnificent gifts, at the sight of which our pathetic reality must immediately bow down in shame. All this came from the representatives of a class, which was not merely divorced from life as a whole, but which was beginning also, in a social way, to die, to discredit living reality—to discredit, too, the struggle for freedom, to impose its own artistic, narcotic Garden of Eden on the other classes, on the youth, on the new rising generation.

Chernyshevsky indeed defended the sacred purity of democracy from all such pseudo-aesthetics, which, although beneficent at first sight, was in fact trying to poison and strangle democracy. This explains Chernyshevsky's suspicious attitude towards art: he was led to deny an art which considered itself a wonderful reflection of a higher existence, because it was a pure phantom, which merely assumed the form of that which actually existed, without its transitoriness, weightiness, firmness or fortuitousness, etc.

---

* K. N. Berkova, *N. G. Chernyshevsky*, Moskovsky Rabochy, Moscow, 1925, p. 114.

Chernyshevsky persecuted all such forms of art as fictious and feeble, and showed that, from a genuinely aesthetic standpoint—the maximum development of life—such forms fall well short of reality and have no real right to exist.

But it does not follow from this that Chernyshevsky considered that art should not exist at all, as Pisarev understood him to consider; neither does it follow that he did not understand that art has an extremely exalted role to play. Here is an extract which shows this:

"In defining beauty as the complete manifestation of an idea in a concrete case, we must inevitably arrive at the conclusion that 'beauty, in reality, is only a phantom, placed there by our fancies'; from this it follows that 'strictly speaking, beauty is a product of our fancies; in reality (or, as Hegel would say: in Nature) there is no true beauty'. From this conclusion it will follow that 'art has as its source the strivings of man to make up for the lack of beauty in objective reality', and that 'beauty, created by art, is on a higher level than the beauty of objective reality'—all these thoughts make up the essence of Hegel's aesthetics and are part of it not by accident but as the result of the strictly logical development of the basic concept of beauty.

"As against this, from the definition 'beauty is life' it will follow that the genuine, highest form of beauty is precisely that which is met in reality, and not that which has been created by art; with such ideas of beauty in reality, the origin of art is only explicable as coming from a completely different source; after this, the material significance of art likewise appears in a totally different light."*

Chernyshevsky showed that man's aesthetic emotions are by no means connected only with

---

* N. G. Chernyshevsky, *Collected Works,* Vol. II, p. 14.

beauty. Of course other aesthetes knew this as well, and spoke about such aesthetic phenomena as the elevated, the tragic and the comic. I shall forebear from analysing the elevated and the comic, because there is little to quarrel with here, but before going on to Chernyshevsky's ideas on the social role of art, I shall linger for a moment on his definition of the tragic. Plekhanov considered this part of Chernyshevsky's *Aesthetics* to be somewhat crude and incomplete.

The prevalent idea of the tragic in Chernyshevsky's time was one which had been inherent in the great tragedians of the ancient world. In his immortal *Poetics* (on which, by the way, Chernyshevsky wrote a special study) Aristotle explained the basic idea of tragedy, as the ancient world saw it. Hegel and Fichte, the kings of aesthetics in the middle of the last century, borrowed much from this idea. They interpreted it in this way: tragedy depicts the fate of a great and significant person, an outstanding figure, who perishes as a result of his tragic guilt. We are sorry that this figure had to perish, because it was a wonderful figure, but we must recognise that justice has been done. What is this guilt? This person represents strength, but he cannot come to terms with his environment; he bears within him something new and original, and he does not bow down before that which is generally accepted, before the law. The Greeks defined this as *hubris*—pride. *Hubris*—the proud feeling of one's own independence, the attempt to place human laws against divine laws—comes precisely from strength, from a strong body, a strong spirit, a strong social position. It is precisely the fact that the person is outstanding which leads to his downfall. In an earlier age Herodotus said that, once someone stands out head and shoulders above the rest, then the gods will inevitably kill him, for they are envious. The gods consider an above-average person a criminal, because they are the guardians of standards. If you have risen above average, you have become interesting precisely because of your abnormality, your above-average position. You will therefore perish because everyone, who exceeds the average will perish.

From where did the Greeks get this idea? Why was it necessary for Greek democracy? For the same reason that ostracism was necessary. In this democratic environment, an extremely unstable and restless one, individual demagogues, no matter to which class they belonged, would try to seize power, to trample others underfoot; one after the other petty and strong tyrants would rise up under different names—now as dictators, now as public orators, now as leaders of an aristocratic mutiny. But the genuine middle-class democracy, with its Areopagus, and all the institutions which arose to protect the nation's stability, created a definite political moral code, with which they fought against this very *hubris*. They said: "If you leave the middle classes and break the laws of your fatherland established by the middle-class democracy (which was dominant in Athens), then you will perish." This was a social antidote, in common with most ethics. They wanted to instil in people a fear of becoming too outstanding. If someone became too significant and famous, he would be expelled from society, and no one would explain why. Here the profound distrust of this unstable democracy is revealed. Fichte, a defender of the individual, who came to the fore with the French revolution, said that even if the heavens and the stars should fall, the moral freedom of the individual would never be abolished. But Hegel erecting the ancient democratic ideal on a new social foundation, said that a person who puffed himself up and set himself against the eternal and lawful progress of the idea was merely laughable.

Chernyshevsky was extremely incensed by all this, and rightly so. He said that great people are sometimes happy, sometimes not. Anything might happen to anyone: you cannot frighten us with your talk. He was amused by the doctrine of the existence of a fate. All this in the end was merely old wives' tales, a feature of religion; it simply scared people with so-called eternal laws, which in fact had been established by a sharply defined social class, in order to fight against human independence. This is not tragedy. Tragedy is to be found in every terrible event, in every terrible ending, in each of mankind's sufferings, even if completely unmerited. And indeed why is it that if someone is guilty and perishes, this is tragic; and yet if he is innocent and perishes, this is not tragic? Gustavus Adolphus, after a series of magnificent victories, was killed in a battle by a stray bullet—why is this not tragic?

According to Plekhanov, when Chernyshevsky declares that everything which is terrible is also tragic, he is not right. There is a difference between the tragic and the merely terrible. There is nothing to be learned from the merely terrible, there is no material for a genuinely tragic work of creation. Hegel and Aristotle, according to Plekhanov, are more correct. Tragedy is death as the result of a law. But its significance is not that the hero perishes by the hand of fate and envious gods, but that the prophets and forerunners of a new world and new convictions, clash with the old world and inevitably perish. This fate which befalls the prophets of a new world seems to us a wonderful one, evoking our sympathy, and yet also an inevitable one, because they are the first swallows of a spring which has not yet established itself—all this is true tragedy.

Plekhanov said that Chernyshevsky's position on tragedy was an abstract one, taken out of its social context, and that he did not approach the subject as, in Plekhanov's opinion, a Marxist should approach it, that is, from a point of view of class struggle.

I should like to object here that tragedy is not always the tragedy of the forerunners; that it is not merely the collision between an individual and society or between a representative of a weaker class and a stronger class. I do not know, in fact, why Gustavus Adolphus's death is not tragic, or why, if a house collapses and women and children are crushed, this is merely an accident, and not a tragedy.

What is the origin of suffering, of a premature and horrible death? It is the result of our weakness in the face of Nature, the result of what is called pure chance. Forces beyond our control sometimes destroy our existence, and these are not necessarily social forces. The bourgeois social order plays its part here: thanks to its disorder, its scatteredness, its disjointedness, we are weak in the face of Nature. Marx said that people would need religion so long as they needed comforting, because they were weak in the face of Nature. When man has conquered Nature, then he will no longer need religion, and this feeling of tragedy which imbues the whole of our existence will disappear. When Engels spoke of the "leap from the kingdom of necessity into the kingdom of freedom", he said that to live in the kingdom of necessity is tragedy. It means to be forced to act against one's wishes, to enclose one's life in a frame which does not correspond to one's desires. The leap into the kingdom of freedom, on the other hand, means that one can mould one's life according to one's desires—that is, first and foremost, according to the laws of one's own existence, and this marks the end of human tragedy. Man is gradually becoming the master of Nature. From this point of view, capitalism appears as a state of affairs when man falls under the power of a disorganised society, under the power of the machine—the weapon which he himself has created for the enslavement of Nature. But capitalism is the final enslavement. When socialism has transformed the machine into a genuine servant of organised society, whose will becomes law, the transition from man's tragic introduction to history to the real, rational history of mankind will have taken place.

This is why I consider that Chernyshevsky was in essence completely right, and that Plekhanov confused a very important but still specific and partial tragedy with a huge general tragedy, which Chernyshevsky quite realistically opposed to the artifices dictated by the class interests of bourgeois democracy.

The idealists will argue, will try to doubt the existence and stability of reality. They will say that reality is "transitory and fleeting", or even "there is essentially no reality; where is it? As you said your last word, it has already gone; that moment which you call the present slips by, and it is impossible to stop it even for a second; you are already living in the future which, in its turn will become the past. Where is it then, this reality? It is simply an apparent, fleeting phenomenon. It is art which attempts as far as possible to halt reality. The rose which an artist has painted lives far longer than the real rose."

Chernyshevsky was aware of this line of reasoning, and this was his reply:

"It would be as boring to relive what one has already experienced, as it is to listen a second time to a funny story, however interesting it might have been the first time. It is necessary to distinguish real desires from imagined desires, which do not really want to be satisfied at all; it is a desire of the imagination, that beauty should in reality never fade. 'Life surges ahead and bears away the beauty of reality in its current,' say Hegel and Fichte. This is true, but as life surges ahead, so do our desires, that is, they alter in content; consequently, regrets at the disappearance of a beautiful phenomenon are the product of our fancy—a beautiful phenomenon disappears, its task completed, leaving behind as much aesthetic enjoyment as the present day could contain; tomorrow will be a new day, with new requirements, which only new beauty can satisfy. If beauty were in reality stationary and immutable—immortal, as the aesthetes demand—it would become boring and repugnant. A living person is not fond of the motionless in life; for this reason he can never look enough on living beauty, whereas he is quickly sated by the sight of a *tableau vivant*, which the high priests of art prefer to living scenes."*

Here are two diametrically opposite philosophies. An apology for peace and quiet: a person has found something he likes, and so he commands the moment: "Abide!", he cries to life: "Wait!" He wants everything to stand still at this instant. Very soon genuine enjoyment, a novice's enjoyment, has gone, and a blissful wonderment will take its place—a sensation which, as the priests promise, we shall enjoy in paradise when we gaze for eternity upon the Lord our God, our souls melting in bliss—Nirvana, a heavenly plunging into non-existence, into oblivion. All these motionless beauties are means of self-hypnosis, as sure a means of dulling our senses as the use of drugs. It is running away from life.

This is not what Chernyshevsky wants. He wants life to pulsate—only then is it beautiful. He wants it to be constantly altering. This is the revolutionary view of life, an idea which is inherent in the genuinely active nature, and only such natures are worthy

* N. G. Chernyshevsky, *Collected Works*, Vol. II, p. 42.

of life. Those people who consider the main thing in life to be peace and quiet can go off to the graveyard—they will find it there.

Let us turn to an analysis of the conflict between these two great writers—Chernyshevsky and Plekhanov—to the question of the significance of art. This is how Chernyshevsky defines it:

"The general characteristic sign of art, which reveals its essence, is the reproduction of life; works of art often have another meaning—an explanation of life; often, too, they are an evaluation of life's phenomena."*

In his opinion art is realistic and reproduces life, those features of life which might interest man. Essential features are depicted in the foreground, while less significant ones are relegated to the background. The effect of this is an explanation of life. Explanation here does not mean commentary, or a translation into rational language. This is what it means: when you have read Gogol's lines on Plyushkin, the meaning of miserly, inhuman and lifeless old age becomes perfectly clear. This will perhaps never be met with in life, or, at any rate, it will not be so clearly understood.

"The reproduction of all that in which man is interested in reality—that is the essential significance of art. But someone who is interested in life's phenomena cannot help, whether consciously or subconsciously, evaluating them; even if he wished to, a poet or an artist, incapable of not being human, could not refuse to offer his evaluation of what has been depicted—it is revealed in his work, and this is the new significance of works of art, by which art becomes one of man's moral activities."**

* N. G. Chernyshevsky, *Collected Works,* Vol. II, p. 92.
** *Ibid.*, p. 86.

So as not to quote too much, let us stop here and put what has been said into order.

What is art, according to Chernyshevsky?

Man is interested in many things in life; he can not only grasp the object of his interest with his intellect, but he can also absorb it, note it, approach it closely, study it with head and heart, and here he is helped by the artist. Belinsky has already established (and Chernyshevsky makes the same point) that when an artist talks about things, he explains them not as concepts but as images. But his images are explanatory images. Why? Because they divert attention from the fortuitous, and give only that which is most important. In this way, life's phenomena become clearer and more convincing. But, of course, conviction is not achieved by the artist saying, for example, "I love this man but not that one," and showing why this is so by a flood of publicist reasoning.

It is true that Chernyshevsky himself does this sometimes in his artistic works, but he considers this wrong. He says that our evaluation of life must come from this explanation by images thrown into bold relief. Whether you love or hate, whether this or that phenomenon, depicted by the artist, evokes pity or respect in you—this depends on your whole set-up, on your convictions, on how you would react to this phenomenon in life. Only in life, perhaps, you would not be able to grasp it immediately and would pass it by, whereas the artist has given you, in his image, the most essential and you have absorbed it.

Can one say that there is anything in this judgement of art, which we could not accept today? But this judgement of Chernyshevsky's—that an artist explains, that an artist evaluates life—frightens Plekhanov, and he declares: As far as the evaluation of a genuine artist is concerned, the philosophical, ethical or social influence of his works on people has nothing to do with it at all. Such an influence is of course possible, but there is no need to try and burden art with these academic aims. Plekhanov, of course, renounces art for art's sake; it goes without saying that an artist is fully occupied by the great ideas of his age, if he is indeed a great man, especially if he is a representative of the leading class. But, says Plekhanov, the enlightener in Chernyshevsky is revealed by the fact that he considers the especial significance of art to lie, not in the artist's images, not in the intuitive, not in that which distinguishes specifically artistic literature from intellectual activity in general, but in that which makes it akin to intellectual activity. Plekhanov points with horror at Chernyshevsky's words, that poetry invariably involves all types of knowledge. It seems to him that Chernyshevsky valued in art precisely that which was least important—mere trifles and trivialities; that he valued that which was there, but only incidentally; it is precisely by not using those elements which relate it with the intellect that art has its most powerful, most genuine and most educative effect.

Plekhanov sees here a flaw in Chernyshevsky's ideas on art which springs, in his opinion, from his notorious intellectualism.

Plekhanov and Chernyshevsky would agree that artistic creation is a moral activity. It is impossible to consider the creative work of a "pure" artist (which both Plekhanov and Chernyshevsky rejected) to be moral activity; if works of art give an evaluation, and if as a result of this evaluation we become wiser about life, more able to discern life's phenomena and receive a fresh stimulus to progressive action, then of course, the artist has fulfilled his moral mission.

What is the big difference between Plekhanov and Chernyshevsky here? It is that Plekhanov fears Chernyshevsky as a rationalist and enlightener; he is afraid that Chernyshevsky, at the back of his mind, wants to force the artist to this moral mission. Plekhanov says: We look on things, how they arise in Nature and in society, and we elucidate their causes. We can see in front of us, for example, a whole epoch, in which artists are not fulfilling their moral mission, but are occupied with what is called art for art's sake; but this cannot be otherwise, just as roses cannot bloom in winter, or snow fall in July. Those people who are divorced from life, who remain unsatisfied by reality, unfailingly turn towards the world of dreams and fantasy. We must understand and recognise this. Every flower has its season—and, in our epoch, flowers will grow, which will correspond to our epoch. But to dictate one's will, to say what art should be, this is impossible. We must forget such thoughts as: we want this kind of art, art must be like this. No, take art as life has made it, and explain in Marxian terms which class has expressed its tendencies in it. This is what Plekhanov says in his article "Chernyshevsky's Theory of Aesthetics":

"In our article on Belinsky's literary views we said that, in his arguments with supporters of pure art, he abandoned the standpoint of a *dialectic* for that of an *enlightener*. But Belinsky all the same looked more readily on the problem from a historical viewpoint. It was Chernyshevsky who transferred the problem once and for all into the realm of *abstract theorising* on the essence of art, or rather, on *what art should be*. 'Science does not consider itself higher than reality, and there is no disgrace in this,' he said at the end of his dissertation, 'neither must art consider itself higher than reality.... Let art be satisfied with its lofty function: to be some substitute for reality in its absence, and to be a textbook of life for man.' "

Plekhanov raises his arms to the sky and says: "These are the views of the purest kind of enlightener. To be a textbook of life means to serve the intellectual development of society. It is in this that the enlightener sees the main function of art."*

Let us take the bull by the horns, and see what it is that Plekhanov wants, first in the sphere of aesthetics and then in the sphere of ethics.

Plekhanov wants a Marxist, analytical and objective viewpoint on things; he says: Prescribe nothing to life, rather, elucidate it. We shall not discuss whether Plekhanov had similar thoughts in every sphere, but he maintained that, in the sphere of art, a Marxist must never say: Art must be such and such, but must always say: Art is such and such, and this is why.

Yes, before Marxism, people had only a vague idea of the essence of social phenomena. Chernyshevsky was a pre-Marxist materialist, so that he could easily exaggerate the power of human intellect and human will. As you know, Chernyshevsky did not believe in the people or the power of the people, and Plekhanov is right in saying that Chernyshevsky was not a Narodnik at all. He loved the people, wanted them to be rid of their oppression, but did not think that the people themselves would achieve this. The people would fight, would rise up for their rights in a universal revolution, only when aroused by another force—the intelligentsia, the leading intelligentsia, with him, Nikolai Gavrilovich, Dobrolyubov and other people of their type at its head. The intelligentsia and its revolutionary organisations could free the people by the incessant spreading of propaganda amongst others like them,

---

* G. V. Plekhanov, *Works*, Vol. VI, Gosizdat, 1925, p. 251.

by agitation amongst the people, and, perhaps, by terror (as you heard at the beginning of my lecture, Chernyshevsky said unequivocally: "I am not afraid of filth or of carnage").

Plekhanov says that this is utopian socialism, and he is right here without a doubt. From this point of view this is the action of an enlightener.* Chernyshevsky was a utopian, but let us consider what Marxism alters in Chernyshevsky's ideas on art.

Marxism has given a correct representation of the laws according to which social phenomena develop. But if we remove from Marxism the idea of consciousness, of the conscious controlling of phenomena, of the active role we play; if we take up the standpoint that we are to look upon social phenomena as processes, and discard any idea of active participation, then this would be Menshevik Marxism, in its most naked form. Is it not true that we are now the vanguard of the huge class, the proletariat, organised into a party, the greatest manifestation of conscious awareness which has ever existed?

We administer a state and comprise a government, which is in itself an expression of the dictatorship of the proletariat. We understand that it is not simply a matter of issuing a decree for everything to be as we want it. Of course not. But can one say that we are not to discuss the form of this or that phenomenon? If so, we would be the purest of pure

---

* In his first book on Chernyshevsky, Comrade Steklov tried to show that Chernyshevsky was not a utopian, but a thinker, whose philosophy almost entirely anticipated Marxism. Plekhanov was right in refuting this point of view and in proving that Chernyshevsky was indeed a utopian. In *Pod znamenem marksizma (Under the Banner of Marxism)*, No. 1, 1928, there is a new article by Steklov: "Was Chernyshevsky a Utopian?" I have not yet read it, but I can see from the title that Steklov is again trying to prove his former line of thought. I think this will be of no avail.

Mensheviks. But we are Marxists-Bolsheviks, Marxist statesmen and we argue as follows: Our first act dictated by Marxism must be the most carefully objective study of the class structure of society, the study of society, the study of the trends of development of productive forces, the study of trade and economics as a whole, a knowledge of the ideology of individual groups—the superstructures above this economic organism. But does this mean that we must merely confine ourselves to a definition of these objective forces? No—we do not spend our time underground, an intelligentsia with no links with the masses, with nothing for us to do except observe the progress of life—to the left or to the right. Our premises, of course, must be the objective data of life; but we are a leading party capable of influencing the course of events to a large extent. We have to sketch out a plan on the basis of an objective and scientific analysis, and there is practically nothing in the life of the country, including its culture, which this plan would not concern. How is it possible to assume, for example, that we can avoid the problem of which kind of literature we should value, develop and support, and that which we should fight against? Everybody knows that the Party Central Committee has issued a manifesto on literature.

To take an example from the sphere of social economics. The development of country life under bourgeois conditions is as follows: the middle layer —the peasants with average-sized holdings—is dividing into the poor peasants and the kulaks. An upper stratum inevitably arises and forms a rural bourgeoisie. But the effect of these laws is quite different under the influence of the dictatorship of the proletariat, under the power of the Soviets. We not only affirm this, but note directly and sharply that it is dependent on us, since we support the poor and unite them into collective farming, bring pressure to bear on the kulak, alienate the middle peasant from him, take away his political opportunities and subject him to high taxation.

A tree which has grown in the forest gives sour fruit, but after grafting it gives beautiful sweet pears. We, by consciously altering Nature's phenomena, are just such gardeners; and we do not have to be miracle-workers either; this is no miracle—it is active use of knowledge, and it is Bolshevik Marxism.

Chernyshevsky imagined that he and his set were already controlling social phenomena, whereas this tiny handful of intelligentsia could in fact do nothing worthwhile socially, could not induce the peasants to follow them, could not organise them. For this reason Chernyshevsky was a utopian. Marx and his disciples established that, for there to be the possibility of a social revolution, capitalism had first to plough the land with a steel plough, thereby creating its own gravedigger—the proletariat, so that the proletariat could become organised. Then in the midst of the proletariat, the Party begins to be formed as its conscious vanguard, whose power lies in the knowledge of the laws by which society develops—a society in which the proletariat plays the progressive role. Marxism, a scientific sociology, safeguards us from fantastic and arbitrary theories and points to the real trend of history. But if, apart from this knowledge, we achieve nothing else, then we shall merely be swept along with the current. In Russia, for example, capitalism only reached a very low stage of development; there were very few workers in the towns, and a social revolution would have become inevitable only after many years. Should we really only have acted within the limits permitted by fate?

The Narodniks,* who wanted to rely on the support of the peasant millions and stir up a revolution, were of course unable to do this. But perhaps the proletariat will prove to have sufficient strength to do what the others could not? This is a step backwards, according to Plekhanov. At the Stockholm Conference Plekhanov shouted to Lenin: "I can sense something old in your new ideas." To what was he referring? To Chernyshevsky. Yet he was wrong if he thought there was anything new in this—it was genuine Marxism. In 1877 Marx wrote the famous letter to Mikhailovsky, which all the Mensheviks puzzled over for a long time, before coming to the conclusion that Marx was joking. But Marx was a serious person and would never have started joking in his letters to Russian revolutionaries. This letter agitated and tormented one of the finest men in the country: Gleb Ivanovich Uspensky. He read and reread it, shedding many bitter tears over it. Why? Marx wrote that Russia had let slip a unique opportunity: a group of her revolutionary-conscious intelligentsia could have stood at the head of a peasant revolutionary movement and changed the course of events, the course of historical development. But now, Marx wrote, the moment had passed, this could not be done, and Russia had irrevocably entered onto the road of capitalism. Uspensky understood this and believed in the truth of Marx's words, but the Menshevik "Marxists" said that Marx was either joking or mistaken. Uspensky took to drink and went out of his mind; amongst other factors, Marx's letter played a part in this. It seemed to Uspensky that as this moment passed, the country would perish. But Marx did not have this in mind at all;

---

* *Narodniks*—followers of a petty-bourgeois trend, Narodism, in the Russian revolutionary movement, which arose in the sixties and seventies of the 19th century.—*Ed.*

he said: Like the other countries, the "unholy" countries, your "holy Rus" has entered onto the road of capitalist development.

In other words, now wait for the proleteriat. Once the proletariat is there, then your time will have come; but without the proletariat there will be no revolution. When the proletariat came, its column of seven to eight million proved to be the real guides and organisers of the hundred-million strong army of peasants.

We have traced the line of this "old idea" of Lenin. Capitalism indeed had not sufficiently matured here, and the proletariat still did not form the majority of the population; but, taking advantage of the historical state of affairs in our country which prepared the way for the peasants' agrarian uprising, we considered it necessary to risk a social revolution.

People have objected: All right, granted that you have succeeded in getting power into your own hands, but what are you going to do with these peasants now? They have got their land and there is nothing more that you can do with them. Surely you do not imagine that you can bring socialism to a country in which most of the population are peasants?

The Marxists-Bolsheviks, however, were not alarmed. They said: We do not think, we *know* that this is possible. It is possible, if we manage to build a firm Soviet state, a dictatorship of the proletariat, which will lead the peasants. In such circumstances it is most certainly possible for the peasants to move forward to socialism by their own, characteristic method—the co-operative method, which here includes both common ploughland and collectivisation; a method which was discussed at the Party's Fifteenth Congress.

It is this distinction between Menshevik fatalism and Bolshevik action, which we must remember in our discussions on literature.

Has present-day criticism the right to talk about literature from the point of view of what it should be? Can it, has it the right to say that writers are bound to write to order, that the best readers demand material to increase their knowledge, to study the life of the classes and social groups of the country, in this transitory period? Have we the right to demand that writers depict positive characters, who illustrate what a young citizen of our republic should be like, to demand that writers be able to brand and show as despicable in our eyes those vices and shortcomings which harm our development? Have we the right to impose these ethical demands on literature? Are we right or not, when we turn our backs on the "sweet sounds and prayers", and declare that our literature must be an ethical force, must aid our self-education, that our literature is in itself a process of self-education for our class? I think that we are right. And who, then, is right: Plekhanov who maintains that it is a great sin to say that our literature must be like this; or Chernyshevsky with his ideas on the writer's moral activity? Plekhanov himself said that each class creates a literature in its own likeness and image, for its own needs; he said that, when a class progresses, all its actions are conscious actions. When, for example, the age of chivalry, at its height, created the chivalrous novel which was to increase the knight's respect for himself, this was not done unconsciously but with a large share of class-consciousness.

Of course, not all the culture of a class arises consciously, but the more conscious, the more organised it is, the more conscious will be all its actions and development.

The proletarian class cannot allow literature to grow like mushrooms in a wood. A gardener's, cultivator's attitude to life is characteristic of the proletariat, the new rising class. Its policy is not only an explanation of reality in the face of the laws of Nature, but also a technical combination which will alter the development of phenomena. This is the active quality in Marxism.

This is why I say that Chernyshevsky's aesthetics, with its impassioned hatred for the concept of art as a substitute for reality, with its deep love for reality, with its desire for the growth, development and flowering of a genuine existence, with its negative attitude towards lifelessness and its claim that art reflects what interests man, and does not simply reflect everything like a mirror—this is why I say that Chernyshevsky's aesthetics is both important and acceptable to us. Chernyshevsky's basic line of thought that art evaluates life—that it evokes from us a definite emotional reaction to what is depicted—and that the artist has a moral influence and helps the rise of culture, is absolutely correct. We declare that, although Chernyshevsky was not a Marxist, we Marxists can accept this teaching. Not possessing the Marxist method, for instance, he would not have been able to explain the reason for the transition in Russian literature from the 20s to the 30s. We have a Marxist spotlight which illuminates the hidden roots of events, the necessary link of phenomena —this is our tremendous advantage. But in possessing the means of scientific analysis, we must not forget the active role we have to play, a role which Chernyshevsky understood so well.

Let us now make a small excursion into the realm of Chernyshevsky's ethics. Plekhanov did not devote very many pages to this subject, but what he wrote is extraordinarily profound and effective. Chernyshevsky's theory of ethics is not particularly complicated and can be summed up in a small number of categorical theses.

In order to determine the essence of Chernyshevsky's ethical viewpoint, Plekhanov takes the following quotation from him:

"When one examines closely the impulses which control people's actions, it turns out that every action, good or bad, noble or mean, heroic or cowardly, comes from one source in everyone. A person behaves as it is most pleasurable for him to behave; he is controlled by a common sense which makes him refuse that which will bring him least advantage or least pleasure, and turn to that which will bring him most advantage, most pleasure."[*]

Here Chernyshevsky anticipated the question: Would he deny the fact that a man can die for his loved ones, for his country, for an ideal, etc? Chernyshevsky would not deny it. Thus it seems that this is a somewhat eccentric egoist, who would prefer his own annihilation, as being more advantageous. Chernyshevsky was not at all put out by this, and said:

"A fastidious person would far rather face starvation than touch food which has been defiled by filth; for someone accustomed to self-respect, death is far easier than humiliation."[**]

This is an extremely important ethical position, bearing witness to the fact that Chernyshevsky's ethics are by no means primitive. He says that there are occasions, when without sacrificing oneself, one dooms oneself to an extraordinarily wretched life; a life which would perhaps be outwardly humiliating —one would be living in fear of something or other, or in slavery, amid humiliation, insult and suffering, etc.; or perhaps one's own self-respect would, as a result, fall to such an extent that all joy of life would vanish. A person who does not consider himself

---

[*] G. V. Plekhanov, *Works*, Vol. V, p. 215.
[**] *Ibid.*, p. 216.

worthy to live, who despises himself, who constantly hears a voice condemning him—such a person has no lust for life, and if he is intelligent, he will prefer to die. Better to die than to live a life full of humiliation.

Plekhanov is quite right when he says that a man's preferences or the way he behaves do not in fact depend on his reason or common sense at all. Even if we took up a rational standpoint, even if we believed that everyone thought before acting, then we would have to say that some, not easily definable quantity enters into his reasoning. Why, for instance, does one man prefer to steal so as not to be hungry, whereas another prefers to starve rather than steal? Can we really say that there are completely impartial scales on which both actions can be weighed and that everybody solves the same problem in the same way? We know that different people solve the same problem in different ways, depending on what they have inherited and how they have been brought up, as Plekhanov quite correctly remarks. Even if we begin to talk about rational behaviour—that which arises out of reasoning—even in this case, what one prefers depends, not on the force of one's reasoning, but on the degree of pleasure, on the value which one places on the advantage to be gained. This depends on character, on the way, in other words, in which a given person has been moulded. From our modern scientific psychological standpoint, we can say that it depends on what reflexes the person in question possesses, on what his prevailing reactions are. Having established this, we shall realise that reasoning is a complex reaction which, very often, never occurs. Action does not always arise out of so-called thought, that is, out of a complex pattern of different reflexes, some of which banish the rest; very often people react immediately, without thinking. A good or bad character, a courageous or cowardly one, depends not so much on the amount of reasoning capacity as on the complex of reflexes.

Plekhanov pays a great deal of attention, quite rightly of course, to the fact that a person's character is formed, not spontaneously, but by society—the example of his family, the street and the school, barracks, the press and public opinion. His social environment is a vast educational apparatus, in which society strives to make man, by nature untamed, into a social being—strives, that is, to distort, or on the contrary, to ennoble his instincts so that they become social instincts, so that society receives the greatest possible benefit from them. According to most people, moral behaviour is that which is of benefit to society as a whole; it can therefore be said that society is bringing constant influence to bear on people, so that, instead of becoming criminal or violating the general rules, they act according to these rules and behave correctly. To induce man to behave correctly and according to the generally established rules is the aim of every society.

Chernyshevsky's reasoning appears from this point of view to be almost childish. A person, whether he reasons or not, acts as a result of the reflexes which have been formed in him, mostly under the pressure of society's educational force; Plekhanov speaks about this as follows:

"Let us suppose that we have a society not divided into strata or classes. In such a society those actions of individuals which coincide with the interests of all will be considered good, whereas those which contradict these interests will be considered bad. In other words, at the source of every judgement on good or evil, will lie what might be called the egoism of the whole, or *public egoism*. But egoism of the whole does not exclude the altruism of each person or *individual altruism*. On the contrary, it is its source: society strives to educate its members, so that they place the interests of society above their own private interests; the more a man's behaviour *satisfies* this demand of society, the more self-denying, moral and altruistic this person will be. Yet the more his behaviour *violates* this demand, the more selfish, immoral and egoistic he will be. This is the criterion which has always—with greater or lesser consciousness of the fact—been applied and is applied, when the question of the altruism or egoism of the behaviour of such and such a person is considered; the vast gulf here, between the one and the other, constitutes precisely that whole whose interests in any one case are placed above those of the individuals. . . .

"Man's education in the spirit of morality means that his behaviour, which is of benefit to society, becomes an instinctive need (Kant's 'categorical imperative'). The stronger this need, the more moral the individual. People are called heroes when they cannot but obey this need, even when its satisfaction goes decidedly against their own material interests —threatens them with death, for instance. The enlighteners, Chernyshevsky among them, did not usually take this into account. It might, moreover, be added that Kant was no less mistaken than the enlighteners, when he maintained that moral impulses have no relation with social benefit. Neither was he able in this case to see things from the point of view of development, and trace *individual altruism* to *public egoism.*"*

Brought up entirely in the spirit of a given society, or a given class, a man acts as if instinctively, and those reflexes which have been instilled into him by social pressure are transformed into instincts. This cannot be doubted. And yet a significant "but" arises here, which I shall now speak about.

---

* G. V. Plekhanov, *Works*, Vol. V., pp. 218-19.

Chernyshevsky says: A man in a dilemma reasons how it would be best for him to act in this instance, and he chooses one or the other action with the aid of common sense. What he chooses might be in no way what he wants. For example: a house is on fire, and a person must decide what is better— to burn to death or to throw himself from the fifth floor. Under normal circumstances he would of course not have to throw himself out, but here he is forced to do so. It does not follow from this, however, that he likes jumping from the fifth floor. In this case it is merely the lesser of two evils. And always, under all circumstances, a person will choose the least evil or the greatest good.

You think it was you who have chosen? Plekhanov objects. No; it was your upbringing and your character which chose for you, and upbringing and character do not depend on you yourself. Much depends on the kind of body you were born with, and even more on the kind of tastes, instincts and concepts which social life, of which you are a part, has developed in you.

This is, of course, true; but from this we might draw the conclusion that, in the sphere of morals, we are also to a greater or lesser extent observers. We watch people act, but it turns out that they are not, in reality, acting at all, that is, they are not committing any acts. A process is being performed, in which it is not the people who are choosing, but something in them which is choosing. This something is a social something; and everywhere, in everything, we see the splashes of the social ocean. In nobody can there be any active desire, any active creation.

Chernyshevsky's point of view is one of human activity. He says that man chooses the least evil or the greatest good, and is controlled by this in life; man for this reason is an egoist. To say: I am a hero, a benefactor, etc., is meaningless. Everybody does what he finds to his liking. If when I like something, others like it too, so much the better. Chernyshevsky considers that an honest, courageous, social person cannot demand any reward for himself. Such a person will receive his reward from the action itself. This is a very fine, honest and pure standpoint, but it is by no means the most important point. What is important is the theory of man's behaviour. Like Holbach and Helvetius, Chernyshevsky thought that man chooses the laws of his behaviour; Plekhanov says, on the other hand, that everything takes place according to a law, and that there is no choice: man has only the illusion that he is choosing, whereas in fact he is choosing according to the laws of his nature, a nature which has arisen as a result of social influences.

Why then do these rationalists, these enlighteners appear? When do they arise? They have arisen, and we must explain this. Why did Helvetius and Chernyshevsky think that everyone was an egoist, a person who chose what suited him best? What does this mean when certain epochs produce people who say: There are no morals, commandments or duties; man is completely free and chooses whatever he likes most of all—and the person who realises this is a genuine person? What is the historical reason for these enlighteners?

It happens when stable morals crumble; when the morals of a ruling class and its whole epoch fall to pieces; when a new class comes to the fore, which has as yet no established morals, but which initially advanced in the form of a revolutionary vanguard, destroying the old system.

These "critically thinking people", who shatter the old system, appear, if you like, as the necessary expression of the process of decay of the old stable world and of the appearance of a new society. One can, for example, say that the Rakhmetovs, the Lopukhovs and all Chernyshevsky's other heroes, that Chernyshevsky himself and Dobrolyubov—none of them had been brought up by one or another class in the spirit of definite reactions. I do not think that their priest's, seminarist environment instilled in them definite reactions, which they understood as a new set of morals. I think this idea is incorrect. They entered life as people who doubted the morals of their fathers—such morals no longer appealed to them at all. They entered life at a moment when the morals of the petty bourgeoisie, out of which they had arisen, had already been shattered. Although they were no longer in its power, the laws of autocracy and the morals of the nobility, etc., were no more acceptable. Against all this they set their freedom.

From the viewpoint of materialist determinism, their freedom was, of course, illusory—but not so from the social aspect.

They declared: We renounce every duty; we do not wish to act according to any commandment, we want to be free. And they wanted their right to freedom to be realised. We know that, even in some ancient societies, there were people who were unhampered by any firm commandments, who declared that man is the measure of all things. Such people were frequently cynical, because as soon as one has denied the existence of God, of the soul, of duties, laws and standards of behaviour, then every delicious feeling and moment must be pursued—"everything is permitted". Remember in Dostoyevsky, how Smerdyakov interpreted this phrase: "everything is permitted"; perhaps Ivan Karamazov is a noble figure, since for him "everything is permitted" is only a phrase, whereas Smerdyakov would commit a vile deed. There is a Smerdyakov in each person: give him freedom and he will behave vilely. This is how Dostoyevsky understands this amoralism. But when people are set onto new paths by a new, revolutionary way of life, they do not have vile deeds in mind at all; they announce their freedom—they need freedom, because they find they possess a special spiritual reserve, or as we would say now, a definite type of reflex.

Vladimir Solovyov ironically stated Chernyshevsky's philosophy as follows: "Man is descended from the apes; after death he will have burdock growing out of him—therefore let us die for the community," and he then roared with laughter, clutching his sides. Surely, if man is descended not from the apes, but from Adam, into whose breast the Lord God breathed a soul in his own likeness and image, then why die for the community? In that case of course, one would have to wait until one's soul, having abandoned its earthly shell, returned to the Lord God and lived there in everlasting bliss. If death did not result in burdock growing out of one's body, but in the gates of paradise or hell opening, then it would be a completely different matter. Solovyov considered that, if there is no soul and death means the end of everything, then we must inevitably be scoundrels and will inevitably commit vile deeds against one another. Only if there is heaven and hell, reward and punishment, will people not commit vile deeds. This is, in essence, a medieval, even a primitive idea. The learned Solovyov fails to understand Chernyshevsky not from the majestic heights where he imagines himself to be, but just like some primitive savage. Chernyshevsky says that if life is a short-lived biological process, then let us make it as happy a one as possible; but it is impossible to make life as happy as possible for the individual because, in the first place, it is fearfully difficult to create your own happiness in an atmosphere of hatred, egoism, pressure from those stronger than you, etc.; and secondly, there is your conscience: it is difficult, agonising, impossible even, to take advantage of your good fortune, knowing that next to you people are dying, and that you are taking advantage of their forced labour, their deaths, just so you can be happy. For this reason, a social revolution is necessary in order to create life which is really rational, a life which will mean happiness for everybody. Once this is so, then the only genuine rational happiness, the only real justification of life, is the participation in a revolution, in working with all one's strength. And if it should turn out that this is impossible in one generation—well then, we will do it in several generations; if it turns out that it will not be we who will fulfil this task, who *can* fulfil this task, let us act in the name of the people. This is how that generation built a bridge from amoralism, from the theory of egoism to service of the people, something of which Vladimir Solovyov is ignorant.

Such feelings are those of someone attuned to revolution, who regards everything critically and wishes to act rationally. Of course, a Marxist, standing to one side as an observer of such ethics, will say: All this is, in essence, an illusion; behaviour is, in fact, predestined according to a law. But as Plekhanov himself, in his brilliant criticism of fatalistic determinism correctly remarks: Given the fact that every step we take is predetermined, that each of our actions is performed according to a law, it does not follow that we act blindly. From the point of view of some future historian, everything will appear as a natural process. But in our eyes, the eyes of people who are actually alive in given conditions, everything is willed, a definite action, a creative activity. We feel this precisely because the process we are explaining is the process of life itself, the process of organic creative activity.

Plekhanov understood this very well, but in this case he went off at a somewhat obtuse angle. He should have taken into account that the ethical ideas of Chernyshevsky and his fellow thinkers not only corresponded objectively to the historical circumstances of the time, but were also the most appropriate, the most capable of developing people's will to action—of jolting man out of his stagnant environment into a life full of bright creative activity—a life hailed by Chernyshevsky, Pisarev and Dobrolyubov.

We all, of course, realise that the formation of a new set of morals, for example, is a complicated social process. But does this mean that we must not at once actively set about examining the fundamentals of morality? Here in front of us is a young proletarian who acts always, without reasoning first, in the proletarian manner. His social upbringing has evidently become instinctive, and for this we can envy him. But this is far from being the case with everyone. The person who lacks such a mature social upbringing, who on the one hand wants to act like a genuine proletarian and yet, on the other, feels his own passions, prejudices and failings pushing him in the opposite direction—this person will be faced with an inner moral conflict. Are we able to educate such people? Yes. The bourgeoisie strives to educate, to transform certain reflexes and modes of behaviour into instincts. We must do this, too. We must do this in the nursery, in the school, by means of direct environmental influence, by influencing each other and ourselves, so that the proletarian elements triumph and become instinctive—so that they are transformed, as Vladimir Ilyich said, into a proletarian morality. We are not saying that the proletariat is building its morality intuitively, like a spider spinning its web. When one set of morals has crumbled and another is still being formed, when you have actively to create the rules of your behaviour, how is it possible not to reason? When someone turned to St. Paul with a question about God, he answered: "And who are you to ask about the Lord our God?" We are not satisfied with such an "apostolic" answer; we want to know, we want to explain why such rules and standards of behaviour are the only rational and lawful ones. Who will say to me: "Don't think about this; man, in fact, does not think, for it is the reflexes formed by society which are speaking in him"? What is this to me, when I need to know how to act tomorrow; whether or not I should steal a book from a friend and sell it. If I do not do this I shall be unable to repay my debts and shall starve; whereas if I do it, I shall despise myself. I am not able to sleep at night, turning from side to side, wondering how to act.

There are always moral conflicts, hesitations and contradictions, but especially when morals are on the decline; when, on the one hand, no obligation or morality is involved and a person must look at things directly, considering things from a purely utilitarian point of view; and, on the other hand, he must ask himself whether it would be better to act from the point of view of his own self-esteem, but not his own interests, or take up the standpoint of his own class, although it would mean the end of him as an individual. If I am told that it is necessary, on each occasion, to act according to certain rules of behaviour, then I demand that these rules of behaviour prove themselves.

Our morality cannot be intuitive, categorically prescribed; it must show that it is right. But is it possible to live without a code of morals? Standards of behaviour are necessary; they must be developed and transformed into norms of upbringing.

If this is so, however, we are approaching very close to Chernyshevsky, because, if we consider that man must reason out and choose for himself the rules of his behaviour, then obviously he must choose the best rules from a rational point of view. Each person, as an egoist, has the right and the possibility to choose that which is best for him; we go up to him and say: I shall explain to you how you are to behave, and I shall show that this is the best way for you to behave. Once we have accepted this, we shall be very close to Chernyshevsky. How is it that Chernyshevsky's theory of egoism, which is, at first sight so naive, and which Plekhanov, it seemed, was easily able to demolish with his penetrating criticism, how is it that this theory has once again come up?

It is because the period in which we are living, the obligations which are placed upon us and the behaviour which this period dictates to us, are like those which Chernyshevsky imagined to be existing in his lifetime.

Chernyshevsky imagined that he was a great teacher, that he would rally around himself a party, a party of the intelligentsia, which would reorganise life and create a new, rational morality; he imagined that he would be able to prove that this was indeed a rational morality, and that any other form of morality was invalid. But his ideas about the period in which he lived and the role he was to fulfil were illusory. We, however, are in such a position. Only recently we were saying that we would not write a code of morality and behaviour, but now it is obvious that we shall not get anywhere without it. Young people are demanding it. We should picture the genuine proletarian to ourselves: what sort of a person is he, and how does he behave in different circumstances? What do good and evil mean to us? We cannot rely on instinct prompting us. We are the people who are educating new generations and attempting to shed the light of reason on every problem—can we really rely upon instinct and say, "Don't worry, somehow everything will turn out well"? No, we cannot say that a young citizen can live without standards of behaviour. Lenin tells us plainly that a code of morals will come, the fundamental position of which will be quite clear: in this transitional period, a period of struggle, each person must ensure that his behaviour corresponds to the interests of his entire class. From this arise very many points which have yet to be developed.

I do not mean that Plekhanov, if he were to think about the moral tasks which face us today, would not say what Vladimir Ilyich said, or what I am saying now. But there is the feeling, when he approaches Chernyshevsky, that he departs somewhat from this position; he seems to overemphasise the fact that everything arises naturally, that actions are not in fact actions, but processes, the result of definite causes. Why is this so? It is because Plekhanov represents the stage in the development of the proletariat and of proletarian ideology, when it was necessary to destroy the subjectivism and the utopianism of Mikhailovsky. This had to be destroyed mercilessly; it had to be shown that, until the groundwork had been laid, until the masses had come to the forefront and acquired the energy and a definite organisation, there could be no progress or victory. So do not imagine that one man can control a crowd, that one man can untie the knots of history. Go to the proletariat, and help it develop and organise themselves; help it to act in conjunction with the forces of history. Only then, only when your own wishes coincide with the laws of social development, will you be victorious.

Everything rational is real, and everything real is rational. Does this mean that what is rational must inevitably become real? But how long will this take? When will today's irrationality mature into tomorrow's rationality? Everything real is rational. But this means that there is an irrational element in present-day reality: something which in fact belongs to yesterday and which is dying away. You must therefore take up the standpoint of tomorrow's rationality, and help its development; only by acting in unison with Nature and by aiding the course of history will you be able to achieve anything.

While Mikhailovsky was forming his toothless subjectivism—his theory that one can change the course of history at will—Plekhanov was the mighty harbinger of truth, the teacher of the wisdom of life. Everything he says is true, but does it represent the whole truth? No; it is perhaps two-thirds of the truth—nine-tenths even—but not the whole truth.

It is necessary to co-operate with reality. When we were underground, the words "unleash the revolution" seemed to the Mensheviks to be improbable and fearfully daring. Why? Revolution is an elemental phenomenon which happens quite naturally like the phases of the moon. Can one speed up the moon's phases? Of course not. Our mind and will can influence phenomena only to a certain extent, can lend a helping hand, as it were. The romantic revolutionaries of the strictly Narodnik type found this vexing; they considered themselves a united force which was leaving its imprint on the epoch. What imprint? One only needed to explain why something had happened, only needed to help old man history on his way a little, for everything to advance. When we were underground, what sort of an aid to history was it, for example, when we had taught the workers of the Obukhov Factory with the aid of the pamphlet *Who Lives From What*? Compare that with what October had to offer! Historical events of tremendous world-wide significance took place—everything was done consciously and in an organised fashion. The moment came with such swiftness, such a huge accumulation of forces, so charged with revolutionary fervour and energy, that it only needed organisation to make it prevail. We Bolsheviks, still underground, knew that this moment would come.

Let me once again remind you of Engels's great phrase about the leap from the kingdom of necessity into the kingdom of freedom. What did Engels mean by this? Once human will is organised, it assumes a tremendous power over the fate of mankind. Marx stressed the point more than once that man believes in gods, etc., because of his confused and chaotic social relationships; but as soon as society has been organised, man will be above social laws and his whole destiny will be subordinate to reason, will be shaped according to reason.

We are already at the turning point. We already have the beginnings of a socialist society and the dictatorship of a politically conscious class—the proletariat; in ourselves we bear the consciousness of the class which represents the summit of human destiny. This means that consciousness, organised consciousness, is acquiring for us greater and greater power. This power is not limitless—it is perhaps very limited: phenomena must first be thoroughly analysed before they can be influenced; they must be correctly evaluated so that there should be no mistakes, but it is nonetheless possible to influence and alter them. Human morals, the rules of behaviour, can be included here. One can no longer say, like Plekhanov, that morals depend on upbringing—as you have been brought up, so you will behave. And yet, according to Plekhanov, that is, through the influence of our society, we must inculcate these rules in people. But since it is we now who are

educating, since every school, the press, the whole
economy and all educative forces are in our hands,
we have to ask ourselves how, in what spirit, we
shall educate, what do we consider to be genuinely
good, and how shall we manage, by conscious and
careful selection, to transform this element of good
into instinct? We must define the methods of education and the means by which we shall instil social,
proletarian morality into a child, develop his
thoughts, make him consider different motives of
conduct and chose that which is of greatest social
benefit.

This explains why we are nine-tenths in agreement with Plekhanov; but over his head we stretch
out our hands to this utopian socialist who ascribed
such huge significance to the power of the human
reason and will. Marxism has cut these factors
extremely short, and has shown that they are themselves subject to objective laws; at the same time
it has shown that, as the proletariat becomes more
organised, as it takes the power into its own hands,
so will the sphere of influence of will and reason
widen more and more—and not as the utopians
imagined it, but in reality.

This is why Chernyshevsky's ethics and aesthetics
and his illusory ideas on the power of man's reason
over reality seem very close to us now, and a great
deal of Plekhanov's criticism of Chernyshevsky is no
longer valid. For this reason, I cannot agree with
Comrade Steklov when he says that Chernyshevsky
was not a utopian; but neither do I agree with
Plekhanov who says that, since Chernyshevsky was
a utopian, his entire system of ethics and aesthetics
was completely useless, that he approached these
problems the way he did precisely because he was
a utopian, and that nothing can be obtained from
his teaching. Chernyshevsky's ideas are important to
the person who is certain of victory, important to us

because we are building socialism, because we have power, even if limited, over events.

This is what can be said about Chernyshevsky's ethics and aesthetics, if judged from a contemporary standpoint in the light of the new conditions. Chernyshevsky himself as a person and everything that he left behind represents the most tremendous and valuable of heritages.

When I met N. K. Krupskaya the other day, she asked me what I was engaged in. I mentioned that, among other things, I was preparing a lecture on Chernyshevsky in the Communist Academy. Nadezhda Konstantinovna said to me:

"There was hardly anyone Vladimir Ilyich loved so much as Chernyshevsky. With him he felt an intimate affinity; he had an extraordinarily deep respect for him." And then after a moment's thought, she said:

"I think there was a great deal in common between Chernyshevsky and Vladimir Ilyich." I do not, in fact, know whether there was much in common— there were differences, as well as common points— but I do know that, in the evaluation of human calibre, of beauty and the shape of character, these two people did indeed stand close to each other. Lenin's heritage and wisdom represent for us and for untold ages to come a rich treasure-house for study. Chernyshevsky, too, has left much behind, which must be recognised, not merely as a wonderful memorial to a definite era, but also as something which ought to be studied.

With this lecture I wished to contribute to precisely such an evaluation of Chernyshevsky.

1928

II

THE idea of instituting the annual celebration of "Pushkin's Day" is an excellent one, for what Pushkin means to the Russian people and to Russian literature is beyond assessment.

Of course, the immensity of Pushkin's genius is beyond question. Nevertheless, it is not just a matter of his immense gifts.

"Better be born lucky than rich," the proverb tells us. One might paraphrase it something like this: be born a genius by all means—but the most important thing is to be born at the right time.

Taine asserted that literature was conditioned by race, climate and the moment, thus, apparently, obliterating the part played by the individual. Goethe, in the foreword to his autobiography says: "Had I been born 20 years earlier or later, I would have been quite a different person." We Marxists also contend that the individual personality is, at least to a very, very considerable extent, the reflection of its own time. Of course, a significant moment of time can only be reflected in a significant individual. It is possible to imagine an epoch which failed to produce an individual adequate to express it (although this seldom happens, for the average artistic potential of humanity varies but little from age to age). In such a case, what we would have would be a poet whose work was interesting in content but imperfect in form. It is possible to imagine a great talent in an epoch when nothing much is happening (something which occurs quite frequently). In this case what we have is great perfection of form allied to insignificance of content.

But, the reader will say, surely there was nothing so very great about Pushkin's epoch? Surely it could hardly be called a happy epoch? Why, it is difficult to imagine a duller epoch, and Pushkin found no peace in it, suffered, dreamt of going abroad, died tangled up in the nets of autocracy, of a soulless society, of repulsive literary relationships, etc., etc.

All this is perfectly true. It was a time of early spring, so early that everything was still shrouded in mist and disease-bearing germs were swarming and breeding in exceptional numbers—a windy spring, grey and rather muddy. Yet those who came before Pushkin were too early to catch a glimpse of the spring sun, to hear the gurgling of the streams. Their hearts had not thawed out, their lips were wry and stiff, and they could only mutter indistinctly in the frosty air. Those who came after Pushkin, on the other hand, were in the position of successors, for the most important words had already been said— by Pushkin.

The classic age of any national literature is by no means always the most brilliant in respect of politics, economics or culture. It is the first age of the first stirrings of what I should call the youthful maturity of the educated classes of any given nation. Just as soon as circumstances permit of a nation's being born, of its establishing itself, just as soon as its talents have scope to develop, it immediately begins to forge a language while the medium is still malleable, still responsive. There is no occasion to juggle, to invent, to be clever-clever. It is enough to take with both hands from the treasury of popular speech and to name things with its help, as Adam in the Bible named all the newly created phenomena of the world about him.

The same applies to content. No one has yet expressed one single live, supple, complex feeling. When those feelings have accumulated in the soul, they break out through all dams and obstacles with a reviving freshness, an extraordinary naturalness. This positive, natural, organic quality is the distinguishing mark of the classic. Though you be the wisest of the wise, though your genius exceed the genius of the classical epoch—you will still be nothing but an epigonus, for you will be using the language which the classics used and, already, that language has become the ordinary tongue of everyday speech. Or else—wanting to go further—you will go too far and fall into all kinds of mannerism, exaggeration, pedantry, provincialism, etc., etc. Time itself becomes more complex in content and more profound in significance in the measure in which the passing years gradually accumulate a vast variety of knowledge and experience. However, if we wish to appear original we may not select the most significant features from all this store. It becomes essential to seek refuge in impressionism, that is, to call attention to the fortuitous and passing, because the essential has already been noted; or in deformation, that is, in a tendency to distort natural phenomena because, as they really are, they have already been superbly reproduced and magnified by the giants of the classic period; or in the mists of symbolism, trying to see beyond the object to those "complex" and "mysterious" secrets of which the soul of the post-classic artist is so richly aware.

Epigonous art is a fearful thing. There is no denying that in the ranks of such artists there may be giants of no less stature than the classic author, nor yet that imitative literature may be extremely elegant, powerful, even deeply moving. Nevertheless, people will always look back, in their best moments, to Goethe, to Mozart, or, further, to other classical periods, to Homer, to Kalidasa—and will feel that here is true, untroubled, profound, restful, healing, ennobling beauty and that all later eccentricities, spasms and fantasies although not devoid of value, do not in themselves add up to progress.

It may be that the great flood of social revolution and the entrance on the scene of the proletariat will prove capable of refreshing art down to its very base and up from its foundations. But this question is still very much in the balance and, of course, it is unthinkable that, in the name of this hoped-for renewal, we should reduce ourselves to the state of a naked man on the naked earth.

The proletariat *is* able to renew the culture of mankind, but in deep-rooted connection with and dependence from the culture of the past. In this connection it may well be that our best hope should be in a hitherto unprecedented phenomenon, not so much in a renaissance as in a Faustian renewal of youth with new strength and a new future—retaining the memory of all that has been, but not feeling it as a drag upon the soul.

Let us leave this question aside for the moment and return to Pushkin. Pushkin was the Russian spring, Pushkin was the Russian morning, Pushkin was the Russian Adam. What Dante and Petrarch did for Italy, the giants of the seventeenth century for France, Lessing, Schiller and Goethe for Germany—Pushkin did for us. He suffered much, because he was the first, although indeed, those writers of Russia who came after him, from Gogol to Korolenko, also, to judge by their own admissions, shouldered no light burden of sorrows. He suffered much because his miraculous, fiery, exquisite genius blossomed in the harsh climate of a Russia where it was still almost winter, almost night. To compensate, he had the "start" on all other Russian writers. He was the firstcomer and, by right of prior claim, took possession of the greatest treasures in all the stronghold of literature.

He took possession of them with a sovereign hand, skilled and tender; so exhaustively, so melodiously, and with such grace did he express the essence of the Russian soul and of feelings common to all humanity that it overwhelms with gratitude the hearts of all those who, in learning the great Russian language, or on sipping their first from the hallowed springs of true art, first taste of Pushkin's verse.

If we compare this greatest artist of our great literature with other founders of other great literatures, with such priceless genii as Shakespeare, Goethe, Dante, etc.—then we shall involuntarily be brought up short before Pushkin's absolute original-ity—an originality, moreover, very different from what we might reasonably have expected.

But so it is. What was it that made our literature so rich and remarkable later on? Its emotional and moral pathos, its almost pathological pathos. Our literature is devoted to ideas because when such an abyss yawns between the understanding of its bearer —the intelligentsia—and the life about them, it is impossible for literature to avoid thought. It is morbidly sensitive, lofty, noble, anguished and prophetic.

Yet, if we throw a quick glance over Pushkin's work without pausing to analyse or to go into detail, then the first thing which strikes us is the freedom, the lucidity, a kind of dancing grace, a limitless youthfulness, a youthfulness which borders on levity. We seem to hear Mozart's minuets; the brush of Raphael darts over the canvas, conjuring images of harmony. Why is it that Pushkin is, on the whole, so carefree, even in his most solemn moments, so carefree, indeed, that people sometimes say: "After all it isn't Shakespeare and it isn't Goethe, they are much deeper, there is more of the philosopher in them, more of the teacher"?

True, those who talk in this way are not right, or at least, not altogether right, for it is enough to raise the veil of Pushkin's all-enshrouding grace to see into those deeps which foreshadow the further development of Russian literature: *Mozart and Salieri, The Feast in the Time of Plague,* certain scenes from *Boris Godunov,* some lyrical outbursts in *Yevgeny Onegin,* the enigmatic *Bronze Horseman* and much else besides—all this is like a wide ocean, calling to mind vertiginous depths and glimpses of lofty heights only barely within the range of the great wings of a Dante or a Shakespeare.

Yet these flashes of intuition, these psychological and intellectual treasures acquired with such extraordinary ease and accorded such extraordinarily scant attention by Pushkin himself—such as, for instance, his astonishing *Faust* where, in one brief scene, he confidently takes his place beside the semi-god of Weimar—are all done almost as if by accident, as though the hand of a master, running over the keys of a piano, acquainting himself and his audience with the full range of magic harmonies which it could produce, might occasionally pick out a few chords, or rather discords, which would strike amazement into the hearts of his listeners.

Whence this felicity of Pushkin's in the midst of his unhappy and difficult life? Perhaps it is a purely personal feature? I think not. I think that in this, too, Pushkin was a member, an element, a part of Russian literature in all its organic historical growth.

A hero of olden times had arisen, and his mighty strength was coursing freely through his veins. Already there was a presentiment of bitterness and sorrow, a presentiment of all the depths and anguish of certain problems—but there would be time enough for them later and, at that moment, they must even have been seen as a joyful challenge. Everything was a joy and a delight, for this radiant season of youth was serene in its own strength. In Pushkin the nobleman, it was not just a class which was awakening to a full realisation of its own potential (although to some extent he certainly bore the stamp of his class)—but a whole people, a nation, a historic destiny. It was from these seeds that in the final analysis, there sprung our own bitter and dazzling revolution.

Pushkin was the first representative of milliards of peoples and of many generations, to greet life and being. Through his lips, they first attained to true self-expression.

Even Dante in the 13th century had had behind him a great culture, his own, scholastic Florentine culture and that of the ancient world. But the Russian people awoke late, fresh and barbaric. Of course, Pushkin, with the rapidity of genius, absorbed Molière and Shakespeare and Byron and, at the same time, Parny and all kinds of other small fry. In this sense he was cultured. But all this lay but lightly upon him, it was not his own past, it was not in his blood. His past, that which lived in his blood, was fresh, Russian barbarity, it was the youth of a waking nation and the dark night of a joyless historical fate, of the heavy, mighty strength of a people which was just beginning to thaw out under the prison-like regime of Nicholas I. And his future was not those few years which he lived out on this earth, nor yet his tragic end, nor even his immortal fame. His future was the future of the Russian people, a vast future which was to decide the fate of humanity from that very mount on which we are now standing, still wreathed in the mists of enigma.

We made a splendid beginning with Pushkin. Fearfully deep and complex, our origin had about it the serene, easy quality of enormous strength. It is a good thing to know Pushkin, for he gives us the most consoling confidence in the strength of our people. It is not patriotism which leads us to this conclusion, but the realisation that, inevitably and of necessity, our people have been singled out from other fraternal nations to perform a rather particular service.

It is a good thing to love Pushkin, and, perhaps, it is a specially good thing to love Pushkin just now, when a new spring is in the offing, following, as it were, hard upon the heels of an autumn far gone in decay. The Russian bourgeoisie, the whole Russian bourgeois social and economic structure, travelled by the shortest of short cuts to the last convulsions of epigonous culture, to decadence, and from decadence into that artistic merry-go-round of absurdity produced by the exhausted cultures of other nations of the bourgeois West.

The new spring comes in with gales and showers, and it is essential that we should pay art that tribute of attention which was possible for the best people of Russia at the time of Pushkin's spring. As I have said before, our proletarian spring, as it will be when the earth breaks into flower, has much more in common with Pushkin's spring than with the gorgeously shaded counterfeit gold which covered the earth before the onset of these present storms and which, in reality, was nothing but a carpet of dead leaves.

1922

DOSTOYEVSKY'S "PLURALITY OF VOICES"

(Re the Book *Problems of the Works of Dostoyevsky*
by M. M. Bakhtin)

1

IN this interesting book M. M. Bakhtin treats only a few of the problems represented in the works of Dostoyevsky. He selects certain aspects of these works and approaches them primarily—indeed, almost exclusively—from the point of view of form. Bakhtin's interests focus on certain *basic* features of Dostoyevsky's method of constructing his novels (and novelle), features which appear to arise naturally—involuntarily, as it were—from the socio-psychological nature of the novelist and which have a decisive effect on the general character of his books. Essentially, the formal methods discussed by Bakhtin all have their origin in one basic phenomenon which he considers particularly important in all Dostoyevsky's work. This phenomenon is *"plurality of voices"*—polyphony. Bakhtin is even inclined to consider Dostoyevsky as the "originator" of the polyphonous novel.

What, then, does Bakhtin mean by this plurality of voices?

"A multiplicity of independent and unfused voices, a genuine polyphony, in which each 'voice' bears a part complete in itself, is in truth the basic distinguishing feature of Dostoyevsky's novels," he says.

And, further ... "The consciousness of the hero is represented from the outside as a distinct, other consciousness. At the same time, it is not objectivised, not confined to itself, not reduced to the status of an object within the consciousness of the author."

And this applies not only to the hero but to all the characters, or rather, to all the *dramatis personae* of Dostoyevsky's novels.

What Bakhtin is trying to say is that Dostoyevsky neither makes the characters he creates into masks for his own ego, nor arranges them in a planned system of relationships designed, in the last analysis, to fulfil some task which he, as the author, had set himself from the beginning.

Dostoyevsky's *dramatis personae* develop quite independently and say what they have to say (and, as Bakhtin quite rightly points out, what they have to say provides, as a rule, the key to the whole novel) without reference to the author, obedient only to the promptings of whatever basic principle of life is dominant in their own character.

Dostoyevsky's *dramatis personae* live, struggle and, most of all, argue, confess, expound their credos to one another, etc., free from all arbitrary interference on the part of the author. According to Bakhtin, it is as though the author granted complete autonomy to every character and, as a result, the whole texture of the novel is woven from confrontations between these autonomous characters, confrontations which seem to occur independently of the author's volition.

Naturally, given this method of construction, the author cannot be certain that his work will, in the last analysis, go to prove what he would like it to prove. In this context, Bakhtin even goes so far as to claim that "at the present time it may be that Dostoyevsky is not only the most powerful influence in Russia, where almost all new prose derives, to a greater or lesser degree, from his works, but in the West also. As an artist, Dostoyevsky is followed by people of the most diverse ideological convictions, many of whom are profoundly opposed to his ideology: the hypnotic power of his art irresistibly subjects all things to itself.... This hypnotic power is not to be confused with the rational appeal of a clear, consciously worked-out ideology. It seems as though all who plunge into the labyrinth of the polyphonous novel lose their way in it and cannot hear the whole for the clamouring of the separate voices. Frequently, there is a failure to make out even the haziest outlines of the whole. The artistic principles which organise the commingling of the voices escape the ear."

To this it might be added that these principles do not only go unperceived but are, in fact, most probably absent. This particular orchestra not only lacks a conductor, but even a composer, whose score a conductor might have followed. What we have here is a clash of intellects, a clash of wills in an atmosphere of complete *laissez-faire* on the part of the author. This is what Bakhtin means by the term "polyphony" when he writes of the polyphony of Dostoyevsky.

True, Bakhtin does appear to admit some higher order of artistic unity in Dostoyevsky's novels, but in what this consists, if Dostoyevsky's novels are polyphonous in the interpretation of the term we have suggested, it is not easy to understand. If we are to allow that Dostoyevsky, from his previous knowledge of the inmost essence of each of his characters and of the material results to which the conflicts between them are bound to lead, could combine these characters in such a way as to form an intrinsically welded whole while preserving the absolute freedom of the individual voice, then it must be admitted that the whole principle of the self-sufficiency of the "parts" borne by the various characters, that is, of their absolute independence from the author, can only be accepted with certain very extensive reservations.

I am rather inclined to agree with Bakhtin that Dostoyevsky—if not at the stage of completion then certainly when working out the first ideas of his novels and the gradual evolution of their plots—was most probably not characterised by the ability to keep to any preconceived constructive plan, that his method of work was indeed polyphonic in the sense that it was a commingling and interweaving of absolutely free individuals. It is even possible that Dostoyevsky himself was excessively and most intensely interested in the outcome of the ideological and aesthetic conflicts between the characters which he created (or which might rather be said to have created themselves through him).

I concede, therefore, that Bakhtin has succeeded not only in describing more clearly than anyone has ever done before the immense significance of this plurality of voices in the Dostoyevsky novel and the part played by this plurality as a most vital distinguishing feature of this novel, but also in defining the extraordinary individual autonomy and self-sufficiency of voices—quite unthinkable for the vast majority of other writers—which Dostoyevsky developed with such shattering effect.

I would also like to stress how right Bakhtin is in another of his contentions, when he notes that all those "voices" which play a truly important part in any of the novels represent distinct "convictions" or "ways of looking at the world at large". These, of course, are more than just theories; they are theories which are as much a part of their exponent as his particular "blood type", inseparable from him, his own basic nature. Over and above all of which these theories are active ideas, they drive the characters to commit definite actions and provide the motive forces of distinct patterns of behaviour, individual and social. In a word, they are of a profoundly ethical and social nature, for they do in fact serve to attract the individual towards the service of society or—as so often happens in Dostoyevsky's novels—to draw him away from such service.

Dostoyevsky's novels are superbly staged dialogues.

In these conditions the profound self-sufficiency of the separate voices becomes, one might even say, peculiarly piquant. One is forced to the conclusion that Dostoyevsky deliberately puts certain vital problems up for discussion before these highly individual "voices", trembling with passion and flickering with the flame of fanaticism, while he himself remains a mere spectator of the convulsive disputes which ensue, a curious looker-on wondering where it is all leading and how it is going to end. To a great extent, this is a true picture.

Although Bakhtin's book centres mainly round the formal analysis of Dostoyevsky's techniques, the critic is by no means averse to embarking on an occasional excursion into sociological interpretation. He quotes approvingly from Kaus's *Dostoyevsky and His Fate* and, in general, agrees with his opinion. Let us examine, in translation, some of Kaus's contentions as quoted by Bakhtin.

"Dostoyevsky is master in his own house, a host who knows how to cope with the most varied guests, who can manage any company, however wildly improbable its composition, never losing control of it or permitting the conversation to flag.... Health and strength, the most radical pessimism and the most fiery faith in salvation, thirst for life and death—all these are locked in a struggle seemingly without issue; violence and kindness, arrogance and selfless humility, the inexhaustible fulness of life, etc. He has no need to coerce his characters, he has no need to pronounce the last word as their creator. Dostoyevsky is many-sided and unpredictable, his works are packed with forces and intentions which one would think were separated from one another by impassable chasms."

Kaus assumes that all this is but the reflection, in Dostoyevsky's mind, of the contradictions of the capitalist world.

Bakhtin gives an excellent exposition of Kaus's basic thesis.

"Kaus maintains that Dostoyevsky's world is the most unadulterated and genuine reflection of the spirit of capitalism. The diverse worlds and spheres —social, cultural and ideological—which are brought into head on collision in the works of Dostoyevsky, were formerly self-contained, isolated from one another, stabilised and justified from within as distinct and separate units. There was no real, material area in which they could, to any appreciable degree, meet and interpenetrate. Capitalism broke down the segregation of these worlds, destroyed the exclusiveness and the inner, ideological self-sufficiency of these social spheres. In accordance with its tendency to level things out, leaving no barrier other than that dividing the proletarian from the capitalist, capitalism tossed these worlds into a common melting-pot as a part of the process of bringing unity out of contradiction. These worlds had not yet lost that stamp of their own individuality which each had acquired in the course of centuries, but they could no longer remain self-contained. The period of blind coexistence, of calm, untroubled mutual ignorance, was at an end, and their mutual contrariety and, at the same time, their interdependence, became increasingly perceptible. In every atom of life trembles this contradictory unity of the capitalist world and of capitalist consciousness, making it impossible for anyone to feel comfortable in their isolation, yet offering no solutions. The spirit of this changing world was more fully expressed in the works of Dostoyevsky than anywhere else."

He himself adds that Dostoyevsky's Russia was the ideal forcing-house for the growth of the polyphonous novel. For "here capitalism was establishing itself with almost catastrophic suddenness and had surprised a multitude of unchanged social worlds and groups, which had not, as in the West, suffered a slow sapping of their individual exclusiveness in the process of the gradual evolution of a capitalist system. Here, the contradictory essence of this society in the process of formation which resisted all attempts to bring it within the framework of a quietly contemplative, assured monological scheme of things, must have been particularly evident while, at the same time, the individuality of these worlds which had suddenly been confronted one with another and knocked off their ideological balance must have shown up exceptionally vividly and fully."

All this is very good and quite true.

What general conclusion is there to be drawn from the opinions of Bakhtin and of Kaus, the former's authority for the sociological part of his analysis? Dostoyevsky, being the child of his time and therefore reflecting in his own personality the colossal ethical shambles brought about by the violent eruption of the complexity of capitalist social relationships into pre-reform Russia,* provided in his art a true mirror, an adequate reflection of all this complexity. Life was seething with contradictions. Various individual philosophies of life were coming into collision; various individual moral codes, sometimes consciously worked out as full-fledged theories, at others manifesting their almost entirely subconscious nature through actions and discordant talk, were being brought face to face. In Dostoyevsky's novels a similar dialectic is in process, an identical

---

* Lunacharsky is referring to Russia as it was before the emancipation of the serfs and other reforms of 1860s.—*Ed.*

struggle. It is as though there were no tuning-fork to set the right pitch to all this cacophony, as though there were no harmony which might have overcome and, as it were, absorbed it, no force strong enough to discipline it into something resembling a chorus.

Bakhtin, however, understands that such a view of Dostoyevsky would not be altogether correct.

Before we go on to set out our further thoughts on the significance of Dostoyevsky's polyphony or attempt to modify or explain further certain interesting points touched on by Bakhtin, let us make a brief comparison between Dostoyevsky the polyphonist and some other polyphonous writers.

Bakhtin maintains that Dostoyevsky's type of polyphony is incompatible with drama. Drama, he believes, cannot under any circumstances be polyphonous, and certain specialists' classification of Dostoyevsky's novels as a new form of drama strike him as completely false.

Bakhtin's grounds for objecting to this classification are most profound. He considers that, although, in drama, there are characters who act and speak in a way which implies a certain clash of personalities or confrontation of ideologies, they nonetheless remain basically mere puppets in the hands of the author who will inevitably direct them according to some preconceived plan.

Is this really so?

Naturally, it is scarcely possible to suspect Bakhtin, who shows sufficient subtlety of judgement in his book, of presupposing all drama (tragedy, comedy, etc.) to consist of plays with a message— *pièces à thèse*. The question of the play which seeks to get across some definite message and of the "free play", which is simply a dramatised, firmly carpentered slice of life, is an old one upon which we have no intention of entering here. Yet it does appear strange that Bakhtin, in insisting on the unfeasibility of polyphony in drama, clearly leaves out of account the greatest of all dramatists—Shakespeare. Of course, it is impossible that Bakhtin should really have forgotten about him. Of course, we repeat, Bakhtin does not really think that all drama is automatically "tendentious". He merely assumes that, since every drama is necessarily a harmonious whole which develops according to certain strict rules, it would be extremely uneconomical, and, indeed, impossible for the author to permit every "voice" to bear its own independent part. This, at least, is the way in which I explain to myself Bakhtin's uncompromising statement on the necessity of monism in drama.

On this point, however, I still permit myself to differ radically from Bakhtin, first and foremost on the evidence of Shakespeare.

Is it not indicative that, for a very long time indeed, it was generally accepted that Shakespeare's plays were utterly devoid of any guiding ideas or principles? As a playwright, Shakespeare is the most "impersonal" of authors; it is scarcely ever possible to say anything about the tendencies he represents. More than this, he is, in the great majority of his works, so alien to all tendentiousness that we involuntarily begin to suspect him of a great conscious or unconscious *revulsion* from such tendentiousness. It is as though Shakespeare were crying out in his every work that life is immense and splendid in itself, even though it does abound in sorrows and catastrophes, and that any opinion expressed on this life must of necessity be insufficient and one-sided and cannot be expected to embrace all its variety, all its dazzling irrationality.

Being thus totally untendentious (according, at least, to long-established opinion), Shakespeare is extremely polyphonic. Here we could cite many extracts from the works of distinguished Shakespearean scholars, and from the sayings of Shakespeare's imitators and admirers, to show their profound admiration for this very ability to create characters who appear to have a life of their own outside the mind of their author, an endless procession of characters moreover, of an incredible variety, all of whom remain incredibly true to themselves in all they say and do.

Gundolf, to whom, at one point, Bakhtin refers, asserts, in drawing a comparison between Goethe and Shakespeare, that the source of Goethe's works (at any rate of the most significant) was always his own experience, while his heroes always embodied aspects of his own personality. In this he sees a contrast to Shakespeare who, in his opinion, was able to create human beings quite independently of himself and of his own experience, almost on a par with Nature herself.

It cannot be said of Shakespeare either that his plays were intended to prove some particular thesis or that the "voices" in the great polyphony of Shakespeare's dramatic world are deprived of their several, self-sufficient parts for the benefit of the dramatic plot, of construction as such.

Yet, when we take a closer look at Shakespeare (helped, perhaps, by the still unproved but very probable hypothesis that Shakespeare was in fact Rutland), we see that his polyphonism is not devoid of a certain organising principle—that he remains, to use Kaus's simile, "master in his own house".

True, everything about Shakespeare is extremely obscure, and this obscurity greatly impedes analysis (which only goes to prove once again how mistaken is the attitude of those historians of literature who maintain that an author's personality and biography are of no help in the interpretation of his works). We cannot even say for sure whether there was in fact one *single* master-mind behind Shakespeare's dramatic world. Leaving aside the numerous borrowed passages, the rewriting of other men's plays and the question of other men's plays which have been attributed to Shakespeare, it is impossible to ignore Gordon Craig's original and profound hypothesis, which attributes a quite peculiar form of polyphony to Shakespeare by distinguishing in his plays the voices of more than one author. All this greatly confuses the question of Shakespeare's polyphony. However, I repeat, if we subject this vast literary phenomenon to closer scrutiny, then we cannot but admit that, behind the works of Shakespeare, we do feel the presence of a personality of some sort, even if it is so many-faceted and titanic as to be hard to define.

What were the social factors reflected in Shakespeare's polyphonism? Why, of course, in the last analysis, precisely those we find in Dostoyevsky. That colourful Renaissance, broken up into a myriad of sparkling shards, which had given birth to Shakespeare and to his contemporaries, was, of course, the result of the stormy irruption of capitalism into the comparative calm of medieval England. Here, as in Dostoyevsky's Russia, a gigantic break-up was getting under way. The same gigantic shifts were taking place and the same unexpected collisions between traditions of social life and systems of thought which had previously had no real contact with one another.

How did the man we assume to be Shakespeare react to all this? Was he nothing but a passive mirror, capable only of reflecting all this tangle of unprecedentedly diverse forces which existed outside himself? I have already said that this is an idea of Shakespeare which has frequently been advanced. We must, however, bear in mind that if a great writer, who is by definition equipped with exceptional sensibility and understanding, is to remain true to the very nature of the human mind with its irrepressible inclination to synthesise separate ideas and facts, to create some system of ideas and critical values, he must, inevitably, seek *not only to reflect the world* but to bring order to it, and harmony, or, at least, to illumine it from some definite point of view.

If this premis is not always born out by the study of individual great writers, it is because we often leave out of account the variety of *forms* which this process of synthesis may take. If a writer is also a poet he is, of course, under no obligation to impose unity and order on society and nature *in practice,* or even to reduce them to any kind of monism by means of philosophic interpretations. He may, for instance (as, for that matter, the philosopher may also) admit the existence of an irreconcilable pluralism. He may consider irremediable the tragedy of the human condition, which, he may be convinced, is the inevitable product of a world of warring principles. With great sorrow, he may determine the existence of this universal want of harmony, he may see no way out. Yet even such diagnosis as this, to whatever conclusion it may lead—whether the inference is that life is not worth while since the world itself is an absurdity, or that, in spite of its disharmony, or even perhaps, because of it, the world is beautiful in its very irrationality, or that life should assert itself heroically in the face of surrounding chaos—even such a diagnosis is, essentially, a *synthetic* conception or a synthetic emotion. Without this capacity for synthesis, it is almost impossible to imagine a truly great personality.

As I shall make clear further on, I have no desire to suggest that such great personalities may not themselves be split, either simultaneously or at different periods of their life, so that their various aspects might almost seem to belong to separate people. When Shakespeare's Hamlet exclaims:

> *The time is out of joint! O, cursed spite,*
> *That ever I was born to set it right*

he is, in my opinion, expressing a profound lyrical impulse on behalf of the author; it must have been Shakespeare's dream to set his time to rights—again or anew. This is his genuine inner aspiration and in every play which does not end in a reconciliation, it is as though he suffers a defeat.

But let us now leave Shakespeare, merely noting that, while he is undoubtedly no less polyphonic than Dostoyevsky and grants an equal autonomy to the self-sufficient individual voice (something which, it seems to me, Bakhtin should find it impossible to deny), the only tendency which the great playwright evinces to pronounce judgement on life, even to change it, shows itself in a manner far removed from all direct contact with the reader.

But is it not clear that such tendencies likewise exist in Dostoyevsky? Once again, Bakhtin will hardly find it possible to deny this. He himself understands that not only Dostoyevsky's characters but their author, too, aspire to the establishment of some new kind of society. He himself writes of this, he himself stresses that Dostoyevsky was characterised by certain ideas on coinherence* and harmony—albeit metaphysical and other-worldly ideas. Dostoyevsky is not just a mirror giving a concentrated and magnified reflection of life and its agonising conflicts. These conflicts are profoundly distressing to him, he has a strong inner desire to resolve them and, for

---

* Lunacharsky uses the Slavophile expression *sobornost,* the root of which is *sobor*—Eng. "Council". *Sobornost* implies "togetherness", "exchange" and "interdependence". —*Ed.*

that matter, he is much *more* concerned with this business, certainly more noticeably so, than is Shakespeare. True, his labours are not crowned with success. But we shall be coming back to that later.

Here, I should like to introduce one more name which Bakhtin does not mention—the name of Balzac. Marx had the greatest regard for Shakespeare as the bard of developing capitalism and of all the infinite variety of the capitalist epoch. He had also a profound admiration for Balzac. Balzac has much in common with Shakespeare. It should not go unnoted that Dostoyevsky, in his turn, was a great admirer of Balzac and translated his works. Balzac's kinship with Shakespeare lies not only in the extraordinary variety of colours in the world around him, where the capitalist order was establishing itself in its more or less final form after the storms of the Great Revolution, but also in his polyphonism, in the freedom and self-sufficiency of his "voices". This again is so true that, although we are thoroughly well informed as to Balzac's biography, it is quite impossible to reconstruct his private opinions. His philosophical and political convictions are of less interest than Dostoyevsky's. It would be permissible to say that Balzac is a thinker of lesser stature than Dostoyevsky. At the same time it is typical that, whereas in Dostoyevsky's novels the author never comes forward as mentor and we never hear his voice pointing a moral, in Balzac's novels we frequently come across long discourses on the facts they describe, woven into the fabric of the story and often making rather dry reading of it. *In spite of this*, Balzac is far less *tendentious* than Dostoyevsky. Is it thinkable to maintain that Dostoyevsky has no "God" in the Chekhovian sense? (I am talking about Chekhov's letter to Suvorin on the absence of God, the absence of any object of reverence or love in the world of the modern writer.) Can it be denied that there is at least a colossal will towards such a "God" in Dostoyevsky and, at certain moments, the conviction that he does indeed possess one? It can be said of Balzac, however, that it is normal for him to drift from one point of view to another and that those points of view are chance-found and even not particularly interesting. Balzac owes his greatness almost exclusively to his polyphonism, that is, to his extraordinary objectivity, his changeling ability to imagine himself in the skin of the most diverse types of the society which he had the opportunity to observe.

This, of course, is why Bakhtin is wrong when he says that Dostoyevsky was the *originator* of polyphony, or even of the polyphonious novel, and of that plurality of voices which allows for the autonomy and self-sufficiency of individual parts.

From this point of view, Balzac undoubtedly goes further than Dostoyevsky. This can, of course, be explained not only by certain distinguishing features of Balzac's talent, but also by many aspects of the society in which he lived, aspects which affected both the material which he gathered from his surroundings and the structure of his own mind and sensibility. As for Shakespeare, whilst perceiving quite definite individual "tendencies" breaking the surface here and there in the works of this great singer of the era of the origins of English capitalism, we are also bound to emphasise his quite exceptional polyphonism according to the definition we have given in this article.

2

To return to the task which we set ourselves before drawing the above comparisons:

We have seen how in Shakespeare, for all his polyphonism, there is an attempt, of profound and anguished concern to the author, to arrive at some kind of objective or even subjective monism. In Balzac we do not even feel this tendency. We feel his works as polyphony in its purest form.

But Dostoyevsky who is, at the moment, of more immediate concern to us than the two West European titans—what about Dostoyevsky? Apart from the polyphonous principle, the desire to assure the free development of independent voices, is he so entirely free from all tendentiousness?

We have already pointed out in passing that Bakhtin himself does not and, indeed, could not deny that there is evidence of tendentiousness in Dostoyevsky's books and that, even if he does not, as author, address himself direct to the reader, the reader is nevertheless quite well aware of the presence of his "host", and perfectly understands on whose side Dostoyevsky's sympathies lie. Bakhtin himself distinguishes, among the other voices, prescient voices which, undoubtedly, in Dostoyevsky's opinion, advocate a higher truth, voices "close to God"—that is, as Dostoyevsky understands it, close to the fountain-head of all truth, "God-bearing" voices.

However, even in those cases when these voices are not in evidence, the whole construction of the novel is worked out in such a way as to leave the reader in no doubt as to Dostoyevsky's own views on what is taking place between its pages. It is, of course, a magnificent illustration of his art that Dostoyevsky does not express these views directly, but we never lose our awareness of the beating of the author's heart, of the spasmodic irregularities as it contracts over what he is writing.

Our formalists keep on dinning into the reader of today—whom they have not the remotest chance of ever convincing—that writers in general, and even the greatest among them, stand quite aloof from their own works, look on them as an exercise in craftsmanship and are interested in them only from the point of view of form. In respect of Dostoyevsky this kind of assertion sounds particularly monstrous. It is evident that Bakhtin has no intention of making any such assertion. Dostoyevsky listens to the great disputes which take place in word and deed in his novels with the most intense excitement, with love and hatred.

Why, then, are we forced to admit a very considerable degree of truth in Bakhtin's contention that it is difficult to formulate Dostoyevsky's final conclusions, if not as theoretician and publicist then in that aspect of his work with which we are dealing here, as a novelist and a writer of fiction? Why did his novels produce on Kaus also the impression of "unfinished arguments"? Why is it as though no one ever carried off the final victory? Why, in Dostoyevsky's conception of the independence and self-sufficiency of voices, is there this deliberate element of withdrawal? Why is it as though Dostoyevsky were to say "I pass" when his turn came to raise his own voice among these other voices which are so far from corresponding to his own convictions, or, rather, to those convictions which he would have liked to have held and which he ascribed to himself? Why, on the other hand, do those voices which obviously command his sympathy (Sonya, Zosima, Alyosha, and others) apparently fail to carry final conviction and so utterly lack the ring of triumph, perhaps even to the considerable exasperation of Dostoyevsky?

In order to explain this phenomenon, without which, of course, Bakhtin's assertion of the self-sufficiency and independence of Dostoyevsky's "voices" would be demonstrably false, we have to take into account not only the fragmentation of the world through which Dostoyevsky's characters move but also *Dostoyevsky's own split personality*.

Without claiming to give an answer to all the

"problems of Dostoyevsky's works" in so short an essay (a task of too great a compass, of course, even for Bakhtin's entire book), without claiming to give so much as an approximately exhaustive idea of this split in Dostoyevsky's consciousness, we would like to call attention here to one basic irregularity—a morbid and horrifying irregularity which, at the same time, made Dostoyevsky profoundly typical of his epoch or, more exactly, of several decades of the history of Russian culture.

The excessive contrast between the social realities of Russia and the intensified awareness which gradually came into being amongst the best people of the educated classes, first among the nobility and then among the *raznochintsy* was an extremely widespread phenomenon the results of which left their mark on over a century and, most particularly, of course, on the great writers and the other leaders of the intelligentsia.

Leaving on one side Novikov and Radishchev, let us look back to Pushkin's horrifying exclamation: "It must have been the Devil's own idea to have me born in Russia with brains and talent". Although Pushkin was a man of exceptional adaptability who could get on in any company and showed himself capable of a remarkably supple policy of spiritual and material opportunism, his life was poisoned, and the social scandal to which he fell victim was the natural result of his whole position between the Decembrists, on the one side, and Nicholas the Gendarme on the other.

In this, it goes without saying, Pushkin was not alone. On the contrary, round about him others were suffering even more, and suffering not only in spirit, but in body. That is common knowledge.

The forerunner of the great wave of intelligentsia recruited from outside the nobility was Belinsky. He, too, was distinguished by a full awareness of the horror of his position. He sometimes speaks of the horror of waking up in full possession of one's faculties in a land exhausted by suffering, in a land ruled by profoundly ignorant and self-assured sergeant-majors, in a land in which there is no serious opposition, no serious support for those who are sufficiently mature to criticise and protest.

If Belinsky remained true to his vocation in spite of all this, he was by no means free of hesitation and doubt: the article on Borodino—however one may explain it by an incorrect interpretation of Hegel, though in fact one can only speak here of an incorrect *application* of Hegel's doctrine—is in fact a profound analogy to the political moods and beliefs of Dostoyevsky. Belinsky very nearly took a header over that same precipice of spiritual opportunism which consists in the acceptance of a series of generalisations and emotional evasions in order to justify one's own reconciliation with the "reigning evil". To this it must be added that Belinsky literally *had the good fortune* to die before he was faced with the terrible trial which fell to the lot of Chernyshevsky and Dostoyevsky.

I shall not try to assert here that Gogol was, at any period of his life, militantly and consciously protestant in his attitude to *all* that was going on around him. Nevertheless, Gogol's unmistakable if gradual transition from satire to the glorification of autocracy and orthodoxy was a spectacle which, we know, Belinsky and society at large contemplated with deep shame and sorrow.

Psychologically, of course, all this came about in quite a different way to that indicated by superficial students of Gogol's life. It is completely misleading to suggest that Gogol had, from the very beginning, thought like a died-in-the-wool conservative landlord. Gogol undoubtedly rose to considerable heights of criticism although, understandably, he did not dare to touch on the highest ranks of society. His renunciation of the part of ideological leader in his own country and the unconvincing, essentially unsatisfying even to himself, exchange of this role for that of faithful subject-cum-religious maniac was, undoubtedly, not only the result of his morbid depression but, at the same time, its most profound cause.

The whole epoch was strewn with corpses and semi-corpses, some of whom had resisted and been broken, whereas others had compromised and remained alive, surviving as spiritual cripples with clearly expressed pathological tendencies.

Chernyshevsky, a very powerful, lucid personality, who, although the stand he adopted was extremely radical, was never in so isolated a position as Belinsky, was nonetheless very sceptically disposed to the idea of establishing a revolutionary order in his own time. A brilliant and heart-breaking monument to this scientific scepticism of Chernyshevsky's is his novel *Prologue*—which has met with so little appreciation from our historians of literature. In spite of everything, Chernyshevsky was foredoomed to the role of redeeming sacrifice, but he tried to do everything in his power to preserve his strength, the strength of one who has deliberately set out to prepare men for a direct struggle the time for which has not yet arrived. Although Chernyshevsky bore heroically with the trials of forced labour and exile, the contrast between the Chernyshevsky who left for Siberia and the Chernyshevsky who returned is no less deplorable than the collapse of any other giants of our thought and literature.

This list might be prolonged ad infinitum. It is always possible to find people who, having woken up in full possession of their faculties, have taken their bearings in the surrounding darkness and, in some way or another, offered battle to their environment, and have, in some way or another, been crushed by it—whether physically, or morally and politically, or both.

Here, however, it is impossible to pass over the sad figure of Nekrasov. When all's said and done, Nekrasov did a great deal for the development of the revolutionary movement, of the revolutionary thought of our country; but the degree of his civic consciousness obliged him to a far more vivid protest which he failed to deliver—in part from weakness of character, but much more because the sacrifices involved appeared almost self-evidently useless. Nekrasov's penitential chant rose to the verge of self-torture after one of his particularly striking and notorious falls—his glorification of Muravyov the hangman. This, one might say, is a startling witness to that tyranny which bent and broke those citizens who had but recently awakened to a realisation of their position in their own country and, first among them, the writers of that country! It was apropos his ethico-political portrait of Nekrasov that Mikhailovsky spoke of these Russians who were "sick in conscience". These men who suffered from "sick conscience" were all more or less deliberate opportunists who had worked out two formulas: either "I see the horror, but I cannot fight it", or "I see the horror but I wish to see some blessing in its stead which would allow me not to fight it and, at the same time, not to lose my self-respect".

Gleb Ivanovich Uspensky had a wonderful gift for portraying such "sufferers". "Defaulters" was his word for the majority of the intelligentsia. The most terrible thing was that he himself died with a split personality, announcing that he was possessed, on the one hand, by the holy martyr Gleb, and, on the other, by a cowardly and egotistic little man called Ivanovich. And this in spite of the fact that Gleb Uspensky was the favourite of the progressive public and in the course of his literary career, had done a colossal amount for the cause which he considered it his duty to further.

Even Lev Tolstoi looms up before us like a crippled titan. His non-resistance to evil is in fact the same old self-defence against conscience advanced by a man who, in his heart of hearts, is perfectly well aware of all the wicked injustice of life, but cannot make up his mind to commit himself to the direct, total struggle which he knows to be beyond his strength.

It is within the framework of this phenomenon—extremely widespread, as the reader cannot but see even from the incomplete list of relevant facts cited here—that we must try to place Dostoyevsky.

The social position of Dostoyevsky which reduced him to the status of the lowest of the low, acquainting him with the bitter lot of the injured and insulted, taken in conjunction with his exceptional sensibility, his gift for suffering and compassion, could not fail to put him on the road to a sufficiently vivid form of protest, on the road to dreams of a radical reformation of the whole social system. Attempts are often made to represent Dostoyevsky's affiliation with the Petrashevsky circle as a superficial and passing aberration, and the fact that he was condemned to death for his connection with this circle as just another, completely unprovoked, absurd juridical atrocity on the part of the autocracy. However, such an explanation will simply not do. One would have to be completely devoid of all psychological sensibility and, moreover, be missing a whole series of politically responsive strings in the instrument of consciousness, in order to doubt (even in the absence of direct proofs) that the young Dostoyevsky was among those who "sought for a city". He was indubitably full of anger against social injustice and so profoundly so that, at some half-hidden subterranean level, this anger continued its vulcanic work throughout his existence. Its grumblings and rumblings can only be ignored by the politically deaf, and the glow it throws up—only by the politically blind.

Dostoyevsky's clash with autocracy took place in the most violent fashion imaginable. To be condemned to be hung—what could be more violent than that! Forced labour came as an "easing" of situation.

The question of the physiological causes of Dostoyevsky's illness and of its first origin has still to be solved. While we are on the subject we note in passing that, in this field, Marxist criticism will have to cross swords with modern psychiatry which always interprets what we choose to call morbid phenomena in literature as the result of hereditary sicknesses or, in any case, of causes which bear no relationship to what might be described as the *social biography* of the writer in question. Of course, we do not mean by this that Marxists should deny the existence of disease or the influence of mental illness on the works of this or that writer, if he happened at the same time to be a psychiatrist's patient. It is merely that all these purely psychological factors do seem to follow very logically from certain sociological premises.

In our own good time we shall return to this rich and interesting theme, but now we just thought it necessary to mention it in connection with this brief analysis of Dostoyevsky's split personality, which is in itself as important a cause of his "plurality of voices" as were social conditions during the epoch of the tempestuous growth of capitalism. After all, other writers, Dostoyevsky's contemporaries, lived under the same social conditions, whereas here we have M. M. Bakhtin proving that Dostoyevsky was the originator of the polyphonic novel—at least on Russian soil.

According to Dostoyevsky himself, his first attack of epilepsy took place while he was still doing forced labour and took the form of a kind of revelation from above after an argument about religion and Dostoyevsky's agonised and passionate opposition to the atheist: "No, no, I believe in God!" This fact is in itself most revealing. Here, too, the social and the biological subsoil seem to bring forth the same fruit, or, rather, combine to bring it forth, not entering into opposition with one another. Driven off to forced labour, Dostoyevsky, who was, like Gogol, extremely conscious of his own genius and of the special role he was called upon to play in life, felt with all his being that autocracy was eating him alive. He did not wish to be eaten. He had to adopt a position which would preserve his prophetic calling and yet not lead to further trouble with the authorities, which could only have ended in immediate catastrophe.

I do not mean that Dostoyevsky tried consciously to become a monarchist, adapting himself to the power that be. Such an assumption would be but poor psychology.

Of course, Dostoyevsky passed through terrible storms of doubt, but "expediency" helped to eliminate, to blur and to soften the "voices" which called him to protest, struggle and sacrifice. The voices which presented the case for the opposition were not those which were over-frank, nor yet those which retained the taint of self-preservation, nor even those which cried "in our present conditions this sacrifice will be in vain", but those which justified an almost opposite position and, on the contrary, found a way to "sublimate" this apparently modest and retiring "expediency".

With the hand of a skilled conjuror, "expediency" illuminated even Dostoyevsky's instinct for self-preservation and the conservative romanticism born of this instinct in a heroic light. Indeed, did not Dostoyevsky have ahead of him a fearless struggle against the radicals and all progressive society? After all, this, too, requires courage.

So the basic foundation of Dostoyevsky's future conciliatory position in relation to the autocracy and the social order was laid in tempests and inner conflict. Dostoyevsky went through hell. To the day of his death he could not convince himself—not only his conscious mind, but his subconscious, his mighty social conscience—of the rightness of this position.

The most superficial analysis of epilepsy, particularly in the form suffered by Dostoyevsky, shows us that aspect which involves a heightening of the sensibility, a kind of exposure of the nerves, and hence, particularly in the difficult conditions of the society in which he lived, constant suffering often petty in origin, but magnified by the nervous condition. On the other hand, the epileptic attack itself is felt, according to Dostoyevsky's inside evidence, as the onset of the macrocosm, of a feeling of harmony, of oneness with the whole creation. In other words, it represents the triumph of a kind of emotional *optimum*.

But how else is it possible to imagine Dostoyevsky's psychology at that time? What *poles* of thought and feeling must have manifested themselves in this constant battle? On the one side—disgust and indignation in the face of reality; on the other—a passionate hope in the reconciliation of all contradictions, even if only in the next world, even if only in the sphere of mysticism.

Dostoyevsky's gifted and passionate nature delved down and intensified the first aspect of his condition to that terrible torturing of himself and of others which is one of the dominant features of his writing. The second aspect it raised to the point of ecstasy.

In this way, social causes led Dostoyevsky to the "sacred illness" and, having found, in prerequisites of a purely physiological nature (bound up, undoubtedly, with his very giftedness) a suitable subsoil, proceeded to cultivate in him a particular view of life, a particular style of writing—and his illness. By this, I do not in the least mean that in other circumstances Dostoyevsky would never have suffered from epilepsy. I am referring to that extraordinary coincidence which makes us think of Dostoyevsky as being so exactly suited to the role which he in fact came to play. At the same time, Dostoyevsky, the first great petty-bourgeois writer in the history of our culture, reflected in these moods of his the confusion of a wide section of the petty-bourgeois intelligentsia and of the more educated members of this class. To them, he was a very powerful and much-needed organiser, the source of that *Dostoyevshchina** which continued, for certain wide sections of that petty bourgeoisie, to provide one of the main ways of self-preservation right until the time of Leonid Andreyev and even on into our revolutionary days.

Religion was bound to play an important part in Dostoyevsky's work, if only because of this "epileptical" character of his social experience and thought. Any mystic system, however, might have served this purpose. Dostoyevsky's choice fell on Orthodox Christianity. It would be interesting to make a brief digression on this subject.

The Orthodox Church, for all the rough-hewn quality of its dogmatic structure (if we are to compare

---

* The suffix "shchina" means much the same as Eng. "ism", but always carries derogatory overtones when added, as here, to a proper name. It implies the superficial imitation of a great man's more extravagant ideas and eccentric qualities rather than a true cult of his work or doctrine. —*Tr.*

it with the refined and durable theory of Roman Catholicism or the sharp spirit of rationalist criticism inherent in Protestant creeds) still managed to play a certain positive role in support of Russia's ruling classes—not only as a basic form of ideological deception for the uncultured masses but also as a kind of *pons asinorum* on the basis of which people of high culture and refined opportunism could work out a philosophy capable of reconciling them with reality. After all, the Christian religion, even as expounded by the Orthodox Church of that time, spoke of love, of equality and of brotherhood. Orthodoxy was understood as an abstraction, as something above and largely beyond mundane life, but, nevertheless, as something which introduced a certain modicum of light, truth and humanity into earthly relationships.

For the ruling classes, the most agreeable aspect of all this was that it required no actual reforms and sought no real reflection in life apart from such trifles as almsgiving, the exercise of charity, monasteries, etc. Everything in life could and should remain as it was: an Orthodox tsar, Orthodox policemen, Orthodox landowners and industrialists, Orthodox workmen and peasants. The former in all the glory of their function as exploiters; the latter—in all the horror of their position as the exploited; but, all together, "brothers in Christ", reconciled, according to the Orthodox Church, by a common ideology, a belief in "divine justice", which makes itself felt both in the torments of this life on earth and in the punishments to be meted out in the world to come.

Now that the standard of thought in our society is so far-removed from what it was in Dostoyevsky's time, this whole concept appears so childish and, indeed, barbarous, that at times one asks oneself: However was Orthodoxy able to satisfy the ideological requirements even of the uncultured masses? But this line of thought, is, of course, largely artificial. For example, on my last visit to Switzerland I caught myself in a state of what I can only call profoundly naive astonishment that in this country churches are being built and believers are conducting religious services according to the rituals of their various cults. I could not resist laying hands on a specifically ecclesiastical journal and was involuntarily shaken with laughter—once again, very naive laughter—to find myself, in this European atmosphere, reading the foolishly contrived arguments and the stale repetitions which flow from the pens of believers. Yet religious thought and feeling show no signs of dying out in Europe; on the contrary, there are even symptoms of a revival in certain circles, particularly amongst the bourgeois youth of France, Italy, etc.

Be that as it may, the idea of heavenly justice, cunning in its very naivety, was able, in the view of many, to justify all earthly injustice and even to provide some genuine relief (mainly in words but occasionally by "charitable actions"). Thanks to this, it could reconcile to reality minds which had just awoken to sharp criticism, hearts which had begun to contract at the sight of social evil but which, in order to avoid a fatal clash with the powers that be, found it expedient to paralyse such contractions or, at least, to modify them.

If we take, for example, three stages of religion's being used in this way in Russian literature and choose Gogol, Dostoyevsky and Tolstoi to illustrate our point, then we obtain the following gradation:

With Gogol the whole business is perfectly straightforward. One has only to think of the great satirist's famous recommendation in his *Selected Passages from a Correspondence with Friends,* in which he advises landowners to read the Gospel to their peasants in order that the latter, having absorbed

A. V. Lunacharsky, 1925

the word of God, might serve their landlord the more selflessly and understand that this service is the purpose of their existence. I do not believe that Gogol's faith was altogether free from flaw, untroubled by inner doubt—perhaps well hidden, or perhaps, only very occasionally troubling his conscious mind—a doubt as to whether all this were really so, as to whether the "word of God" were not, in fact, a handy invention for the benefit of the landowners. As far as I know, there is no direct evidence for this. If anyone really wants to accept Gogol's faith as something monolithic, there is nothing to prevent him doing so. But even a monolithic faith is still a form of inner adjustment to the outer world and, for Gogol, whose critical genius, winged with laughter, might at any moment have brought him into violent collision with the autocracy and the landowners, it was in the highest degree essential to find a reconciliation with reality, particularly one so sweetly scented with frankincense and myrrh*.

At the other extreme of the period we have selected—in the works of Tolstoi—we apparently have something totally different. Tolstoi discards Orthodoxy as such and takes the field as the declared enemy of the Established Church. He is not only fully aware that this Church acts as an apparatus for the stabilisation of slavery, but it is for this reason that he detests it. However, it is necessary to bear in mind that the chief purpose of religious adaptation in such cases is to paralyse, or at least to modify, any possible conflict between conscience and evil. Tolstoi leaves precisely as much religion as will serve

---

* Dostoyevsky, whose whole approach to the matter was more complicated, made fun of Gogol's prophetic mission and, in particular, of these lines from the *Selected Passages from a Correspondence with Friends,* putting them, almost word for word, into the mouth of Foma Opiskin in *Selo Stepanchikovo (The Friend of the Family).—Author's note.*

to justify his theory of non-resistance. A consistently rationalist view of life (had Tolstoi ever got that far) could not possibly have served as a logical basis for this doctrine, which is in fact an outright rejection of all violent forms of combating evil.

To a certain extent, Dostoyevsky occupies a position betwixt and between. He is much less naively Orthodox than Gogol. On this point it will not even occur to anyone to deny whole simoons and sandstorms of doubts and agonising inner debates.

Dostoyevsky very seldom seeks support in the outward forms of Orthodoxy. This is not important to him. Important to him is the more profound, "inner" understanding of the Church which opened the way for him to contrast it, at least partially, to the state. Indeed, in Dostoyevsky's books, the Church does not only justify the state by its very existence, the altar does not only hallow and justify the palace, the dungeon, the factory, etc., but it is also shown as a power which, in many things, is opposed to all ways of life outside its own jurisdiction.

Dostoyevsky is, of course, perfectly well aware that the Synod and all the priesthood are officials in the service of the throne, but it is not enough for him that these priests hallow the activities of ministers and district superintendents. It still seems to him that as least the best of these officials of the priesthood and the very "spirit" which informs them are, in their own way, "revolutionary".

"Come, oh come!" exclaim the inspired monks of Dostoyevsky's works. What is it they thus invoke? What is "to come" is that the Church, with its charity and brotherhood, should, at some stage, overcome the state and all society founded on property, that— at some future time—the Church would build some special, almost unearthly socialism. This ecclesiastical Utopia will be based on that coinherence of souls by which Dostoyevsky tries to replace the once-glimpsed and later rejected ideal of political socialism expanded to him by his friends of the Petrashevsky circle.

However, Dostoyevsky's "ecclesiastical revolution" takes place in an atmosphere of even greater humility than Tolstoi's sectarian revolution. It is a task which will take many hundred years, a matter for the distant future, perhaps even for the next world. It is possible that Dostoyevsky, like Tolstoi, is led by the very logic of his thought to perceive this harmonious coinherence as a purely nominative ideal, as something which will be realised only in eternity, in infinity, in the sphere of metaphysics.

In this way, God, Orthodoxy, Christ as a democratic, individual, purely ethical principle of the Church— all this was quite essential to Dostoyevsky, for it gave him the opportunity to avoid a final spiritual break with socialist truth while, at the same time, justifying him in anathematising materialist socialism.

These positions also gave him the chance to assume a profoundly loyalist attitude in relation to the tsar and to the whole tsarist regime. At the same time, from the altar end of the Church, the end facing the congregation, it was possible to embellish these ecclesiastical modes with all kinds of effective graces. In this way, Dostoyevsky's Orthodoxy is at once a profoundly conservative principle and, at the same time, a kind of maximalism. Maximalists in the sphere of religion have always been in a position to say to materialists: "You will never dare to include the right to immortality in your programmes? You will never be able to demand absolute bliss and the merging of all men into one 'all-spirit'? We, on the other hand, can manipulate these beautiful, delicious things as much as we like, representing them as the true reality."

A less tragic nature than Dostoyevsky's might, perhaps, have been quite satisfied with this kind of cunningly worked-out self-comforter. But Dostoyevsky, a genius of fathomless profundity, was tormented by his immense conscience, by his acute sensibility. Dostoyevsky challenges his foes again and again under various guises, and these foes are not only philistinism, not only vice in all forms but, first of all and above all, this damnable, self-assured materialism. In his own soul he has killed it, buried it, rolled great stones across the entrance to the tomb. But it is not corpse which is immured behind these stones. Someone is always moving about, someone's heart is beating loudly, giving Dostoyevsky no peace. Dostoyevsky continues to feel that it is not only the socialism outside of himself which will not let him rest, not only the developing revolutionary movement in Russia, Chernyshevsky and his theory, the proletariat in the West, etc.; above all he is tormented by materialist socialism in his own self, which must on no account be allowed to emerge from the underground, which must be spat on, trodden into the mire, humiliated, made to look insignificant and ridiculous. This is what Dostoyevsky does do to it. Not once and not twice. In *The Possessed* he loses all self-control in this respect. And so what? A little time goes by, the smoke of argument dissipates and the mud of insinuation wears off, and the uncompromising disk of real truth begins once again to shine and to beckon.

Of course, after his experience of forced labour, Dostoyevsky did not for one moment have a genuine faith in his materialistic phantom. Yet it was enough for him to feel the stirrings of doubt to lose all peace of mind. On the other hand, he devoted all his genius for thought, feeling and character-drawing to the erection of altars to heaven. There is something of everything: the subtlest sophism and the faith of a charcoal-burner; the frenzy of the "fool in Christ" and refined analysis; the poet's facile gift of winning over the reader by the acute insight attributed to the religious characters, etc. Yet Dostoyevsky returns in doubt again and again to survey his many-storied edifices, understanding that they are not built to last and that, at the first underground tremor caused by the movement of the fettered Titan whom he has buried in his own heart, the whole pile of spillikins is going to collapse.

It seems to me that only if we adopt this approach to Dostoyevsky will we understand the true substructure of that polyphony which Bakhtin has noted in Dostoyevsky's novels and novelle. Only Dostoyevsky's split personality, together with the fragmentation of the young captialist society in Russia, awoke in him the obsessional need to hear again and again the trial of the principles of socialism and of reality, and to hear this trial under conditions as unfavourable as possible to socialism.

However, if this trial is not given at least an appearance of unbiassed fairness, the hearing of it loses all its comforting, soothing properties and cannot be expected to calm the tempest of the soul. So a long line of characters—from revolutionaries to the most superstitious reactionaries—as soon as they emerge from Dostoyevsky's inner world and are allowed to run free, immediately get out of hand and begin to argue each in his own voice, and to prove each his own thesis.

For Dostoyevsky this is a pleasure, an agonising pleasure, all the more so because he realises that, as the author, he retains the conductor's baton, remains the host in whose home all this ill-assorted company have foregathered, and can, in the end, always restore "order".

In that higher artistic unity which Bakhtin senses in Dostoyevsky's works, but does not define and even appears to consider almost beyond definition, there is always this juggling with the evidence—delicate, subtle, fearful even of itself, then, suddenly, every now and again, at various points in this trial which goes on and on through every novel and every novella—a quite uncamouflaged, coarse policeman's trick.

Nevertheless, the unheard-of freedom of "voices" in Dostoyevsky's polyphony which so strikes the reader is in fact a result of the limitations of Dostoyevsky's power over the spirits he has conjured. He himself guesses this. He himself realises that, although it is within his power to restore "order" for the benefit of the reader on the stage of his own novels, behind the scenes there is still absolutely no way of telling what's what. There, the actors may escape his control, there they may continue to develop the contradictory lines of thought which they began to trace on the visible horizon and may, in the long run, tear their author to pieces.

If Dostoyevsky the writer is host to his characters and master in his own home, is it possible to say as much for Dostoyevsky the man?

No, Dostoyevsky the man is not master in his own home, and the disintegration of his personality, its tendency to schizophrenia, arises from his desire to believe in something not suggested by what he really does believe and to refute something which refuses to be finally refuted. All this together renders him as an individual peculiarly suited to create the agonising and essential image of the confusion of his epoch.

The only true court of appeal against Dostoyevsky is not to be found in any contemporary writer nor, as yet, in any later writer, but only in the turn taken by events in the world after his death, in the entrance of new forces onto the social arena and in the creation of a completely new historical situation.

However, even our present situation, in which we see all problems from a different angle, does not leave us indifferent towards Dostoyevsky. If we ourselves find no positive ideas in Dostoyevsky we must remember that we are not as yet a majority in the country. Many groups and strata of our society will continue to seek support for their ideas in Dostoyevsky and to suffer from his illnesses. Dostoyevsky is not yet dead, either here or in the West, because capitalism is not yet dead, still less the survivals of capitalism (if we are to speak of our own country). Hence the importance of devoting careful study to all the tragic problems of *Dostoyevshchina*.

1929

THIS winter the Stradivarius Quartet gave a series
of chamber concerts by the famous Moscow composer
Taneyev.

Taneyev is known in Russia and Europe as the
author of the most profound and extensive work on
counterpoint. This work and Taneyev's merits as an
artist have earned him the greatest respect as a
unique mathematician of music.

However, this, too, was the reason why Taneyev
was grossly underrated as a composer by the general public. What I mean by this term is the public
that attends concerts, is interested in music and is
familiar with it, but does not belong to the small
circle of highly qualified persons with an exceptionally
erudite knowledge of music.

A little rumour has been circulated about Taneyev
to the effect that he is a "brainy" musician who
solved his musical problems as a mathematician
would solve his, and that is why, they say, he can
only be of interest to professionals, but leaves his
audiences cold.

The Stradivarius Quartet performed in rather
small halls and thus their concerts could not acquire
the nature of mass propaganda of Taneyev's achievements in a field that was his forte: chamber music.
But it is important to note that these concerts
invariably met with enthusiastic acclaim. I know
many persons, intelligent and well versed in music,
who (lacking a true knowledge of his works before)
have now as a result of these concerts changed their
opinion of him entirely.

I believe that more should be done to provide a
re-evaluation of Taneyev. In but the recent past it
was considered quite proper to call Tchaikovsky a

sentimental, tearful intellectual, whose music could allegedly be of no use whatsoever to our generation. I believe that the writer of these lines was the first to come out against such an opinion of a great composer who has a place of honour in Russian music which, as is now quite obvious, beginning with Glinka and ending with our own young composers, justly occupies a prominent place in world music.

The great Scriabin has long since been restored in favour and adopted as it were by the revolutionary epoch. I believe it is imperative that the same impetus should be given to a similar process in respect to Taneyev. It would be most rewarding to organise a performance next year of his great oratorio *Upon Reading a Psalm* and his laconic, stirring and truly tragic opera *Orestes*.

At the request of the Stradivarius Quartet I spoke on Taneyev, introducing their concert series. The present article is the edited stenographic report of my speech.

II

I would like to say a few words about Taneyev the man.

In both his way of life and appearance Taneyev was a typical Russian gentleman, outwardly with something of Oblomov about him as well; he liked the quiet life, the provincial calm of his remote corner of Moscow; he was rather indifferent to politics, though he was not only a liberal, but a democrat with radical leanings who welcomed the 1905 revolution, for example, quite joyously and reflected it to some extent (indirectly) in several of his works.

Though apparently in possession of a well-thought-out philosophical system in which he made ends meet quite harmoniously and without the aid of a god, in whom he flatly refused to believe, he never insisted upon nor even expressed his opinions. They were undoubtedly reflected in his music but, once again, indirectly. Taneyev was a very kind man, he tutored poor pupils without renumeration, he helped them financially from his own small income; he was never concerned with his own welfare and was satisfied to lead a modest, quiet life.

However, one must never forget that this quiet, tepid way of life, calling to mind Goncharov's Oblomov, has nothing at all in common with Oblomov's vacuousness. For Goncharov himself had very much in common with Oblomov and much of his great novel was autobiographical. Yet, a very different sort of heart beat beneath Goncharov's robe, and a whole world of images lay concealed by the lazy, dreamy expression on his face, so far removed from the silly sentiments which encompassed the entire world of his famous character.

Taneyev was of the same breed as Goncharov, as Turgenev. The seeming sluggishness and disorder of their lives was compensated by a tremendous, forceful inner creativeness. The work of men of this type—a type soon to be relegated to the past, perhaps—is of especial value in its fruitful, contemplative nature.

A slowness, a sweet pensiveness, a journey through ideas and emotions "in a horse-drawn carriage" is simply a poor showing in untalented persons; but with talented persons this produces an unusual soundness in everything they create, a depth and completeness in their work.

In our neurotic age, when history itself is dashing on headlong and the commotion of city life has reached a stage of terrible confusion, and people are so high-strung that it seems their nerves have been pulled taut and are vibrating at a thousandfold acceleration, in this age art has plunged through impressionism to futurism, momentalism, etc. This process is quite natural, but it does not necessarily mean it is progressive.

Such fleet and instant art undoubtedly produces definite impressions; it can achieve that which is impossible in the carriage of ethereal, slow-spun ancient classical art; but much has been lost on the way.

Taneyev lived in a world of music, but he did not regard music as a world unto itself, a world ruled by its own strange laws. He did not regard it as a complex sphere of higher mathematics, as would a scholar in his ivory tower.

Taneyev was a musical philosopher in two respects. In the first place, he tried to set his musical forms into a single graceful structure by a profound, slow and sure process of thinking based on a tremendous knowledge of music. Secondly, he imbued this creation with the essence of his deep and sensitive intellect; his own world outlook, his thoughts about the Universe, life, etc., were expressed in his musical forms. I do not believe that anyone, even those who are indifferent to Taneyev, would ever take it into their heads to deny this forceful presence of a rather austere and compelling intellect that reigns in his music.

But this is not all. Taneyev was a very warmhearted man, affected by all the passions of man's intensive life. No matter that the old bachelor's life appeared devoid of storms and passions; grief and hope, indignation and love, loneliness and the joy of communing with Nature and his fellow men and many, many other emotions made this stout, yet sensitive heart tremble both in his youth, when Taneyev seemed such a hearty fellow, and in his grey-haired maturity, when those who knew him well all but worshipped him as a saint and sage.

That is why it is stark barbarism and sheer

ignorance to judge Taneyev as a man devoid of passion. The fact of the matter is that Taneyev never stooped to sentimentality, that he was a stranger to the slightest hint at Gypsy bathos, which sometimes, especially if performed with affectation, we even find in Tchaikovsky's music.

Taneyev is wise; he entrusts his emotions to music only when they have become clear to him, when they have been crystallised in music. This does not mean that Taneyev merely presents an outline of emotion; no, his emotions are very much alive. After all, no musician can convey real sobbing or laughter, no artist can incorporate his own real nose in a painting. Music, as no other creative sphere, demands a reminting into the *special* gold coin of *one's own* material. Taneyev's minting, of the highest quality, devoid of alloys, is, at the same time, vital throughout and well designed throughout.

Taneyev was a gentleman, a gentleman of slow pace, a gentleman who was drawn into himself, a gentleman who, through tremendous diligence and great talent had acquired a culture that was unique, a gentleman who had reached the apex of wisdom.

We have no use for lords of the manor, we cannot stand lordliness and, perhaps, we despise Russian lordliness above all, but we cannot close our eyes to the fact that in the "cherry orchards" of the landowner fragrant flowers sometimes blossomed, when an exceptionally cultured person, who could not have existed outside the lordly manor, led a life of complete cultural dedication, when a person gave himself up utterly to an aesthetic problem—when, at the same time, he rose *above* his class and began to see reality in a different light. There resulted people who were exceptional in artistic merit, often combining a wonderful philosophical and social train of thought with art that was of fine emotion and forceful architecture.

The greater part of our classical literature has been created by such lords. They gave us such men as Herzen, as Plekhanov. It is difficult for me to imagine a man like Taneyev coming from any other background, and not from the quiet streets of old aristocratic Moscow, which, nevertheless, were open to all the winds blowing from the West; and I would stress that this native son of Moscow is extremely important to us, and in our review of our inheritance we must regard with special care the amazing musical canvases woven and embroidered by the patient hand of this composer and sage.

III

In order to better understand Taneyev's special place in music, I shall draw a parallel of sorts between him and Scriabin, a parallel which rests upon another parallel, one deeper and more general.

Much has been said about the differences between "mood" music and "architectural" music. These musical poles are but sides of one and the same music and complement each other in varying degrees. But this does not detract from the fact that we are faced with two streams of music: the objectively-architectural (epic would be more correct) and the emotionally-sensuous, or lyric. However, the words "epic" and "lyric" are less suited for an understanding of the true meaning of this difference than the terms "architectural" and "emotional".

Music originated as an expression of human emotions. We cannot for a moment doubt that it was born of man's cries of emotion. We know wherein the "music" of the animal world originates. Erotic music is the most objective example since, besides its cries of naked passion, it includes some elements of *enticement*, attracting the female by *a serenade* of sorts. In the nightingale's song we find not only the emotions of the male, but an art that is self-contained, unfolding in the mating process and reaching, not in the individual, but in the species as a whole, true perfection.

Every other type of song has apparently developed along similar lines: sobbing gave rise to lamentation, which in turn became a dirge; the wild shrieking of warriors before a battle resulted in military marches, and so forth. The whole significance of transforming emotional cries into music, or, more probably, into singing, lies in the fact that a purity of form was acquired, that there gradually evolved clear tones and their set combinations, the skill of producing melody, etc.

In following this course, music eventually became most complex. Man found expression for the personal or social emotions that burned in his breast in the use of the most varied instruments.

There is good reason why in recent times, say, beginning with the middle of the eighteenth century, there has been such an unprecedented blossoming of music, which continues to this day. On the one hand, the individual became a most complex entity at the time, especially with the appearance of the typical petty-bourgeois intellectual, i.e., an individual who was unsettled socially, divorced from the guild, with a complex, quite individual soul, with a highly developed brain and nervous system and often with a great amount of suffering in his life. The gradual progress of democracy and individualism created this type of individual, and Jean Jacques Rousseau was one of its first bright manifestations. I believe that a careful analysis of an individual like Rousseau will do much towards providing an understanding of the central and most significant type of intellectual as an ideologist, including and perhaps primarily the artistic ideologist of society in modern history. The emotional, diverse and painfully unbalanced personality of the new man, "the psychopath", in the true psychiatric meaning of the word, became ever more complex as social relations became more complex. At the same time, this personality reached the apex of sensitive self-analysis and, finally, the most unusual flexibility and virtuoso skill in expressing all the ins and outs of its most complex inner life. Here we come upon Schumann, Chopin and their followers; however, social emotions at times became turbulent and multiform. Thus, Beethoven was, of course, not only the spokesman of the complexities of his own personality, but reflected most forcefully the storms of the Great Revolution.

One can regard Scriabin in some ways as the supreme representative of this type. At a time when the French school of impressionists, headed by Debussy, seemed to have reached the limit of musical momentalism and miniaturisation, Scriabin, with no less diversity of emotion, was possessed by a tremendous desire for social expression, for social, national and even cosmic dimensions, which came of his being a man of a nation which had gone through the great revolution of 1905 and was now on the way towards the greatest of all revolutions.

Perhaps modern Western Europe, fast becoming Americanised, is gradually beginning to lose this form; however, it is not always replaced by an architectural one, of which I will now speak, but is quite often mechanised instead.

The tendency of some contemporary West European composers to embrace machine-inspired rhythms, mechanical dance forms and music deprived of its soul but "electrifying" instead, a very normal tendency in the era of arch-capitalism and imperialism, is doubtlessly fatal for music. It is possible that the proletariat will be carried away by this movement, but it should be warned against it, *for the basic principle of the proletariat is the complete subordination of machine to man,* while the basic principle of hyper-capitalism is the complete subordination of *man to machine.*

Architectural music is something else again. Perhaps its roots lie elsewhere; perhaps its source is instrumental music, i.e., man's admiration of the sound of a singing bow, or the ringing of a clay pot, or a metal object.

In this instance sound did not express a definite emotion. Undoubtedly, man contributed something of his own interpretation here as well: from the very start, he sensed the spirit of the singing bow and the rolling drum; in fact, he animated his surroundings, in accordance with his animistic outlook, to a greater extent than we do today. Nevertheless, he was dealing with *objective* beauty here, as in his gradually extending range of colour, and the human voice could now join the voices of his instruments and be regarded primarily as a source of beautiful sound. Here we have the beginning of a process which Weber called the *rationalisation* of music.

The music of all peoples who have achieved some small degree of culture is a refinement of the world of sound, singling out elements and then constructing various combinations from these elements to correspond to man's desire. Just as man builds cathedrals, palaces or tombs from tangible and visible material, so does he build monumental works from sound; combines them with dances or other ceremonies, especially of a religious or court nature and also with the epic themes of the first heroic songs, of individual or choral hymns to the gods.

This music does not develop of its own accord. It satisfies definite social demands, as does monumental construction. Primarily, it increases the pomp of religious and royal ceremonies. One must remember that these ceremonies have a very definite social significance: to strengthen and elevate the importance of the rulers, and astound and conquer their subjects by the magnitude, beauty and perfection of the state and heavenly systems, as reflected in art. It is striking that just as it was possible to create great architectural works of art on this basis, thus was it obviously possible for great masterpieces of music to be created.

Indeed, the ruling class in its more or less golden age wishes its architecture, and its musical architecture as well, to express solemn grandeur, a deep sense of inner stability and harmony. There was good reason why the aristocrat Pythagoras, who strove to establish a dictatorship of a group of the most highly placed families, stressed the great significance of the structural principle in music. It was he who expressed most clearly the idea of the existence in the heavenly world of true and magnificent order which is distorted in the earthly world. Pythagoras attempted to express this order in terms of musical harmony.

Such is the social origin and social significance of architectural music. It could not but develop wherever there was a well-established social order. That is why the Catholic Church made such extensive use of it, as the Protestant Church did later, relying on the magnetic powers of music: the organ and the congregation singing together.

Unfortunately, social order has until now usually been expressed in a religious form, in the form of a monarchy, more rarely in the form of various religious and knightly orders, guilds, etc.

It is not difficult to see that a socialist society is destined to create the most grandiose collective order. It is not difficult to foresee as well that this grandiose order of an entirely new and unprecedented type will call to life truly exhalted music which

I call architectural, i.e., the majestic combination of chorus and orchestra to produce an idealised expression of the gigantic agreement of forces.

We should note in passing that this can be presented most fully only in contrast to some negative entity which it has conquered or which threatens it, and which, in accord with the victorious light of harmony and unity, usually constitutes the essence of all architectural-musical structures.

The advances to socialism and a true realisation of the present lack of unity and ills of humanity inspire its finest sons to a mighty surge towards this order. They realise that there is a world of wise, exalted life in their dreams, a world without racial and class contradictions. They may not realise this, they may even deceive themselves and relegate this ideally construed world beyond the grave, to another world or to an *imagined* celestial time and place. At any rate, the appearance of such musicians who strive for order is possible and even inevitable in our time.

It is most peculiar to see that the Western *bourgeois* world is likewise striving towards order, and that the social expression of this is reflected in the neo-monarchist, fascist, etc., movements. This has found its expression in music as well. Vincent d'Indy, who stressed so eloquently the two poles of music I am speaking of here, who censured Debussy and considered himself to be an architectural musician, was actually an active monarchist.

The new tendencies in Western art, especially in French art (neo-classicism, purism, etc.) may be a reflection of the bourgeoisie's desire to supplant democracy and individualism with a dictatorship; but the tendency of the proletariat to exchange a capitalist system for a truly social system, i.e., a well-ordered socialist system, can also lead to architectural music.

Scriabin, so greatly influenced by Chopin, but who later fanned Chopin's fire with such unusual passion that it became a roaring holocaust, is undoubtedly a musician of mood.

He himself writes of the great pleasure he derives from the knowledge of his power over musical matter, the unusual force with which he can make the obedient sounds reflect the deepest emotions.

It was the experience of an artist, capable of transmitting his passionate change in mood so swiftly and forcefully into objective reality, into music that charmed the souls of others, that suggested the strange philosophical wanderings that provide the key to the music of Scriabin's second and third periods.

The essence of Scriabin's philosophy is now well known. Scriabin believed that the universe was the free creation of a certain personal spirit, a creation, however, full of contradiction and tragedy, a sort of sorrowful, passionate, bitter, exciting game of the spirit with ghosts it itself had called to life.

Scriabin conceded the existence of a god-artist and considered the universe to be the work of this artist, created by his dream as it were for his own exalted "pleasure".

But how does a creative individual, Scriabin himself, his ego, appear in respect to this god? In viewing his own personal world, his ego as a creative centre, and his surroundings as his own game, Scriabin, as is often the case with idealists, descended to genuine solipsism, i.e., to imagining that this god was none other than Scriabin himself and that in relation to his ego the rest of the universe was his own free but terrible artistic game.

Proceeding from these concepts, which he kept in secret from the public, Scriabin built his dream, truly bordering on the insane and in scope surpassing the flights of the imagination of composers of all time.

Scriabin believed he could create a musical mystery which would actually evolve into the solemn chords of conciliation, of the triumph of the spiritual essence of creation, so that after the fantastic performance of this all-encompassing mystery, there would actually be no reason for the universe to exist any longer. The colourful phantasmagory would shrivel and vanish, and the spirit would enter a new phase of existence which would be an extension of itself, its complete self-knowledge and, at the same time, its release from the glittering, seductive nightmares it alone had created.

If this construction of Scriabin's is translated into a social language, we shall see the social experience that is reflected in his philosophy, in his musical plans and, therefore, in his works.

Scriabin sees the world and primarily, the human world, as a unique and exciting kaleidoscope of events, in which diversity is bought at the price of rupture, ugliness and suffering.

The world Scriabin perceives through our present bourgeois civilisation attracts him, on the one hand, by its wealth, its noise, its combination of pleasures and horrors and, on the other hand, it seems to be a temporary, unacceptable world that must undergo a basic revolutionary upheaval which would replace it by universal calm and order.

Thus, we see in Scriabin an interest in the very tempo of life, both internal and external, in the chaotic era of imperialism, a deep understanding and the ability to respond to all the exciting and burning contradictions of psychological and social life; and, on the other hand, a tremendous desire for order. However, Scriabin perceived the one and the other in his own individual way. Scriabin enjoyed the way objective life, so tormenting and dizzying, played on the strings of his unusually sensitive heart and how the flutterings of this heart were later reflected in music. He perceived this picture as his own creative dream, as his own self-delight and self-torture and, therefore, the serenity and order which his soul yearned for he also perceived as *his own* serenity and order, as his personality absorbing all the vagaries and contradictions, as *absolute self-assertion*.

However, it is most characteristic that Scriabin approaches this state of serenity in a revolutionary way, i.e., he does not visualise a situation in which his creative ego would *gradually* reconcile the universal discord or in which he would build another structure in music, one of stately harmony, to counteract the noisy confusion of the universe, and humanity in particular. Nothing of the kind! It was characteristic of Scriabin that he considered self-incineration in the fire of excesses, which he visualised during his greatest interest in solipsism, as the incineration of the world.

Scriabin's god is one of self-incineration who, in the fire of passions that have reached their peak, destroys his own body and frees his true essence; that is why the great mystery which Scriabin perceived in somewhat hazy outline took on the nature of just such a wild frenzy of passions, such a wanton orgy, when the elements of the soul and, therefore, the universe, began to disintegrate at a definite stage, and only after this extreme *explosion* of destructive passion would there dawn a new calm morning of other-wordly order, quite unfathomable to us.

What social force, what social experience is reflected in *these* features of Scriabin's work?

Undoubtedly, the revolutionary experience of 1905, the imminent revolution. This was refracted by Scriabin through a very original prism, perceiving a world charged with a tremendous force, at one and the same time both destructive and directed towards supreme order, a force which in exploding would destroy the neurotic, uneasy kaleidoscope of the world.

But once again, as an individualist, Scriabin perceived this simply as a mood, as a definite trend of emotions and conveyed it with unusual, half-insane and brilliant boldness, as the identification of this force with his own personality. It was *he* who was the great revolutionary, it was *his* work that would destroy the world, it was *this work* that would produce the harmony.

Scriabin, however, was not mad. Essentially, he was a very sane and intelligent man.

Later (not long before his death, unfortunately), he realised his mistake and in clear and logical entries in his diary he destroyed his solipsism and confessed that the world exists objectively, that, therefore, other human beings and other creatures, and other organisms, bodies and things exist—undoubtedly, actually exist; if this is so, then he would obviously have to say good-bye to the mystery, to the belief that one mighty work, one individual could change the world. Scriabin then wrote the *Initial Act* instead of his mystery; true, it was still overflowing with individualism and idealism, but the very fact that he views his new majestic musical poem of the world as a solely *preliminary* movement to something else is most significant and gratifying.

But when Scriabin thus freed himself of the extremes of individualism and realised that the world is an objectively existing ocean of matter, when he more or less came to understand mankind's place in it—did he then reject his idea of the tortuous kaleidoscope of our present social life, of the necessity of an explosion within it, of the necessity of achieving a true, wise order in life? I do not think so. Naturally, I do not have direct proof of this, but I think that Scriabin, channelling his thoughts towards a healthy outlook on life (from subjectivity to objectivity, which could have later taken him from idealism to materialism), was forced once again to translate his hopes and plans from the language of *mood* into a *social* language.

At any rate, Scriabin did not do this as a musician: as a musician he remained the only genius of his kind, i.e., in constructing music as something entirely personal, as mood music, "Chopinising", as it were, he imbued this subjective music, owing to the peculiarities of his philosophy, with social and even universal force. Moreover, the entire world, seen through Scriabin's moods, acquired the features of a stirring fanfare, terrifying though delightful in its diversity and strength, the features of the concerted struggle of the elements—with the elements of human consciousness in the forefront, naturally—among themselves and the rush of this entire mass to an imminent explosion, which will be tortuous but will be a final absolution. A new, truly harmonious order is the final goal of this ravaged universe (society!).

Thus Scriabin, despite his individualism, advanced towards a portrayal of the revolution or a prophecy of it through the portrayal of passion. He prophesied it in music and herein lies his social significance. Inasmuch as the reader will agree with this analysis, he will accept the fact that this significance is great, indeed.

V

From what I have said of Taneyev it is apparent that he was a very different type of man.

First of all, Taneyev, unlike Scriabin, was an architect in music.

Taneyev does not regard music as an expression of tumultuous passion, it is not a human cry, transformed, yet bearing all the features of its origin.

Taneyev considers music to be a self-sufficient element with its own inner laws, its own order, which must be clearly defined lest one be led into wretched contradiction. One can build more or less freely in the wonderful and shining material of music, but the more perfectly the artist knows the laws of his material and the closer he conforms to them, the greater his freedom. The matter that is music seems to seek combinations of its own accord, to align itself into a beautiful, convincing and logical structure.

Even if man were simply to play with these singing combinations as a child plays with blocks, without thwarting the inner qualities of these magic blocks, in a way that would guide his creative hand according to the will inherent in the musical forms themselves, even then the result would be elements of a very special world, far more orderly and pure inwardly and, therefore, more beautiful than ours.

Music is the transformed life of matter which Taneyev considered to be striving towards order in its very essence.

In his works most complete and most in keeping with his philosophy, he raises his own concealed moods to the pinnacle of music. He transforms the world of human passions, he does not let it ring out acutely to all but wreck the golden forms of music, he tries not to deprive the fits of despair or terrible clashes of the elements of their force, but translates them *in toto* into the exalted language of music.

When one listens to the more *pathétique* passages in Taneyev's quartets and trios, one realises how masterfully he used the elements of suffering, gentle sorrow or heroic struggle. Taneyev understands and accepts them; but when Taneyev the *musician* depicts all this, you feel that the fingers of a master have touched the waves of the storm, knowing beforehand that these waves are as yet the unpacified and unco-ordinated elements of a given whole which cannot but be co-ordinated.

Taneyev did not really think there was a world beyond in which supreme happiness would be achieved; he did not really believe in a providence that would provide a happy end; and, least of all, did he suppose he was a magician like Scriabin who thought he could solve, for his own benefit, the discord of existence in one thunderous chord of a magnificent finale.

No, Taneyev considers music and his deep knowledge of music as proof that the Universe *is already* just in such a state of harmony, that the world and Nature are actually a symphony, a state of accord, although at present this world is passing through certain stages of development which tend to remove it from its own true essence. I believe that Taneyev's outlook is probably closest to that of the great German idealists, to Fichte, Schelling, and especially Hegel. As is known, Hegel insisted that his idealism was an objective idealism, i.e., that in his opinion idea as a concept is not in opposition to matter, to the world; that the development of the idea proceeds concretely within the concrete phenomena of the concrete universe.

Returning to our simile of magic blocks, one can put it thus: the world is actually a magnificent system of such blocks, as is music. It lends itself—perhaps to multiform, if not singular—construction, i.e., to the realisation of accord and happiness on various levels; but the builders are clumsy, and the magic blocks seem scattered about in confusion. Taneyev feels that a musician possesses a different set of magic blocks than those of which the real universe is built. A musician's magic blocks are simpler, clearer and in closer harmony with each other. It is much easier to construct the higher forms of accord and happiness from musical magic blocks. They can do away with disintegration and discord and transform all griefs and sorrows into happiness.

This is the musician's true calling. That is why he can be a *pure* artist and why he must be a formalist-musician. He must give precedence to form, because it is the formal side of music that determines the social role of the musician as one who advocates the elimination of contradictions. At the same time, Taneyev firmly believed that music is a *socially significant* phenomenon and was always a staunch supporter of *meaningful*, ideological, philosophical music.

This brings me to the following conclusions: if Scriabin depicted so brilliantly the pathos, the passions without which no revolution is ever possible, Taneyev revealed its other side, which in the present year of 1925 is no less close to our hearts: the constructive side, the side of eliminating contradictions, achieving harmony, unity and the creation of the highest form of order.

Despite Scriabin's passionate dedication, we do not find this state of order. He is too much of a romanticist. However, the revolution is not only romantic, but is classical in its constructive nature.

Taneyev the classic evolved a truly musical philosophy of usefulness and order which included freedom as one of its elements. But there are times when Taneyev lacks Scriabin's passion. If, on the other hand, Scriabin achieved a certain degree of objectivity *in his way of thinking* towards the end of his days, in his life and in *his music he remains an individualist*. Taneyev, on the other hand, relegates his personality to the background, he is to a very great extent an objective and epic personality.

We have in Scriabin's music the greatest gift of musical romanticism of the revolution, and in Taneyev's music the greatest gift of the same revolution—musical classicism.

I would like to add several remarks on the social role and social significance of Taneyev's music which I find necessary even in such a brief essay as this.

I have already said that Taneyev was a formalist and I praised him as such. Nevertheless, any reader in the least bit familiar with my writings knows that I am a sworn foe of formalism and consider it to be one of the sins of a decadent culture.

But here one must clearly draw the line between two types of formalism. The ruggedly individual formalism of an artist-competitor in an era of the decay of the ruling classes takes on the nature of a mad race for originality, ostentation and affectation.

This race for originality is all the more disgusting, because the eccentrics are not after originality of thought or emotion, but *solely* after peculiarity of form, i.e., after a bizarre effect, shock value and sometimes even sensational nonsense. The last link in this type of race are the various Dadaists or outright charlatans, and there are various degrees of this which not only smell of decay, but which are fully decomposed already. That is why Hausenstein, an excellent historian of German literature and a Marxist, in attempting to defend expressionism was later forced to admit it was undeniably decadent in form.

Taneyev's formalism is something else again. In his letters to Tchaikovsky, which are in themselves of tremendous interest, he tries to explain the great work he has done in studying the origins of music and its classical canons. "Why am I searching in the seventeenth century," he wrote, "why am I seeking an established language, why am I seeking a well-defined, complete form of music? Because this is not scholasticism at all, but the more significant, well-moulded treasures. Each form, evolving organically from generation to generation, has a complete universal significance and, in the end, rests on the foundation of folk art."

What does this mean? It means that Taneyev is not trying to produce a bizarre effect at all; it means Taneyev wants to learn the language of music, which he regards first as a product of the collective creative effort of a people, then of generations of skilled masters, of entire guilds, and, finally, of a number of brilliant individuals who lived, however, in an organic era, who did not jump from place to place, but derived their logical conclusions from the work of their predecessors in this gigantic, collective, objective undertaking.

A scientist is a poor one, indeed, if he does not grasp the whole of his science as just such an organically growing tree, nurtured constantly by new experiments. If one is a scientist of great erudition, it does not at all mean he will have nothing to contribute himself. On the contrary, it is possible to add something organic—at times even great perhaps—to that which has been created by humanity only if this past has been fully understood. One can judge how lawful this continuity appears to us Communists from the fact that even the gigantic rupture that comes with the proletarian revolution does not disrupt this continuity, and Lenin, the world's greatest revolutionary, triumphantly states once again that the process of building a culture of the new class, the process of changeover to an entirely new universal culture, can only take place on the basis of a complete understanding of the old culture.

Thus, Taneyev is a formalist in the sense that he does not set his all-too-transient personality—as the skilled contemporary Bohemian heroes do—in opposition to the age-old structures, but, on the contrary, he arranges and generalises the creative achievements, he does not invent a personal abstruse language but studies the great language of the people, its laws and its infinite wealth, and, naturally, his purpose is to further enrich it.

In another letter to Tchaikovsky, Taneyev says most significantly: "He who does not understand the inner, ideal language of music will certainly create dead values." Thus, there can be no break between form and content in Taneyev's works. The musical form itself is full of meaning. This was the nature of Taneyev's research in music *for himself* and for his pupils in order to fully understand the *true* meaning, the psychological and social significance of each musical formula.

Some music critics noted with surprise that Taneyev first completed the various parts of a composition and then seemed to join them along the lines of the magic blocks I have spoken of.

But why are these music critics (Karatygin, for example) surprised? Because they are used to evaluating music from a lyrical, emotional point of view. Naturally, such music must come from several basic determinants, it must grow organically, as a plant from its original seed. Architectural music is something else again. If a critic would have approached the Cathedral of Milan when it was under construction, he would certainly have been amazed by the fact that in one place they were working on a plinth, in another they were carving a statue, in a third they were cutting stones of the most capricious shape and form, etc., but all this was being done because these various parts were just that—*parts* of a planned *whole*.

Taneyev could borrow much from completed musical material and could slowly prepare rational forms for his subsequent constructions, because he knew so well that these forms belonged to some higher unity.

VII

And so, we revolutionaries can expect future titanic songs of revolutionary passion, but for the present will not find a more passionate musical language not only in Russian music, but perhaps in all of world music, than the language of Scriabin in such of his works as *Prometheus* and others, similar to it.

As builders, as champions of the communist *order* and enemies of the pseudo-democratic chaos of capitalism, we will yet hear great songs of construction and the accord of peoples, but perhaps even in world music we will have difficulty in finding songs of such deep, significant and constructive wisdom as those which Taneyev has given us.

1925

ALEXANDER BLOK

Chapter One

*The Class, Time and Personality
of Alexander Blok*

EVERY writer speaks for one class or another.

This does not mean that every writer is the spokesman for his own particular class, the adequate and unadulterated expression of the whole plentitude of its content—its traditions, culture and interests. The classes themselves have each, as one might say, their own social biography. They go through various stages and may be at any given moment at their conception, nearing their prime or on the decline. The biography of a class may even comprise several such peaks and declines. Class background is not always the same for corresponding classes from one country to another. In one country a class may be more markedly in evidence than in another. However, if a class be taken at some specific epoch, it is possible to find among those who may be accounted its spokesmen (usually, of course, more than one, even many different people) some whose work is indeed more or less adequate to express its essence—who seem to have grown out of the very heart of the class in question, whereas others appear rather on its periphery, where they are more subject to the influence of other classes.

It is essential to take into account all those shifts and modifications in that subsoil of class which— in social time and social space—is the breeding-ground of ideology, and at all costs to avoid the pitfalls of oversimplified Marxism or, more exactly, anti-Marxism, which considers class as an indivisible and unchangeable formation and which, for this reason, has difficulty in defining the true social essence of this or that ideology (in relation, for instance, to the works of any particular artist). In this way, a whole series of such artists can be assigned to the same generalised class category and the differences between them are no longer seen as having their origin in social causes. This approach leads either to such differences being ignored or to their being explained by transient and socially fortuitous elements.

Blok is a spokesman of the nobility (the *dvoryanstvo*). He should be regarded as a scion of the line of the nobility's ideologists and his place is—to extend the metaphor—at the end of that line. With certain reservations he may be considered the last great artist of the Russian nobility.

In so far as his place is at the end of the line of the nobility's historical development, Blok reflects the nadir of its disintegration. Profoundly infected by the traditions of the nobility, he is, at the same time, a bearer of anti-bodies. He is charged with hatred for his milieu and for his class. In so far as he finds these in a state of enfeeblement, of disintegration, and is himself a product of such disintegration, Blok is debarred from seeking salvation in that aristocratic nucleus which still, to all appearances, formed the acknowledged "establishment" of his society: i.e., in the hard core of reactionary bureaucrats and firmly entrenched landed gentry.

One of the characteristic features of the decline of the nobility was, incidentally, that its more or less progressive representatives tended to break away from this central core.

In Russian literature we find a whole series of authors belonging to the nobility who are consciously or half-consciously defending their culture against the most terrible immediate foe of their class— against the bourgeoisie, against capitalism. Nonetheless it is no longer possible for these defenders of aristocratic culture openly to champion the Blimpish platform of the nobility as a class. On the contrary, they are well aware that this kind of aristocratic traditionalism is the most vulnerable joint in the armour of their class. Morally, they shun this hard core of their own class as though it were a black, dirty smear on its face. To this moral revulsion is added a frequently vague but nevertheless anxious premonition that such mechanical, violent, 'Black-Hundred'* methods of self-defence are doomed to defeat, and that the more ruthless the defence, the more ruthlessly will it be defeated.

In essence, all the nobility's Narodism was rooted in the desire to defend their hereditary culture from the advances of capitalism and from those inevitable results of the development of capitalism, which the more intelligent representatives of the nobility at least partially foresaw. To this end, they sought to bring into play not so much the attitudes of the landowners as those of the peasantry, which were complementary to them.

Truth and justice, as the peasant understood them, were in many ways akin to the ideals of his master and came to be adopted by the latter as if they had been his own. The landlord hid behind the peasant, tucking his estate away behind the village, and, from this point of departure, proceeded to work out his own "peasant" ideology according to the promptings of his own class-consciousness. Bakunin, for instance, interpreted the peasant in a spirit of elemental romanticism; Herzen stressed his inborn affinity with certain home-grown germs of socialism; Tolstoi approached him from a lofty moral angle in an exceptionally disinterested religious spirit, and so forth.

---

* The Black Hundreds were monarchist gangs organised by the tsarist police to fight the revolutionary movement. They assassinated revolutionaries, attacked progressive intellectuals and perpetrated Jewish pogroms.—*Ed.*

Blok came upon the scene to find his own class in a state of extreme disintegration (its central core dominated by Pobedonostsev or post-Pobedonostsev* attitudes). The bourgeoisie, on the other hand, were at the height of their power and vigour, although, at the same time, uneasily aware of mortality in face of the unexpectedly rapid, tidal advance of their antipode—the proletariat.

For all his hatred of the bourgeois world, Blok feared the end of the bourgeoisie and the onset of a new era without historical precedent. Nevertheless, even he managed to construct something resembling a personal philosophy out of the tatters of aristocratic tradition, a romanticised conception of the peasantry (the element of "the people"), and a confused, harsh, anxious, burning sympathy for the forces of revolution—a philosophy in which he tried to find the solution to the growing storminess of the social scene.

Class (at a distinct stage of its development and in a distinct subsection of the class as a whole) was the determining factor of Blok's general platform as a citizen, as a political thinker (in so far as he can be considered from this aspect), and as a philosopher (again within his own limits). This particular subsection consisted of the most educated members of the ruined, *semi-déclassé* landed gentry who were at that time having to seek a living from other sources than the land and rapidly becoming indistinguishable from the professional petty bourgeoisie (as, for instance, in the case of Blok himself, who was for all practical purposes reduced to earning a living by his pen).

---

* Pobedonostsev—reactionary tsarist statesman, Procurator-General of the Synod, actually head of the government and chief inspirer of the savage feudal reaction under Alexander III. He continued to play a prominent part under Nicholas II.—*Ed.*

The fact that Blok happened to be a poet, however, and that, as a poet, he achieved wide recognition and became the mouthpiece of fairly considerable circles of the Russian intelligentsia was, to a considerable extent, the result of his own, strictly individual qualities.

Blok's way of thinking, I repeat, is entirely conditioned by matters of class and time. Personal to him—at least to a considerable extent—is the fact that, although his thought found a more or less adequate medium, in his publicistic articles, his diaries, letters, etc., it was first and foremost in poetry that he achieved a supremely individual form of self-expression. Only personal to him to a certain extent, of course. Let us explain:

Blok became a poet because he was extraordinarily sensitive. A heightened sensitivity is a prerequisite of the artist's calling, as of his success. It is possible, however, to imagine an artist in whom the process of thought is highly developed. The images such an artist creates are distinguished by clarity of outline. Almost as clearly as does the language of ideas only, of course, more immediately, vividly and emotionally, they offer an *interpretation* of that reality in contact with which the artist's imagination brings them into being. However, the nobility had no need of such a poet in Blok's time and, even had such a poet intact appeared at the same time as Blok, he would not have been greatly admired even given considerable talent. On the contrary, the extreme nervousness, the uncertainty, the shaky hold on reality and the failure to perceive a clearly defined way through this reality—all ensured a peculiarly enthusiastic reception for a poet such as Blok for whom poetic images are not so much an interpretation, not so much the expression of the artist's profoundly poetical *understanding* of reality as, on the contrary, a manifestation of his inability to understand it, and, as a direct result of this inability, of his hostility towards it.

Hostility towards reality (covering, to a considerable extent, one's own subjective awareness of things and one's own psyche) leads, inevitably, to despair. Blok often came very close to despair. However, he was not a poet of unadulterated hopelessness. On the contrary, at almost all periods of his work he was trying to find—for himself as for his "flock"—some message of consolation.

Yes. Reality is incomprehensible and abhorrent, but there is always the hope that it is nothing but a filthy covering behind which is a high mystery. Perhaps the occasional glimpses of beauty in Nature, man and art are simply mysterious pointers towards something which exists eternally in some other sphere and beckons man to itself, filling him with hope? Perhaps it is possible to touch on these other worlds not only in a flight of white wings towards a dream of holiness, perceiving their blurred contours in the imagination "as in a glass, darkly", as the Apostle Paul has it, but also amidst the dregs of vice, of all that is satanic in life, in the oblivion which comes of drink and debauch. Perhaps, in a word, it is possible, at the very bottom of the "abyss", to enter into a similar communion with this same eternal power which, itself beyond good and evil, yet promises to whirl man away beyond all hard decisions, troublesome rules, hesitations and anxieties, and to plunge him into the flaming ocean of the supratemporal and supraspatial music of true being?

It may even be, finally, (Blok's third period) that the squall of revolution, whose approach can already be sensed, will, on closer inspection, turn out to be the onset of that very divine dance of the violent, wild and primitive element which is destined to burst like lava through the prosaic, boring crust of everyday life.

With regard to existence in its everyday manifestations, Blok is always a revolutionary. He tries to see this existence either as an obstacle to be overcome, or as a symbol, a hint at some other, radically different state of being. He cannot, however, find comfort in any definite religious system. For that matter, he could scarcely have "consoled" his sceptical and sophisticated contemporaries with the aid of any definite religious doctrine or of any pedantically constructed metaphysical system (whether Vladimir Solovyov's or any one else's). This hint of the inexpressible, however—now seen as a glimpse of whitish-blue heights, now of yellowish-black, now of burning red, devoid of all definite form but rich by virtue of its breadth and vast scope and beautiful with the beauty of the ill-defined—this alone might mount to the head like the wine of truth, even though that truth be revealed only to the prophetic mind.*

On the other hand, because Blok chose to play the part of a prophet who cannot, or will not, speak out clearly, but who uses the word as though it were a note of music, because he elected to become a *musician,* who operated words and images to suggest a yearning for that which is beyond speech and varied the approaches and the glimmering, half-caught visions in many keys, he became more than the spokesman and the seducer of those of his own class who felt as he did. He appealed not only to the degenerate, déclassé, nobility with their intensely refined culture, but also to wide circles of the bourgeois intelligentsia, for, at that time, the triumphant bourgeoisie—the detested enemy of the nobility—had itself begun to sing sad songs foreshadowing its own approaching end. It had itself begun to fear

---

* Lunacharsky is referring here to one of Blok's best-known poems, *The Stranger,* in which the poet plays on the tag: *in vino veritas.—Tr.*

reality and, in its own, far clumsier manner, had begun to peer anxiously into the beyond in order to distract its own attention from uneasy contemplation of the historical prospects which were opening up before it.

Certain individual features of Blok's personality were, of course, a *sine qua non* of such popularity. However, even these purely personal traits were not without a class foundation. Also, they were subject to class control. I shall explain:

Blok was the scion of several noble families. There is no need to trace his pedigree back too far. His father was not altogether normal. He was a professor of some talent and an original thinker whose unbalanced, nervous temperament made itself felt even in his writings. That daemonic unease which is invariably mentioned in reminiscences of Alexander Lvovich Blok was undoubtedly inherited by his son. Together with a certain, perhaps typically German, physical toughness, kindheartedness and sentimentality, truly Blokish traits in the full sense of the word (Blok's ancestors were Germans who had been granted titles of hereditary nobility in Russia), Blok's father, possibly through the Cherkasovs, his maternal ancestors, bequeathed to his son a slightly sadistic kink, an exaggerated sensuality, a tendency towards extremes, a tenseness always near to breaking-point. This daemonism was the basic factor of Blok's paternal heredity. But neither can the Beketov line be considered altogether healthy. The Beketov style of living was profoundly ingrained in Blok, for, in his childhood and adolescence, he had grown up under the dominant influence of his mother's family.

"Beketovism" might be described as a well-balanced, harmonious version of the way of life of the cultured nobility. The Beketovs—once rich but, by the time of Blok's birth, considerably impoverished aristocrats—had found an outlet into the world of scholarship, where they were held in considerable esteem. Without breaking either with the traditions of religion or with their attachment to the homeliness and pleasant customs of the country-house idyll, the Beketovs seem to have experienced no difficulty in reconciling all this with a liberal outlook and a rosy belief in enlightenment in a spirit of respect for Art and Science with capital letters.

The Beketovs were thoroughly decent, gentle people with a social conscience. In spite of a certain measure of essentially harmless progressiveness, they were profoundly traditional. All this had the effect of strengthening in Blok those very aristocratic features which attached him to his class. At the same time, however, we know that Blok's mother was inclined to mysticism, that she was an epileptoid, subject to more and more frequent attacks towards the end of her life. So, on the side of the Beketovs also, we find a heightened nervosity and pathological tendencies.

All this taken together and ploughed back into the stormy and bewildering life of the period went to form the subsoil from which grew Blok's profoundly morbid dreams, the flowering of which was the reflection of that life in his own psyche.

On the one hand, Blok's psycho-biological predispositions were in many ways just what might have been expected in a class such as the nobility of that time had come to be. On the other, the social milieu which forms the poet is always on the lookout for a spokesman, for an instrument as perfectly adapted as possible to produce that music the creation of which is the peculiar task of its artists.

When a poet begins his service to society, when he publishes his first songs, and while he mounts the next few steps of the ladder, his fate is in the balance: he may either be rejected or acknowledged.

167

Whether or not the poet is acknowledged by certain sections of society, which sections are the first to recognise him and the extent of this recognition, are all contributory factors of enormous importance to his further career and even to his development as a writer.

Blok had every qualification to become the prophet, dreamer and latter-day romantic of the nobility, a kind of Novalis singing the sunset of the landowning intelligentsia—and this is just what he did become. Had he not been burdened by his own specific psycho-biological preconditioning, had he been—healthier, let us say, more definite, more balanced, then his work would have passed more or less unheeded by his contemporaries, at any rate by those circles of the intelligentsia who were at that time to some extent the mentors of public taste and who, in fact, took up his poetry as their emblem.

If Blok's way of thinking was the product of his class and his epoch, then his way of expressing his thoughts, or not even so much his thoughts as his emotional complexes, was preconditioned by his psycho-biological nature which, in its turn, was predetermined by a heredity that was itself a reflection of the psycho-biological instability of his class (the product of the growing uncertainty of its position in society). Added to this, his class (together as we have already said, with the kindred masses of the bourgeois intelligentsia) accepted him as their spokesman in his own time, gave him fame, inspired him to become the poet of his epoch, that is, to express certain great and necessary truths. It was the very abnormality—or, to put it mildly, the extreme originality—of Blok's psychological make-up which fitted him so excellently for the writing of that symbolist poetry, which—wavering between the poetic arrogance of high despair and a dream which took many forms groping in the darkness after some kind of salvation from the horrors of life—was most suited to meet the requirements of his public.

Chapter Two
Blok the Musician

Maria Beketova, who knew the poet intimately and well, says in her reminiscences of Alexander Blok that, in the generally accepted sense, he was not musical. He loved music, it affected him very strongly, but he himself could not play any instrument and did not have a good ear, i.e., he was simply not able to reproduce the music he heard. However, Maria Beketova adds immediately, Blok had a remarkable sense of rhythm. He himself confirms this statement to some extent in a letter to Andrei Bely: "I am hopelessly lacking in all understanding of music, nature has given me absolutely no ear for it," he writes. "I cannot discuss music as an art from any point of view whatsoever." Here, however, he adds something more important than Beketova's remark about his feeling for rhythm. "In this way," he says, "I am condemned never to be able to exteriorise the singing which is always going on within me."

By this, Blok is confirming that inside him lived a perpetual song, some kind of musical element which we can hardly think of as being melodically organised but rather as consisting of a rhythmical alternation of emotions, of their rising and falling away, in other words, of some dynamic more or less organised life of feelings, moods, fits of passion—very close, it may be assumed, to what Blok experienced when listening to music.

Since the real music that one hears with one's ears makes its effect not so much through the actual material medium of sound and tone as through a dynamic interaction of the breaking-down and the establishment of repose, it is evident that Blok, for all his ill-developed aural apparatus (whether as listener or performer), was nevertheless equipped with an exceptionally fine-set, emotionally super-responsive, dynamic apparatus. Music aroused in him deep, varying, overwhelmingly powerful waves of feeling. He was subject to such waves even when he was not listening to music. They required an outlet but, not finding one through the purely tonal medium, found what they needed in words.

Goethe once made an extremely original, if not altogether accurate observation. He said that people with a great inner need to express themselves through art, who lack plastic or musical talent become poets and are reduced to describing in words those visual images or those worlds of sound which they would prefer to recreate more directly, without filtering them through the intellect, for the immediate delectation of eye and ear.

This is, on the whole, true of poets of the musical type. Blok, of course, is more than just a poet-musician. He is also artist and sculptor, playwright and thinker. Nevertheless, there can be no doubt that Blok's visual descriptions and plastic imagery, as also his thoughts and his objective renderings of the clash of human passions and actions, lag far behind the musical impact of his poetry. To some extent, Blok's poetry is a substitute for music. He would probably have been a happier man had nature endowed him with a composer's talent. At all events, the musical element in his work gains complete control over the word in its quality as the name given to a specific object, subordinates it to its own require-ments, seeming to fade out sharp outlines, trans-forming them into fluid shadows which intertwine fantastically, merge and dissolve, obedient to the poet's inner, lyrical and musical impulse.

Blok himself was fully aware of this particular characteristic of his poetry. Remembering Verlaine's famous *ars poetica* with its demand that poetry should be *"de la musique avant toutes choses"* and its advice to the poet to *"tordre le coup à l'éloquence"*, Blok says of the earliest period of his work, which he refers to as "prehistoric": "I was brought up in my mother's family. Here, there was great love and understanding for the word; on the whole, traditional ideas on literary values and ideals dominated in the family. In popular terminology, as Verlaine would have had it, the preference was given to *éloquence*; only my mother was distinguished by a perpetual rebelliousness and an anxious interest in the new, and, in her, my aspirations towards *musique* found a supporter. . . . However, I shall be grateful till my dying day to that dear, old-fashioned *éloquence* for the circumstance that, for me, literature did not begin with Verlaine or, for that matter, with any form of decadence."

Had it been merely a question of reaffirming the fact that, in Blok's poetry, the emotional and rhythmic musical elements are of more importance than the thought or the plastic image, it would not have been worth while to assign so important a place to the idea of Blok the musician in this brief attempt to define his essential sociological and artistic significance. The heart of the matter lies much deeper. Blok was a musician through and through and he apprehended the world in terms of music.

We have already discussed why Blok's class and epoch required of their poet that he should provide them with a reflection of reality in which all the contours were blurred, a reflection which would not admit of any genuine realism, which emptied reality of true content, either seeking therein some symbolic clue to a world beyond, or else seeing it as a damnably opaque veil drawn over the essence of things to hide their ideal substance from the human eye.

This essence of things, this world beyond, this so-called real world offered a kind of feeble but nonetheless real hope of the possibility of appeal against those injustices which real life was inflicting upon the disintegrating class.

Blok's symbolism would not have had the same power had it been based on dry allegory or on some such artificial system as Steiner's which, for some strange reason, exercised such a prolonged and complete tyranny over Bely, a far more rational and metaphysical thinker than Blok. Blok's power lay in the fact that he created symbols which were above all, musical. Even judged by the canons of symbolist values, no single image of Blok's, from whatever period of his work it might be taken, has the weight of something complete in itself, of a clearly minted cultural coin which could, under any circumstances, become a seriously accepted form of social "currency". Yet, as these symbols combined to form a single weave, entering into the mainstream of the musical torrent of Blok's poetic melodies, so they took on a quite extraordinary charm, a peculiar, hypnotic power, a tremendous charge (illusory, of course) of profound significance—particularly for the reader who was eagerly looking for such profound significance beyond the confines of real life.

In this respect, Blok's meeting with the philosopher Vladimir Solovyov and with a group of his young followers merely served to pour oil on a fire which was already well ablaze. Bely writes of the impression made on these symbolically-minded young people by Blok's first volume of verse: "For us youngsters Blok was a unique phenomenon; at that time it was possible to come across 'Blokites', who saw in Blok's poetry a turning point in the fate of the Russian Muse; Blok had raised a corner of the veil which covered her face: this face was seen to be that of Sophia, the Divine Wisdom of the ancient Gnostics. In this poetry, the theme of earthly love was interwoven with the religious-philosophical themes of the Gnostics and of Vladimir Solovyov. The symbolism of that time found its ideal representative in the person of Blok. . . ."

All his life, Blok's feeling for the world remained musical and he held serenely to the conviction that the inmost essence of being is musical—not tonal, that is, but essentially emotional and dynamic and, therefore, subject to its own system of laws.

Blok does not only hear those melodies and chords which sound as a distant accompaniment to the events of his own and others' private lives, to the boring and everyday as well as to the vivid experience, and which constitute the true value and meaning of all that happens. He sees the whole Universe as a kind of crust, a cold and gloomy outer covering beneath which rages the element, the fire of the musical principle which has its own destiny and controls the fate of the outer world. For Blok, the history of mankind, too, was governed by this inner musical burning. He believed, however, that from time to time the flame of music would waver and sink, the crust would thicken and freeze, and anti-musical epochs would result, epochs which Blok considered empty of talent, sombre, hateful.

Here, it is worth noting in passing that these ideas of Blok's were far from exceptional, particularly during his lifetime. Spengler maintained something very similar. It is possible to find elements of an analogous view of the world in Nietzsche (his concept of Dionysius). Ideas of much the same sort play a tremendous part in the work and thought of Scriabin. Many other names might be mentioned here, among others—Bely's. It was in a letter to Bely apropos of the latter's article "Mir iskusstva" ("The

World of Art") 1902, that Blok, calling this article a "revelation", first clearly expounded his theory of music as the fundamental principle of being.

This whole philosophy of music, which, of course, far from being a whim or passing phase, was the key to Blok's character both as man and poet, is set out in his diary for the spring of 1919. At that time, Blok was absorbed in the problem of the intelligentsia and in the related problem of humanism. It seemed to him that humanism was dead and that the intelligentsia itself had outlived its time. All the circumstances of the moment combined to constrain him to place all his hopes in the ability of the masses of the people to introduce some new kind of culture. This it was that led Blok to germulate a whole series of extremely interesting observations which he noted down in his diary.

The entry for March 27th reads: "The summit of humanism, its culminating point—is Schiller. A broad, dusty sunbeam beating down through a rose window to illumine an enormous baroque cathedral— the Europe of 'the age of enlightenment'. It is because Schiller does illumine us in this way, because, for the last time, he united art with life and science and man with music, that he is so infinitely close to us now. Immediately after him, man and music were parted; mankind, of whom the Marquis of Posa sang in the full light of the dusty sunbeam, went on its own ways—ways of statecraft, politics, ethics, law and science."

From then on, music "flowed on along a course of its own" and further: "Kant the Terrible established the limits of cognition. In response to this challenge flung down by a declining humanism, breaking the surface of the humanist world come licking the first, flaming tongues of music which, in another hundred years' time, will consume the whole European world with fire."

Blok allows that the best artists (musicians in the true sense of the word or people with the gift of musical apprehension) have preserved some gleams from the musical fire which has shrunk far back and down beneath the crust and left mankind in darkness. Then, however, the showering sparks of revolution begin to break the surface. The element, majestic and untamable, is reminding us of its existence. "The face of Europe is illumined with a completely new light as the 'masses', the people, the unconscious bearer of the spirit of music step out onto the arena of history. The features of this face are distorted by a foreboding which grows with the century."

Later, Blok returned to this same theme.

On March 28, in an extremely interesting passage on whether or not an artist should be apolitical (at which we shall take a closer look under separate heading), Blok stresses that politics, as he understands the word at present, i.e., as a synonym for the people's revolution, are dear to him because they are "musical". "No," he writes, "we cannot remain 'outside politics' because in doing so we should be betraying that music which only becomes audible when we completely cease to hide. For instance, to take one particular case, the secret of a certain anti-musicality and reediness of tone which we find in Turgenev lies in his political apathy."

Finally, on March 31 of the same year, Blok writes an entire philosophical treatise in miniature on the same subject:

"In the beginning was Music. Music is the essence of the world. The world grows in supple rhythms. Growth is retarded and then 'comes on with a rush'. Such is the law of all organic life on the Earth, of man also, and of mankind. Pressure heads of volition. The growth of the world is culture. Culture is musical rhythm."

Here, Blok even attempts a sketch of the history

of human culture from this point of view, which corresponds roughly to the briefly outlined thoughts of March 27 which we have already noted.

An extint culture, no longer animated by the spirit of music, is civilisation, rationalism; and here Blok gives full reign to his hatred and contempt for rationalism, for the "brain"—which was not his own strongest point, and for which, as the last offspring of the nobility, he would, when one comes to think of it, have had little enough use. "Scientific progress takes on a positivist and materialist character; it breaks into hundreds of separate movements (methods, disciplines). The reason given is the manifold variety of the object of study—the world. But the hidden reason is the withdrawal of the spirit of music."

Further, Blok goes on to demonstrate his total failure to understand the Marxist contention that "the idea without the masses is impotent, the masses without the idea are blind". The contribution which learning, transformed according to new class principles, has to make to the revolution, is beyond his comprehension. This "music" is a closed book to him. According to the picture painted by Blok, civilisation and its learning have become the heritage of an exclusive circle of specialists, and he contrasts these with the masses of the people whom he imagines ignorant. Yet it is in this very ignorance that he perceives their sacred significance.

The aristocrat in Blok can appreciate art, but knowledge, in his opinion, is a bourgeois affair, and the artistically-minded aristocrat, ignoring knowledge, stretches out his hand towards the crowd which, to him, appears "sacred in its ignorance", and in whose storms and tempests he acknowledges something akin to his own romantic spirit, to his own lack of self-discipline, to his own self-indulgent whims.

But this is not what concerns us just now—we shall return to Blok and the revolution in the next chapter. What we are trying to establish here is that Blok saw this revolution as a supremely musical moment in the history of culture and of the cosmos. It is possible to catch Blok in the pose of a contemptuous aesthete, capable of such remarks as: When will our chattering fellow countrymen get it into their thick heads that art can have nothing in common with politics? But here, in 1919, when politics had "risen before him as an explosion of the musical element", he writes: "I fear any manifestations whatsoever of the 'art for art's sake' tendency, because this tendency runs contrary to the very essence of art and because following it we end by losing art; for art is born of the perpetual interaction of two kinds of music—the music of the creative personality and the music which sounds in the depths of the popular soul, of the soul of the masses. Great art is born only when these two electric currents are connected. Deliberate disregard for political values is the same old humanism, only turned inside out, the division of the indivisible; like a garden without a mixed border; a French park and not a Russian garden which always manages to unite the useful and the agreeable, the beautiful and the homely. Such a garden is lovelier than the finest of parks; the work of great artists is always a beautiful garden with flowers and weeds, and not a fine park with well-kept pathways."

Blok remained essentially true to this musical, intuitive, side of his character throughout his life. Various critics have tried, when writing about Blok, to represent him as torn between his mystico-romantic impulses and the search for greater realism. I reject this point of view on Blok outright. Of course, if under the heading of mysticism we are to understand a tendency towards the high-flown, a yearning for sanctity, purity and spirituality, then it is indeed indisputable that the domination of this particular type of idealistic, ascetic mysticism over Blok was very short-lived. But what did Blok oppose to it? Elements of realism proper in Blok's poetry are negligible, with the possible exception of a few thoughts and evocative phrases on the subject of coal and a New America, and one or two other things besides. On the whole, though, Blok, in reacting against the pink-and-blue type of mysticism, plunged straight into another drunken, sensual, debauched mysticism. This has been noted by many students of his work.

Alexandra Ilyina, for instance, writes: "All Blok's life was full of an inner desire to break away from mysticism and romanticism," but adds immediately: "but, as time went on, every such break-away in the direction of realism (?) was expunged by a new, formless wave of ill-defined maximalism."*

If by "maximalism" we are to understand those sensual orgies which Blok himself describes in his diaries and notebooks, the constant, hopeless drinking, the trips out of town in order to drink, etc., meditations on how he had reacted to the other "hundred, two hundred, three hundred women I have possessed" besides his wife, then all one can say is that the application of the term is most unusual. To Blok it seemed as though Bolshevism, committed to refashioning the world on entirely new foundations, was insufficiently "maximalistic", but he could not even begin to formulate his own ideas as to what the truly maximalistic revolution of which he dreamt should really be like. It is therefore quite out of order to balance the poet's misguided Left Socialist-Revolutionary sympathies against his wild "maximalistic" gropings for some kind of release through the lowest forms of depravity.

---

* Alexandra Ilyina, "On Blok", "Literary Saturdays at Nikitina's".—*Ed.*

Blok did in fact begin with high-flown mysticism. Having been brought up in a fairly religious spirit and in the Beketov tradition of pure and chaste family relationships, Blok perceived his first love for his future wife through a prism of angelic wings. Added to this was the circumstance that the youthful disciples of Vladimir Solovyov wove a genuine cult about this romance, attributing allegorical significance to Blok's love for Lyubov Mendeleyeva and declaring his bride to be the earthly reflection of Sophia, the Divine Wisdom. In the most ridiculous fashion, these young men would sit over their country-house breakfasts at Shakhmatovo* and, wide-eyed and mouths agape, follow her every movement, her walk, her speech, her gestures, investing them all with mystic significance. Even comparatively reasonable and sober people fell victim to this extraordinary self-deception. When you read the eloquent pages which Blok's aunt, Maria Beketova, devoted to the description of his wedding and her assertion that a certain young Pole, overcome by so ecstatic an experience, eventually entered a monastery, it is impossible to keep a straight face. To any normal, sober man all this poetical mysticism must have seemed sheer farce from beginning to end.

In 1912, Gumilev wrote in the literary monthly *Apollon*: "Many guesses were hazarded as to the true identity of Blok's Most Beautiful Lady: people wished to see her now as the Woman clothed with the Sun, now as the Eternal Feminine, now as a symbol of Russia. However if we were just to suppose that She were quite simply the young girl who was the poet's first love, then, it seems to me, not one poem in the whole collection would prove incompatible with this supposition, and the actual

---

* The Beketov family estate in the country north of Moscow, the management of which devolved upon Blok after the death of his grandparents in 1902.—*Ed.*

image, having become closer to us, will become even more wonderful and will gain immeasurably from the artistic point of view."

I would not like to say whether or not Blok's *Verses About the Most Beautiful Lady* do gain from such a realistic interpretation, but at least there can be no doubt that a real country-house romance was indeed at the bottom of all the incense-burnings, inspirations, mysteries and religious devotions which go to make up this book.

In Blok himself, however, a directly opposite principle was at work. Very probably this was—first and foremost—the manifestation of a certain healthy German sobriety which was one of his characteristics. Maria Beketova tells us that Blok enjoyed physical work: "Blok was very fond of physical work. He had great physical strength and a good, straight eye. Whether scything grass, felling trees or digging, he would do everything very neatly and always make a good job of whatever he had undertaken. He even used to say that work was always work, 'whether it be laying fires or writing verses...'."

There was a period of Blok's life when he went through a craze for gymnastics and even attributed an enormous importance to the principle they represented. He himself said of the time when he was writing the *Verses About the Most Beautiful Lady*: "The sober and wholesome people by whom I was at that time surrounded succeeded, it would seem, in protecting me from the infection of mystic charlatanism."

Blok was losing faith in the doctrine of Vladimir Solovyov. He began to feel that these monkish, troubadour warblings were, in some way, hollow, emasculated.

Having wrenched himself free of all these pallid phantoms, however, Blok fell victim to the elements of his own sensuality. It was not the physical vitality of which we have already spoken, but an exaggerated sensuality only partly connected with natural energy and, in essence, pathological, which drove him to seek experience in the underworld of tavern night-life. Here, beyond doubt, was the source of inspiration for the second and longest period of Blok's poetry with its burning evocative power, its all-pervading eroticism, its despair, its mystic aspiration to attain, through sin, to the very heart of nature.

His erstwhile allies such as Bely exercised a biting irony in their assessment of Blok's departure from the fold. Bely writes: "Blok's verses came into bloom like silken roses, from behind them glimmered 'a vision, beyond the scope of mind'. But, when the roses opened—in each rose there was a caterpillar, a pretty caterpillar, true, but nevertheless, a caterpillar; the caterpillars were transformed into all sorts of devil's spawn and little priests of the bog* who fell hungrily on the petals of the poet's sublime dawn; from that moment his verse began to mature. Blok, who had formerly seemed a true mystic, had turned into a poet of stature, a beautiful singer of caterpil-lars: on the other hand, as a mystic, he had turned out to be a fraud."

Bely, of course, is quite wrong to say that the Blok of this period was a fraudulent mystic. Of course, Blok's mysticism here was no longer monastic. Ironically, he recalled the well-known saying: "If you never sin, you will never repent; if you never repent, you will never be saved." For Blok, the very vortex of excess, the burning of the flesh in the sweet torments of sensuality were, in some sort, a source of mystic experience. Drunken debauchery, spicy infatuations, wild affairs with

---

* Bely is here referring to a poem by Blok from the series *Bubbles of the Earth,* entitled *Bolotny Popik (The Little Priest of the Bog).—Tr.*

easy women—all these phenomena seemed to bring
him much nearer to the "essence of things" than a
well-ordered life in his quiet, white country-house.

The duality which, at this stage, became evident
in Blok—the contradiction between chivalrous,
monastic aspirations largely absorbed from the outside and the gypsy poetry of the café-chantant which
he represents as a distinct element in the make-up
of the world at large—had already been noted in a
shrilly discordant poem which somehow got slipped
into his first book of verse:

> To worship in the Lord's high dwellings
> With heart abased is my delight.
> Where sacred canticles are swelling,
> In shadowy throngs I merge from sight.
> I fear my Janus-soul perfidious,
> And keep the visored helm of Grace
> Most carefully closed upon my hideous
> And diabolic, second face.
> But when, in prayerfull superstition,
> The sure defence of Christ I ask,
> Then simulation and perdition
> Smile to themselves behind the mask.

But Blok was already at the mercy of another
duality. Again, he was torn not between the rival
claims of drunken romanticism and realism, but
between the quickly exhausted, and exhausting
tarantella of the senses and a growing passion, not
devoid of anguished foreboding, for Russia—a
Russia perceived, on the one hand, through the base
of all this clamour and debauch, and, on the other,
wreathed in the flames of approaching revolution.

It is not my intention to provide here a more
detailed analysis of the pagan period of Blok's
poetry. Much has already been said and written
about it. Blok himself characterises the period when
he cries of the "broken and piercing note of mad-

ness", of the "shriek for salvation", of how he "trod down despair, searching for truth in wine", etc.

Bely, also at the very beginning of this period, found the right words to describe the turning point: "In 1903, Blok addressed 'us' with words of hope:

> Let us join our hands in silence
> Fly away into the blue.

"In 1905—he breaks off short: The hands had not been joined; no one had flown away into the blue; the ships had not come; we had been left behind; and we were left sitting there like fools on the damp tussocks of the marshes; we were 'a disease', 'the playthings of the elements'."

In a word, it was to a considerable degree, a personal break-down. The fantastically successful dream of perceiving something sacred and mysterious in the features of the Stranger, of the unknown woman glimpsed in a low tavern, could not soothe his profound uneasiness any more than the dream of perceiving Sophia, the Divine Wisdom, in his own beloved and perfectly real bride had been able to do.

Blok's third period is most closely connected with the revolution. There, it is Blok's love affair with the revolution which is the dominating factor—a very strange romance which requires interpretation.

D. Blagoi, in his interesting article "Alexander Blok and Apollon Grigoriev", having noted the inevitable stalemate of Blok's daemonic quest, gives an excellent definition of the third way which then opened up before him (Blagoi calls it the second way, since he leaves out of account the service of the Most Beautiful Lady) in the following words:

"There is a second way which promises a radical cure—a way which, as was to be expected according to the historical dialectics of his class, exercised an invincible attraction over the poet, even as it attracted so many other 'descendants of heroes', representatives of the 'rotten', 'dead', 'finally extinct' Russian nobility all (Blok's own epithets): 'flight' from the alien, unfamiliar, 'terrible', doom-laden town, back home, but not back home to their own small, tumble-down 'white house', to their 'nest of gentle-folk', but flight towards a roomier dwelling, 'to the fields', 'to the boundless Russian plain', to the people, to Russia. Blok clutches at the possibility of such a way with all his might."

Blok's third period, his blunderings along the ways of revolution, taken together with a kind of prologue inspired by the tempest of 1905 and the ensuing years of reaction, is at the same time the last period of his life and work.

Chapter Three
Blok and the Revolution

Blok was very conscious of belonging to the nobility. His whole private life was closely connected with the traditions of the country gentry. He had received a sufficiently thorough education, particularly in the sphere of literature, to know the history of the culture of the aristocracy and to take pride in its most brilliant achievements. In many of Blok's judgements on events and people there is a hint of aristocratic arrogance, although this is softened by his sincerely democratic principles and by a certain flavour of Bohemianism. However, Blok was also conscious of the curse which hung over his class. The official representatives of the nobility, those, that is, who were the prop and stay of the throne and who set the whole tone of the country's political life, appeared to Blok as a dark, even criminal force. Blok was brought to this conclusion not only because he belonged, through the Beketovs, to the liberal and enlightened wing of the nobility, but also because he was half déclassé and, by the end of his life, had practically nothing left in common with the real landowners and became increasingly dependent on his pen and subject to all the troubles common to the professional intelligentsia and his brother writers.

Like Pushkin, Lermontov and Nekrasov, Blok was, on the one hand, passionately devoted to his native land and, on the other, acutely aware of the terrible state it was in, of its lack of culture, of the neglect of its rulers and leaders and of their guilt towards it. Without hesitating, he calls this Russia, to whom he openly declares his love ("My wife, my life"), an "unhappy" country—"befouled by bureaucrats, dirty, downtrodden, drivelling—the laughingstock of the world". Naturally, the blame for all this does not lie with the people but with the ruling classes.

In verse and prose, Blok looked back with hatred to the regime of Alexander III, to the days of Pobedonostsev, though he had sufficient experience of all the "delights" of reaction in his own lifetime. He was well acquainted with the Stolypin* administration and was to write of it: "Those were times when the autocracy could do whatever it set its mind to: Witte** and Durnovo*** had the country roped in a stranglehold, Stolypin wound the end of the rope firmly round his sensitive, aristocratic hand. . . . All this was of only a few years' duration, but those few years lay heavily on us like a long, sleepless, haunted night."

---

* Stolypin—Chairman of the Council of Ministers, 1906-11, an extreme reactionary. The suppression of the revolution of 1905-07 and the period of severe political reaction that followed are connected with his name.—*Ed.*

** Witte—an influential minister in tsarist Russia; was for many years (1892-1903) Minister of Finance. The measures he adopted in the sphere of finance, customs, policy, railway construction, etc., were in the interests of the big bourgeoisie and promoted the development of capitalism in Russia.—*Ed.*

*** Durnovo—one of the most reactionary statesmen of tsarist Russia. In 1905 he was Minister of the Interior and took drastic steps to crush the first Russian revolution.—*Ed.*

Blok's reference to the "sensitive, aristocratic hand" was no slip of the pen. In condemning that nucleus of his class which still retained its power, the official representatives of the nobility, Blok was not only totally unsympathetic towards their closest rivals, the bourgeoisie, but, on the contrary, felt the utmost aversion towards them from the top of the social scale right down to the bottom.

In the depths of the trough which divided one revolutionary epoch from another, in the year 1908, Blok asserted with profound sorrow: "The Russian nobility has finally died out. A new ruling class has appeared in place of the Russian nobility."

But Blok understood very well that *this* ruling class had brought no relief to the country, that it implemented its rule through the same landowners, the same bureaucrats, the same autocratic machinery of state, but that it had not the strength in itself to produce such people as Pushkin, Tolstoi, Turgenev. On the contrary, throughout all its own hierarchy from the upper middle class down to the petty bourgeoisie, it was scarcely capable of producing a higher cultural ideal than that of Artsybashev's *Sanin*.

Blok demands bitterly: "Is there or is there not a class in Russia capable of carrying on the splendid work of the nobility?"

For Blok no doubt existed but that neither the tradesmen and industrialists nor the professional intelligentsia, nor yet the artistic intelligentsia had the necessary strength. If the nobility had collapsed, then everything had collapsed. The only hope lay in the mysterious "people".

Here, I would like to go rather more deeply into Blok's hatred for the "detestable victor"—the bourgeoisie. Blok had inherited this hatred from his class and, in particular, from that group to which he happened to belong, which had suffered more than others from the advance of capital. In this respect Blok has much in common with his father.

V. D. Izmailskaya in her article "The Problem of 'Retribution' " describes the elder Blok's attitude in the following terms:

"It would be quite useless to look for scholarly impartiality on the pages of this book about Russia, which is a scathing denunciation of the vices of the bourgeois system. A.(lexander) L.(vovich) brings a publicistic impressionism to the expression of his contempt for the 'boring mediocrity', the 'bourgeois narrow-mindedness' and the 'bourgeois morality' of the European middle classes, whom he considered to be devoid of high ideals. Their ideals he thought fit only for the attainment of some special 'English happiness' (ridiculed by Tolstoi). Most certainly, he saw no connection between them and the 'universal happiness' dreamt of by Dostoyevsky."

His son goes further. His conception of the bourgeois age is given in the long poem *Retribution*. So felicitously and completely is Blok's judgement on this epoch pronounced here, that we take the liberty of quoting a lengthy extract.

> *O nineteenth century, O age of iron;*
> *In very truth a cruel century!*
> *Into the darkness of a starless night*
> *Has man, from trouble free, been cast by you!*
>
> . . . .
>
> *Along with you, succeeding other plagues,*
> *There entered neurasthenia, boredom, spleen.*
> *The age of foreheads beating on the wall,*
> *The age of economic theories,*
> *The age of meetings, federations, banks,*
> *Of dinner speeches, phrases smartly turned,*
> *The age of shares, annuities and bonds,*
> *And but a little live intelligence. . . .*
>
> . . . .

It is the age of wealthy bourgeoisie,
Of evil growing by unseen degrees
Despite equality and brotherhood
As watchwords, dark affairs have ripened here.

And what of man? He lived bereft of will;
Not man was master but machines and towns!
So bloodlessly and painlessly has "life"
Now racked his spirit, as ne'er happ'd before—

But he who with his guiding hand controls
The figured marionettes of every land,—
He knew what he was doing, when he spread
The mists of humanistic reasonings;
There, in the leaden mist with dampness sodden,
The flesh is withered and the spirit quenched;
Even the angel of the sacred strife
Seems from our presence to have taken flight. . . .

The Twentieth Century's more homeless still,
And still more terrible its gloomy life;
For even blacker and with vaster reach
The shadow spreads from wing of Lucifer. . . .

. . . .

The ceaseless roar outpouring from machines,
That forge destruction through the day and night,
The fearful knowledge of the fraud that marks
Our petty thoughts and all our past beliefs,
The first ascent of aeroplane in flight
Into the void of undiscovered spheres—
And a revulsion from this life of ours
And yet a frenzied love for life itself,
And passion and a hate of fatherland. . . .*

---

* This extract is taken from the late Sir Cecil Kisch's
unrhymed translation of *Retribution.* Sir Cecil Kisch,
Alexander Blok, Prophet of Revolution, Weidenfeld and
Nicholson, London, 1960, pp. 164-67.—*Ed.*

Like the nobility of old, Blok felt an intense repugnance for any kind of financial transactions, for buying and selling, for hiring out his labour. "I was at the bank today," he notes in his diary. "The very touch of money corrupts the soul."

The landowner, thrown out of his idyllic country life, has long since forgotten his own natural economy. He is déclassé; he has lost his last possession, his home, his country-estate, the "beloved earth", so assiduously sung by good, bad and indifferent literary luminaries of the nobility.

Blok felt this very poignantly. In 1906, immediately after the revolution, he wrote in the article "Stagnation":*

"I see a sight to make the gods laugh: the world lies green and blossoming, but on her bosom the towns—corpulent spiders—are sucking in the growing things all about them and exuding din, fumes and stench. . . .

"What is to be done then? What *is* to be done? There are no homes left. . . . Chaste customs, serene smiles, quiet evenings—all these are coated with cobwebs. . . . Joy has decreased, hearths are cold. . . . Doors stand open to the snowy square. . . . We live in an era of doors standing open into the square, of dead hearths. . . . Tramps are appearing among us. Idle and homeless loiterers are to be met within the public squares of the town. . . ."

Several journeys abroad provided Blok with a great deal of pleasure by bringing him into contact with old cultures of a more or less vividly expressed aristocratic or patrician character. All bourgeois Europe, on the other hand, filled him with horror and revulsion. He writes of the "monstrous

---

* Bezvremenye (Russ.)—an untranslatable word indicating that times are so dull—or so hard—that all the clocks appear to have run down.—*Tr.*

meaninglessness to which civilisation has been reduced". He says that, in Europe, "everything is over". He senses there a "moribund inertia".

A feeling of profound aversion for the triumphant bourgeoisie aroused in him something approaching physiological disgust. In the autumn of 1911 he wrote home from France: "No person in the least fastidious would agree to settle down in France."

During the war, long before his famous *Scythians,* he prophesied gleefully: "Let Europe go on fighting, let her, the unhappy, bedraggled cocotte! All the wisdom of the world will run out through her fingers, stained as they are with war and politics, and other people will come and will carry her 'whither she would not'."

He made no exception for the intelligentsia, the Russian intelligentsia included. It was, he maintained, caught up in the life of the time as a whole, it was in a state of decomposition, it was not musical in the metaphysical sense of the term. Blok begins his diary with a whole series of remarks on the distressing thoughts aroused in him by his nearest neighbours—the intelligentsia: "Literary circles in Petersburg are in a state of final decomposition. The stench is already appreciable." He is constantly warning himself against having too much to do with professional writers: "Keep literary friendships down to a minimum—you will only poison yourself and fall ill."

Despairingly, he adds after these words: "And I myself am no better than those who I am writing about."

His penetrating artist's eye hates the depravity of the "leaders" of the intelligentsia. He writes: "Milyukov, who was recently seen edging his way to the front with a candle at Stolypin's memorial service ... in whom and what are we here to place our trust?"

For the reader who wishes to acquaint himself further with the depths of Blok's malice towards the intelligentsia and the bourgeoisie, we would recommend a study of the vividly described episode noted in his diary for the 14th November, 1911: "All the crowd on the Nevsky Prospect is like that," Blok concludes. "The ugly mug of Anatoly Kamensky is like that."

Evidently Anatoly Kamensky, an insolent writer who always played for easy popularity, seemed to Blok a kind of arch-type of the bourgeois intelligentsia.

"Everything is giving at the seams," Blok wrote at that time. "The stitches are rapidly rotting from within ('decaying'), but the outer appearance is still preserved. It would be enough to give a little pull, though, and the Persian lambskins would fall apart—and reveal the dirty, filthy, animal face of a bloodless, exhausted and violated corpse."

From this it is evident that, in Blok's view, things were in no better shape "with us" than "in the West".

The war, which Blok was able to observe from comparatively close at hand, increased his distaste for all that was happening. He saw it altogether as an element of the bourgeois civilisation he so detested.

"Why is it that up till this day no one will believe me that the world war is nonsense. . . . Some day that will be understood. I do not say this only because I myself am rotting away in all this nonsense."

"Europe has gone mad. The flower of humanity, the flower of the intelligentsia, have been sitting about in bogs for years now, have been sitting, with the utmost conviction (is not that symbolic?), along the whole 1,000-verst length of a narrow strip which is known as 'the front'. . . . It is hard to say which is the more repulsive: the bloodshed or the idleness, boredom and vulgarity all of which carry the titles

'The Great War', 'The War for the Fatherland', 'The War for the Liberation of the Oppressed Peoples'— and how many more? No, under this sign we shall liberate no one."

We see that Blok was charged with a colossal energy of negation against the established order. He was occasionally reduced to complete despair. In a letter sent from Milan in the spring of 1909 he says: "More than ever before, I see that I shall never until I die accept anything of the modern way of life, that I shall never knuckle under to it. Its shameful order fills me with nothing but disgust. It is too late to change anything—no revolution on earth would have the power to change it."

It is clear on the basis of all this that Blok, exhausted by his tavern-type mysticism, having found nothing—either on his heavenly or his infernal mystic quests—but "charlatanism" and "terrible weariness and boredom", was maturing towards a great readiness to throw himself to meet the oncoming tidal wave of revolution, in the belief that here he would be able to wash himself clean, that here all the world would be able to wash away its uncleanness.

Blok did not believe that the period of reaction was destined to last for long. 1917 found him ready and waiting. In his extraordinarily powerful address "Culture and the Element" (end of 1908), he prophesied that the bomb was due to go up in our time, although it was generally taken to be nothing but an innocent orange: "All of us are imbued with a feeling of sickness, alarm, catastrophe, rapture."

"Russia, having heaved herself out of one revolution, is already gazing avidly into the eyes of another, perhaps more terrible still."

From these words, it is clear that Blok himself fears this bomb, this advancing element, but, unlike many others, he is prepared to welcome it.

Here we must make an attempt to sort out Blok's attitudes to the revolution, both positive and negative, on the basis of his own expressed opinions from 1905 onwards.

The revolution of 1905 made a great and positive impression upon Blok. We know that he even got himself mixed up in one of the demonstrations and carried a red flag at its head.

However, the period of reaction which came after the great splash of the revolution produced a still greater impression on him. Unlike many other representatives of the intelligentsia who sank back into various reactionary moods and dark philosophies, Blok, whose reaction to the explosion had been extremely morbid and had led to an intensification of his "gypsy", "daemonic" element, still, at the same time, found strength in himself to meet with the utmost indignation the gaze of the Gorgon of political reaction which was threatening his country and, from time to time, to raise his voice against it in resounding, ireful lines which are among the best political verses in Russian poetry.

The period of reaction was, for him, "a long, sleepless, haunted night".

In 1907 he writes of suffocation and notes: "Even among the young it is only very seldom one meets with one single person who is not mortally bored and unhappy, hiding his true face under the sickeningly familiar grimace of pampered delicacy, refinement, exclusive self-love."

At that time, Blok was himself close to this kind of state, which he described as "Russian dandyism". He was, however, very well aware that such attitudes were the product of political reaction.

In those years the intelligentsia really did inspire him with the most acute distaste. He was a genuine rebel in their ranks. Alongside his "café-chantant mysticism" he felt the pull of active citizenship, awoken in 1905, the same sense of citizenship which, later, when the "revolutionary element" was to ring out again as the dominant musical theme of existence, was to reveal its face so fully and to show some features of great nobility and others, more blurred in outline and less easy to define.

Very characteristic of Blok at this time, disillu- sioned but filled with contempt for the misleading stability which was settling down over the country, was an article he wrote in October 1908 for the news- paper *Rech (Speech)*.

"The verses of any one of our new poets are unnecessary and, almost always, harmful reading. . . . It is wrong to foster admiration for writers who lack the social halo, who have not yet earned the right to consider themselves heirs of the sacred literature of Russia. This is harmful, taken by and large, not only because it produces an atmosphere of commonplace vulgarity—worse than that: the soirées devoted to the new art . . . are coming to resemble *centres of social reaction.*"

While he was taking part in the religious-philo- sophic debates of the intelligentsia's "élite" he wrote of their significance—more truly, of their lack of significance—with exhaustive virulence: "Now they have started up this chattering once again; yet all these highly educated and embittered men of culture, going quietly grey over their arguments about Christ, all their wives and wives' female relatives in high- necked blouses, all these hard-thinking philosophers and all these priests with their oily shine of self- satisfaction know that the poor in spirit, whose need is for deeds, are standing outside the doors. Instead of deeds—a monstrous juggling with words. . . . All this is now becoming fashionable, within the grasp of university lecturer's wives and charitable ladies. . . . But outside—the wind blows, prostitutes shiver, men are hungry, they are being hung; and reaction broods over the country, and life in Russia is hard, cold, vile. Why, even if all those chatterers were to wear themselves away to shreds in their searching, of no use to anyone on this earth other than to 'refined natures', nothing in Russia would be one jot the worse or the better for it!"

Blok's poetry attained maximum political significance towards 1914, in his *Iambi*. True, these verses were not published together as one book until much later, in 1919, but they represented a powerful undercurrent in Blok's poetry. We shall limit ourselves here to reminding the reader of one poem, written in 1911:

> Here then the call of inspiration;
> Albeit my soaring muse is free
> She's drawn towards humiliation
> And dirt, and dark, and poverty.
> Drawn further, further, humbler, lower—
> That Other World's best seen from here. . .
> Have you seen beggars, though, in winter?
> Or children in a Paris square?
> On life's impenetrable horror
> Come open, open wide your eyes
> Before the holocaust arise
> To devastate your home for ever.
> Prepare for work. Roll up your sleeves.
> Let righteous wrath mature and smoulder,
> You cannot?—then let mount and moulder
> Your spleen and boredom's seared leaves.
> But call no truce with this existence!
> She's false. Rub off her greasy rouge!
> Adopt the timid mole's resistance—
> Get you to ground. Nor breathe, nor move,
> But nurse your hatred of life's horror
> Not heeding how the world may go. . . .
> Though you may not behold the morrow
> Say to the present—firmly: No!

Blok's just anger and his sympathy for the masses, born of his disillusionment with a society which had no place for him and of his "metaphysical" hope in that new music which, he believed would be brought into being by the advance of the lower orders, were, therefore, at their height during the period of reaction. Blok really did string his lyre with brass. However, although he tells us how cruelly he hates and despises life as it is, he admits that he "may not behold the morrow"—does not, in other words, perceive what is to come. It had seemed to him that, from the crest of the next wave of revolution, he had caught a glimpse of some hazy but radiant future; but Blok's eyes were so constructed that it was impossible for them to see the real contours of the actual great revolution which was in fact to take place, of the completely new future which was in fact approaching.

Full of doubts, anxieties, bitterness, vague hopes, Blok, even in these moments of his life, during the years of reaction when he was most actively occupied by questions of social change and upheaval, still did not feel that his personal fate was bound up with the fortunes of that class from whom he awaited regeneration. He was always aware of himself as a representative of that same intelligentsia which he so abhorred. In the article "Russia and the Intelligentsia" this admixture of real dismay in the face of revolution is expressed with a curious sharpness.

In 1908 he wrote: "In casting ourselves upon the neck of the people, we are casting ourselves under the hoofs of a runaway troika, to *certain destruction.*" In 1913, speaking of Pushkin, he noted, ". . . yet again we experience this shock of fear, remembering that our rebellion may also prove to be 'insensate and ruthless'."

The mood which descended on Blok during the revolutionary days of 1917 in February and after October has been described often enough. It is a prolongation of what went before, although in a different, more vivid outward form, corresponding to the grandiose quality of events. Blok is very explicit on this period and his position at that time is quite clear. It is clear in its very lack of clarity.

It seemed to Blok that his ideas corresponded to those of the Left Socialist-Revolutionaries because they too believed in the "elemental", were extremely diffuse and liked to speak of Revolution with a capital "R" and to think of it as something immensely lofty while remaining completely alien to its class essence and its real aims.

Of course, one might say that Ivanov-Razumnik, who became a friend of the poet's at about that time, had a bad influence on him. But such ideas should be put aside, for the truth was that Blok simply found in Ivanov-Razumnik confirmation of his own attitudes.

The revolution, when it came, was tempestuous and magnificent—and Blok, in a series of remarkable articles, called on the intelligentsia to put off their "a-musicality" and to appreciate the sublimity of this great symphony. He defended the revolution against charges of isolated though frequent cases of vandalism and violence. He spoke of the great flood which was bearing a mass of flotsam along with it on the surface, but which, in itself, was great and fruitful. The intelligentsia, he said, must accustom its overrefined ear to the musical roar of this flood.

It is as though the déclassé professional writer of noble origin, Blok, were trying to forget himself and to wash away all memory of the unclean and tormenting experiences which he had undergone in the degenerate, rotten life of the last years of the Old World.

Recalling the hatred of the bourgeoisie and of bourgeois Europe, he was able to draw out impressive notes in his address to her (the famous poem *The Scythians*). He contrasted the immensity and world-wide significance of what was going on in the Eurasian plains of Russia to the narrow reaches of bourgeois ideology.

He turned to the West with love and threats in the name of his extraordinary people in whom he had long since, as he believed, descried traits of furious energy and incipient greatness beneath the outer shell of apparent wretchedness.

I remember an extremely characteristic incident when, having just arrived in Paris in 1923, I had occasion to meet up with a group of surrealists, representatives of the déclassé intelligentsia, who nurtured a particularly virulent dislike of the bourgeoisie. Naturally, these people who, at that time, were on the verge of joining the Communist Party and were planning to take over Barbusse's organ *Clarté*, had no knowledge of Blok, but their whole attitude was so extraordinarily akin to his that it was a living illustration of the similar social foundation of both phenomena.

While we were talking, the surrealists whose leaders at that time were Breton and Aragon, addressed me with a declaration which went something like this.

"We, surrealists, are first and foremost anti-bourgeois. The bourgeoisie is dying, but it is dying slowly and poisoning the air about us with the reek of decomposition. Which feature of the bourgeoisie do we, the intelligentsia, consider the most detestable, the most deadly? Bourgeois rationalism. The bourgeoisie believes in reason. It looks upon itself as reasonable and considers that the whole world is built on principles corresponding to its own colourless, prosaic and terribly narrow logic. It is as though the world itself had submitted to bourgeois logic. But, in actual fact, under the outer shell of reasonableness there is a huge and mysterious elemental sphere, which one has to have eyes to see, which cannot be seen with the eyes of reason. This is why we defend the principle of intuition. The artist can and should see things in their surreal significance. We need the revolution in order to overthrow the sovereignty of the bourgeoisie and with it the sovereignty of reason, to recall the great sovereignty of elemental life, so that the world may dissolve in the true music of intense being. We honour Asia as a continent which, up till now, has drawn the life force only from these true springs and has not been poisoned by European reason. Come, you Muscovites, and bring in your wake countless detachments of Asiatics, tread our European 'after-culture' into the ground. Even if we ourselves are to die beneath the hoofs of the wild steppe horses, then let us die! Only let reason die with us, and calculation, and the deadly, stifling principle of bourgeois life!"

This is an almost exact transcription of the sense of what was said and of the images in which the young French poets clothed their thoughts at that time. It cost me a great deal of trouble to overcome their astonishment and even their indignation, when I answered that they had got a completely wrong idea of the revolution; that the revolution was the champion of the cause of reason; that we looked for support from European civilisation, that we considered Marxism but as its best gift, as the apogee of reason—true, not of logical, but dialectic reason; that we seek to absorb all that is best of European culture, all that the European bourgeoisie has rejected; and, finally, that not only are we ourselves seeking to build up our country on the basis of this doctrine which we consider the culmination of European learning, but we wish to spread the light of this same reason in Asia also, and have no intention of becoming the bearers of the influence of Asiatic mystic metaphysics in Europe.

All this most probably seemed very unpoetical to them. Had Blok been there in my place, he would almost certainly have come to an understanding with the surrealists at once; they would have found that they spoke the same language.

However, even as Blok hearkened to the storm of revolution as he understood it, admiring the vast scale on which events were proceeding, and expecting, as a result, some sudden metaphysical changes for the better which would transform all the foundations of being, he still felt the old fear.

On June 19, 1917, Blok wrote: "I shall not be surprised if the people, clever, calm, and gifted with an understanding of something the intelligentsia will never understand (that is to say, with a socialist psychology, completely, diametrically different), should suddenly begin (though not, perhaps, very soon) just as calmly and majestically, to hang and to despoil the intelligentsia (so as to establish order, so as to clear the brain of the country of rubbish)."

On the 30th of June he adds: "If the proletariat comes to power, then we shall have a long wait for 'order', it may not even be established in our lifetime, but let the proletariat wield power, for only children could make anything new and interesting out of that ancient toy."

And so the proletariat is represented as an irrational force, as an unthinking, inexperienced child, incapable of establishing order; but this is all to the good; perhaps, in playing, he will succeed in creating a new world.

The revolution, meanwhile, went its own way. Professor Tsingovatov gives an excellent analysis of

Blok's attitude towards it in his valuable book *A. A. Blok*. He writes:

"Blok accepted the October Revolution as a long-desired way out from a dead end—personal, social, European and international—but he accepted one particular aspect of it, seen in the light of Left-wing Narodnik dreams of utopia and mystic, apocalyptic ravings. The way out—quite real in itself—was perceived so subjectively, that it turned out to be a hopeless delusion—a mixture of Christian communism and Scythian Pan-Mongolism. This incurable poet-symbolist saw many things in the revolution: Christ and the Twelve Apostles, Scythians and Asiatic hordes, and orange-groves—and Catilina arose before him in the guise of a 'Roman Bolshevik'. Blok only failed to see one thing, something it was impossible that he should have seen through his romantic spectacles: the real October, the real workers' and peasants' revolution, governed by the inevitable laws of the class struggle, which had come into being as a stage in the process of the development of the means of production and socio-economic relationships."

In the meantime, the revolution had begun to assume certain features of this same order which Blok had not believed the working class capable of establishing. True, it fell to Blok's lot to live through those years (and he did not live to see better) when the proletariat was at grips with the most stringent shortages which made themselves felt in every branch of activity as the result of ruinous wars. Blok's most immediate experience was, therefore, this immense destitution which invaded his own private life as well. True, Blok bore these unavoidable hardships heroically enough. To carry wood up to the top storey, to have to think of ways to make ends meet, of how to obtain food was all in the day's work, but it went on for so long that all this disorganisation of everyday life, to which Blok could foresee no end, could not but have inclined him towards pessimism. The main factor here was that Blok had absolutely no understanding of the economic aspect of the revolution. Although he dreamt of a Russian America and began writing some work or other which was to centre on coal, etc., he was still so completely alien to economic questions that the task of building socialism as a new economic system seemed to him something remote and academic—failed, in fact, to make any impression on him whatsoever.

Blok overlooked Lenin. He heard no "music" in Lenin's speeches. On the contrary, it seemed to him that even the Bolsheviks were simply one of many kinds of flotsam on the surface of the profoundly disturbed masses of the people. Lenin and his reasonableness evidently seemed to Blok a mere offshoot of the intelligentsia's cult of reason, a theoretician trying to graft his plans on to the great, mysterious tree which had suddenly shot up from the depths of the people.

This is why Blok's last years passed in an atmosphere of immense bewilderment. It seemed to him that the music was again draining out of the revolution, that the only sounds now were the wild discords of an unsettled day-to-day existence and isolated outbursts of open rebellion. He felt that the revolution was gradually being overcome by the element of Soviet statesmanship. In this element Blok heard no music. Rather, he distinguished a near-bureaucratic, near-bourgeois spirit, although, as it were, turned upside down.

Blok's whole character, everything about him which made him the beloved and desired singer of the doomed, everything which enabled him to see and to show the bitterness of life and to bring comfort with confused symbolic prophesies—all this became a hindrance to him, something which had to be overcome if he were to understand the revolution.

Revolution, of course, requires passion and enthusiasm, but it requires these qualities in a particular, cooled and tempered form, which does not for one moment cloud the reason of that scientific socialism under whose banner the very element which Blok adored had come into being. To understand this doctrine requires the utmost mental effort. The true greatness of the Bolshevik revolution lay in the fact that, while exercising the maximum influence over the course of the element of revolution as such, it at the same time directed it into clearly defined creative channels so that its course became more and more harmonious.

But Blok had no ear for this kind of harmony. He no longer recognised it as music. Only in the indefinite, only in the chaotic, only in the blinding splendour of high-flown and imprecise mystic light or in the dubious flickering of infernal flames could Blok perceive anything akin to his own nature. In this was his condemnation.

All that has just been said can be most clearly understood on the example of the history of Blok's famous poem *The Twelve*.

Maria Beketova tells us that in January 1918, when *The Twelve* was being written, Blok was in a state of joyful, extremely high tension. Blok was not worried that people like Merezhkovsky considered *The Twelve* to be a betrayal of culture and a glorification of the Bolsheviks. Demonstrative snubs of this sort there were in plenty, but there was also no lack of demonstrations of enthusiasm.

Bolshevik circles, naturally, accepted *The Twelve* with certain reservations. In the first place, it was quite clear that Blok was again approaching the revolution from the wrong angle. His heroes were purely elemental bearers of the revolutionary principle. The revolutionary element raises them very high in their quality of the true, plebeian "advance guard" of the revolution but, according to Blok, this element is heavily soiled by hooligan tendencies of a near-criminal character. There can be no doubt that such figures did get themselves mixed up with the revolution, and, at one time, even made a certain contribution, but, of course, they did not represent the strength of the revolution.

The Twelve could scarcely be further removed from the position of the Communist Party, because Blok felt allegiance to the Party to be something quite unrevolutionary, something alien to his whole make-up, whereas in fact, as the whole future went to show, it was the true leading principle of the revolution. Apart from this, the sudden appearance of Christ at the head of the Twelve, that mystic touch which Blok himself did not fully understand, came as a shock.

Chukovsky writes in his reminiscences that Blok, in answer to Gumilev's remark that the mystic finale appeared to be artificially tacked onto the end of *The Twelve*, had said: "I don't like the end of *The Twelve* either. I wish the end had been different. When I finished it, I was surprised myself: Why Christ? Was it really Christ? But the more I looked, the more distinctly I saw Christ. . . ."

So it appeared that Blok had created his Christ "in a wreath of white roses" quite involuntarily, almost as though under the influence of a revolution. It seems to me that the main motive force here was a combination of childhood memories which taught him to identify Christian religious concepts with the idea of the highest conceivable morality, sanctity, inviolability and—more important—of Dostoyevsky, who loved to finish off his utopian visions of a future which, in his books, is always the work of atheists, by the irruption of Christ into their world, returning to man in an unexpected moment to hallow the just "lay" order of life which they have established.

It is, however, typical that Blok had no intention of lowering or even of diluting the revolutionary tension of *The Twelve* by the introduction of this figure. In his notebook for January 29, 1918, we read the very significant lines: "That Christ is going on before them is beyond doubt. It is not so much a matter of whether or not 'they are worthy of Him', but the terrifying thing is that, once again, it is He who is with them and that there is still no other; should there not be Another—?"

These lines show that somewhere in Blok's creative laboratory thoughts were fomenting as to the importance of raising the revolutionary principle above the "wreath of white roses", but that he could not find the required synthesis.

Probably, Blok would have opened his eyes wide in astonishment and fear had anyone suggested to him that this "Other" was already living; that he was the great teacher and leader of the proletariat, at once a real man and the true embodiment of the greatest ideas which had ever developed on this earth and which made the sayings of Christianity look naive and old-fashioned; that he was that very Vladimir Ilyich Lenin whom, perhaps, he had occasionally encountered at meetings or in the street.

At least, it is clear that, in the poem *The Twelve*, Blok wished to give a true picture of the real might of revolution, fearlessly to point out its hostility towards the intelligentsia, to show the wild, almost criminal forces which served it, and at the same time, to bless them with the greatest blessing at his command. What Blok wrote about *The Twelve* in April 1920 for the Volfila (Free Philosophic Association), therefore, represents a great falling away from this height.

Here, he completely denies the political significance of *The Twelve*. He says that he "does not disown" what was written "in tune with the element", but that "only the blind" could see "politics" in his poem.

Blok continues: "At the same time it would be wrong to deny all connection between *The Twelve* and politics. The truth is that the poem was written in that extraordinary and always brief moment, when the revolutionary cyclone which is passing overhead whips up a storm in every sea—in nature, life and art; in the sea of human life there is also a smallish creek—something like the Marquise's Pond*— which is known as politics; and there was a storm raging in that teacup, too. It is easy to talk: they were talking of putting an end to the diplomatic service, of a new legal code, of stopping the war, which at that time had already been going on for four years!—The seas of nature, life and art were running high, the spray flew up to form a rainbow over us. I was looking into the rainbow when I wrote *The Twelve*, that is how a drop of politics remained in the poem. We shall see what time will do with it. It may be that every kind of politics is so dirty that one drop will cloud and spoil all the rest; it may be that it will not destroy the sense of the poem; it may be—who knows after all?—that it will prove to be that fomenting agent thanks to which *The Twelve* will still be read in some time not our own. I myself can only speak of that now with irony; but do not let us take upon ourselves to pass final judgement just now."

This tirade is horrifying. That same Blok who once in a gesture not devoid of grandeur had declared that to retire from politics was to betray the most profound essence of poetry and to leave out of account a most important part of it, now, in the face of the

---

* A part of the Gulf of Finland.—*Ed.*

greatest events which the world has ever seen, announces that politics is a "marquise's pond", reduces all politics—including, that is, the revolutionary policies of the proletariat—to some kind of "dirty principle", etc. What we have here is a manifestation of complete political idiocy.

Although Blok, in his best moments, had been able to perceive the greatness of the movement of politics through the customary mists wreathing about him and making all the objects of the outside world lose their sharpness of contour in contact with his poetry and take on the outlines of fantasy, now, weary and not understanding what was going on around him, he was ready flatly to deny all connection with the storms of politics. For him, the revolution remained nothing but an elemental cosmic manifestation.

True, he does not belittle his past ties with the revolution. He even puts an interrogation mark to the question as to whether such a poem as *The Twelve* will be of value in the future because of or in spite of its political message—but this is cold comfort.

The revolution had dealt Blok himself some extremely painful blows. It had finally dispersed the last remnants of the landowner which had still clung to him. It had subjected him—a matter of bitter regret to all of us—to long months of real need. But, more than all this, it had not brought him satisfaction. Instead of cosmic wonders and Left-S.-R.-cum-aristocratic surprises, instead of grandiose romantic pathos, it had begun to show its constructive aspect. Perhaps if Blok had lived until such time as this aspect really began to be clearly distinguishable, when its features took on more distinct outlines even for those who were standing afar off, he might have found some return bridges back to the revolution. But at that time, in its embryo forms of constructive work and given Blok's essential socio-psychological qualities, there was no hope of that.

While we are on the subject, when Blok was told of the sack of his beloved Shakhmatovo where he had passed the happiest and "most sacred" years of his life, he reacted with something like indifference. In 1919 he wrote: "Now nothing remains of that home where I spent the happiest times of my life. Perhaps the old limes are still whispering there all alone in the wind, if no one has stripped off their bark." But he considered this event a manifestation of "historical retribution". "A poet should not possess anything—it's as it should be," he replied to those who offered him their sympathy.

In the article "The Intelligentsia and the Revolution", he develops the following courageous ideas under the influence of this event.

"Why do the people befoul the treasured estates of the landowners?—Because peasant girls were raped here, and thrashed; if not at this landowner's, then at his neighbour's.

"Why are they cutting down parks which have stood for centuries?—Because, for centuries, the masters have been making their power felt under the spreading limes and maples: have flaunted power under the noses of paupers, education under the noses of bumkins. . . .

"I know what I am talking about. There is no getting round this.—It's no use trying to pretend this was not the way things were; yet this is just what everyone *is* trying to pretend.

"After all, are we not answerable to the past? We are links of a single chain. Or are the sins of our fathers not to be visited upon us? If this is not felt by all, it should, at least, be within the comprehension of the 'best people'."

Blok maintained that he had always been aware of the doom hanging over the estates of the nobility:

A. V. Lunacharsky, 1932

"That all is not well there, that the catastrophe is approaching, that the storm is already battering at the doors, is something I have known for a very long time, since before the first revolution."

At the same time, it would be extremely superficial to assume that this final destruction of Blok's material link with the nobility and with its whole way of life passed him by painlessly. On December 12, 1918, he wrote: "Why was it that tonight I woke from dreams of Shakhmatovo with my face bathed in tears?"

Chapter Four

Conclusions

Before us, therefore, is a poet of erratic personality. His social position is extremely unstable and tormenting. He feels that his class, his type of man— is doomed. He detests the reality around him and his immediate conqueror—the bourgeoisie and all it stands for. He seeks a way of life in high-minded mysticism into which he channels the youthful experience of a pure, ardent love. But in the depths of these "white roses" a caterpillar is already hidden. The caterpillar element of wild debauchery, the element of aristocratic rakishness emerges in a peculiar form. These ravings of the blood are experienced as a quest for truth at the bottom of a glass, as an attempt to arrive at some special meaning of life through sin, as an orgiastic search for Dionysius, perhaps even for Christ.

These aspects of Blok make him a particularly suitable vehicle to express the moods not only of all those who belonged, like him, to the moribund aristocratic intelligentsia, but also of the bourgeois intelligentsia who, at that time, were already standing on the edge of the precipice which was to prove the terminus of their social existence—so short-lived in our country. The "music of revolution" sounds through all this. In this music Blok seeks something profoundly akin to his own elemental searchings, to his desire to look beyond the bounds of being. This revolution of the Russian peasant, of the Russian rebel, this peasant principle of revolution, this peasant justice had, of old, served the Herzens, Bakunins and Tolstois as a refuge from the despair of a doomed aristocracy. Blok romanticises the revolution. He "ennobles" it in the sense that he gives it kinship now with his "sacred" quest, now with his sinful searchings. He finds both in the inebriated emotional sweep of *The Twelve* and in the accompanying figure of Christ. With these elements he interweaves and confounds the revolutionary principle.

Unable to see any other way out, Blok was ready to believe that the way out was the revolution, specially prepared and taken with a stiff dose of romanticism. He admitted the idea that this romantic revolution, like a runaway troika, might finally crush his class, and perhaps, himself, but Blok was ready to bestow his blessing on this forward rush, for he could see no possibility of his own social group advancing in any way.

Thus the poet, in his own way, cried, *"Morituri te salutant"**. But what it was exactly for which Blok was prepared to lay down his life became less and less comprehensible as time went on. Blok saw only —on the one side—a kind of grey disorganisation, neglect, untidiness of life and—on the other—the incomprehensible and alien plans of the Bolshevik Party which had taken the wheel of events firmly into its own strong hands. Blok was almost ready to curse this revolution which, according to him, had become an "unmusical" revolution, having lost not

---

* "Dying, we salute thee" (Lat.)—Roman gladiators' greeting to the emperor from the arena.—*Ed.*

only its aristocratic features but what he thought of as its tremendous, Razin-like* features, a revolution which becoming more and more "European" before his eyes had become prose.

Blok's works and, therefore, his whole personality are of considerable significance for us, an object lesson in history. Here we have a perfect specimen-product of the last, decadent stages of the culture of the nobility and, to a certain extent, of the whole of pre-revolutionary Russian culture (aristocratic and bourgeois). At the same time, it is interesting to note a profoundly positive and admirable feature— the ability of this last child of a long line to perceive and to understand something of the greatness of the revolution, to greet it with full courtesy, to be ready to cast all the values of the world which, though his own, he had grown to hate, at the feet of the wild horses of the revolution, galloping he knew not whither. No less instructive, however, is the evidence of the limits which Blok's class consciousness imposed on his understanding of the revolution.

The last poet of the landed gentry might sing praises to the red cock**, even though it were his own house that was aflame. Senseless and cruel riots, however much they might horrify him, could nevertheless command his blessing in the name of some utterly vague perspective, of some kind of purification by fire from an uncleanness which he knew only too well and from only too intimate experience.

But the proletarian revolution, its iron revolutionary logic, its clear ideas of enlightenment, its grasp of the laws governing social phenomena, its stubborn

---

* Stepan Razin—leader of a peasant revolt in the seventeenth century.—*Ed.*

** The red cock—Russian folklore appellation of fire much dreaded in a country where wood was the principal building material.—*Tr.*

and intense work to lay the foundations for a new, planned economy—none of this could possibly hold any immediate appeal to the heart and mind of the last poet of the gentry. All this seemed to him to be part and parcel of that bourgeois world which he had so deeply hated.

And why should that be thought surprising? Tolstoi, battling powerfully against the onset of the capitalist element in the name of the nobility, dissolved his nobility in the peasantry almost without residue— yet the genuinely revolutionary forces were on the other side of the barricades. He might occasionally say a few words of sympathy for the disinterested heroism of the revolutionaries, but they were profoundly alien to him. Their philosophy of life seemed to him an abomination, seemed nothing but a new mask for the same old daemon of civilisation, which provoked all his conservative, aristocratic hatred. These same aesthetic, rebellious principles had been responsible for Herzen's revulsion from Marx, for Bakunin's having become the declared enemy of socialism. All this was in the order of things.

Blok, at the moment of the physical death of his class, exhibited the maximum revolutionary impulse of which the consciousness of the nobility was capable. This maximum was enough to produce a few brilliant, interesting, though turgid and confused works of art. Nevertheless, it left Blok on the threshold of the true revolution, amazed, bewildered, unable to appreciate the real rhythms of its march, the "music" of which had remained inapprehensible to him because already sounding through it could be heard elements of a great and reasonable spirit of organisation, a spirit utterly alien to that past in which Blok's whole nature was so deeply rooted.

1932

FORTY years in the literary career of a great writer will always cover a large area on the ever-growing map of world culture. It is only at a distance that such a mountain range can be evaluated as a whole.

The results and full significance of Maxim Gorky's work as concerns our epoch and Russian and world culture as a whole, and his relative place on the great map of human achievement will only become clear at a future date. All the more so since the mountain range that is Gorky has not yet been completed, and we hope to see him grow most wonderfully and gigantically for many years to come.

And yet, forty years is a long time. When a person who has worked for forty years looks back from the vantage point to which life has brought him he sees a long and winding river whose source appears as remote as ancient history, while the ribbon itself acquires an integral significance which such a person wants to discover and establish for himself, and sometimes for others as well.

It was approximately after forty years that Goethe, for instance, felt the irresistible need to comprehend the meaning of his life and his work and tell others about it.

I do not know whether Gorky now has a desire to embark on a similar preliminary summing-up of everything he has experienced and accomplished.... He is not devoid of an inclination to autobiography, and it is responsible for a number of books which are truly the pride of Russian literature.

Neither does Gorky lack a sense of retrospection, for what else is the great structure of *Klim Samgin* if not a very original panorama, a sum-total of his recollections in the course of several decades?

But we cannot wait until Gorky himself gets down to writing his *Dichtung und Wahrheit*.

The golden bell of the grand fortieth anniversary is ringing, reminding us literary critics of the great Marxist-Leninist school that we as yet do not have a major work which would at least present a series of clear, concise photographs from all the chief angles of the mountain range Gorky has erected in forty years.

Such a work must be written. It must be written soon. I do not know whether this should be done by an individual or by a group of authors. At any rate some preliminary work has been done.

I am far from the thought of presenting in this article, which finds the allotted space too restrictive, a sketch or outline of this likewise preliminary Marxist book on Gorky.

I am merely pointing here to the far horizon, where Gorky's might mountain range rises above the sea level, above the glades and the forests. I am merely pointing most sketchily to its vital foundation, to the elemental deposits from which it "grew".

I am merely drawing an outline for the reader to help him recognise the profile of the mountains lost high in the clouds.

II

Perhaps the great majority of outstanding literary phenomena and significant writers appear as a result of major social changes, of social catastrophes. Literary masterpieces mark these changes.

Lenin, in his magnificent works on Tolstoi, which no Marxist literary critic can afford to ignore, defines the basic elemental, social, unavoidable reason for Tolstoi's appearance, for the existence of Lev Tolstoi *per se*, for the scope of his talent, his triumph in Russia and throughout the world, for the immortality of his artistic achievement and the poverty of his philosophical and social ideas: this was the colossal catastrophe which shook Russia at the time. The old Russia of peasants and landowners was perishing under the pressure of the relentless onslaught of capital.

The Russian peasant was the hero and, unfortunately, the passive hero of this terrible bloody and tear-drenched drama.

There arose then a great cloud of tears, grief, moans, destitution, cries of despair and anger, passionate, heart-wrenching bewilderment, a searching for a way out; a fiery question mark rose over the land as a terrible nightmare: where was one to find the truth?

While tormenting the peasants, this crisis dealt the landowners a terrible blow as well, sending them down to the bottom. All the old ways began to shake, as things do in an earthquake.

And a man came forth whose background, education, culture, sensitivity and gift for writing made him capable of transforming the peasants' grief and the peasants' bewilderment into works of art. This man was a landowner, and, therefore, there were many scenes of aristocratic life in his works, although the peasant spirit predominated and the peasants' suffering dominated the Count's every thought. This did not divert Lenin's keen insight to a superficial evaluation of Tolstoi as a writer of the nobility. No, Tolstoi's fiery revolutionary spirit, ready to sweep away thrones, altars and the nobility itself, was not of the nobility; nor of the nobility was the essentially noxious and most harmful spirit of submission, patience and non-violence, which for centuries had been the faithful helpmate of every executioner in the heart of the peasant himself.

In like manner, Maxim Gorky signifies a tremendous step forward in the history of our country at a later date.

The bourgeoisie came to power, it asserted itself as the dominant class, though it still shared its power with the lions of the nobility. But these were new noblemen—the very same ones whose first representatives Tolstoi described with such loathing in *Anna Karenina*.

On the whole, the moneybag now ruled the country. However, it only fulfilled its rather relative cultural and economic role to a very small degree. It was carnivorous and grasping. Naturally, it created something, but it destroyed much more.

The historical experience of other countries and its own instincts indicated that the stylish European parliamentary dress which fitted the foreign big bourgeoisie so well was not made for it. And though well-fed Russian capitalism would from time to time mutter something unintelligible about a constitution, it relied above all on the gendarme and the priest.

Nevertheless, this capitalism, which oppressed the country both by its maturity and immaturity, was dangerously ill. It was grieved. It was tortured by terrible premonitions. It was full of fear and divarication. It had its connivers, its oppressors and pessimists, but all of them carried the stamp of doom on their faces. This giant in golden armour, but weak of heart, had not been born to a long and happy life.

The further growth of capital continued to oppress the villages mercilessly. But it was not their groans that filled the new and powerful artistic organ and the many organ pipes of the young Gorky.

His social standing made him more familiar with the stagnant, swampy, tortured society of the city petty bourgeoisie, gripped as it was by rigid routine and overflowing with strange characters.

They were Gorky's first subjects. He chose as his theme one of the city's strangest phenomena, the tramps, and then, in time, turned to the proletariat.

As we listen keenly to Gorky's music, from its very inception, we can but laugh as we reject the superficial and, I would say, silly little theories that Gorky was a writer of the lower middle classes.

Following in Lenin's giant footsteps, we can say that Gorky's indomitable, turbulent, rainbow-bright joy of life, which burst forth from his very first lines, was not of the lower middle classes. Nor is his merciless indignation at the ruling evil of the middle class; nor is his firm belief in man, in his mighty culture, in his coming victory; nor is his bold call for courage and his stormy petrel, heralding the coming revolution, of the middle class. None of this is of the lower middle classes—all is of the proletariat.

III

The social change which gave birth to Tolstoi, and which can be defined as the destruction of old Russia by the swift advance of capitalist industry, was a change that was one-sided and irreparable.

Tolstoi made his ideological escape from his class, which was doomed by history, to the peasantry. But there was no way out for the peasantry, either. It was only much later that a way out would be found for the impoverished peasantry, and only the victorious proletariat would be capable of showing this way to it.

One can rightly say that the proletariat, as such, did not exist for Tolstoi. The revolutionary democrats, representatives of the progressive peasantry, and their great leader Chernyshevsky, appeared in a distant haze as dim but most unpleasant silhouettes. He considered them to be children of the same

Satanic city, madmen who wanted, by using violence to quench violence, to further increase the hellish confusion of the advancing pseudo-civilisation and who strove in vain to tempt the simple folk by their crude promises of plunder, distribution and the false carnal sense of well-being.

The change of which Maxim Gorky was born was, on the contrary, of a dual nature and provided a way out.

Though the full, leaden weight of capital had descended upon the country, this great mass, as we stated previously, had already begun to crack, an indication of its impending doom. Even in literature the triumph of capitalism was reflected not so much in triumphant songs as in a groaning and creaking, while such portrayers of life in a capitalist society as the seemingly capable and observant Boborykin began their descriptions of capitalist life with its inherent defects, crashes and inner doubts.

Is it not strange that in all of Russian literature it is difficult to find a writer at all famous who might be called the bard of capitalism? I believe that Pereverzev's attempts to delegate this place to Goncharov are most unsuccessful.

Capitalism, on the other hand, had its own proletarian lining on which history was later to base all of society.

True, that which the chief literary giant of the epoch, Maxim Gorky, found most obvious was yet another side of capitalism. As we have already noted, the discordant, wretched howling of the suffering lower middle classes, over whose bones the capitalist chariot was rolling just as it was rolling over the bones of the peasantry, was the first wild, spontaneous dissonance of which the mighty chords of Gorky's rage were born.

Yes, Gorky came to literature dressed in peasant boots and a peasant shirt, tuberculous, yet mighty, having drunk deeply of the cup of grief, yet yearning for happiness; he came to the sunny offices of the magazines which were salon editions compared to his native cellar, to tell the full and terrible truth about the "moles" and their blind, filthy, horrible life. This was Gorky's great mission, this was his great speech of indictment. This determined his biting, sarcastic, merciless realism.

Gorky condemned Luka (*Lower Depths*) as a man who consoles the suffering by hastily stuffing their mouths with a narcotic pacifier of lies. Gorky did not want to lie to the poor, whom he considered to be his brothers, as "Chizh who lied". In his absolute honesty Gorky rejected the false solace, "the exalting deceit" which at times seemed to be on the tip of his pen. This honesty, this courage was the quite subconscious reflection in his early writings of the approach of a new type of music: the march of the advancing proletarian battalions.

Who knows but that, if spring and revolution were not in the air as a result of the increasing numbers and growing social consciousness of the workers, Gorky would not have fallen a victim to the blackest pessimism? We know that he was dissatisfied with the frayed idealism of the Narodniks. And does not his pen-name, Gorky,* seem a threat to pessimistic moralising?

One thing certainly could never have happened to Gorky. No matter how much soot from the icon-lamps and the various strange religious fantasies had accumulated in the middle-class cellars where he had spent a part of his life, he had quickly developed an immunity against "God" in all shapes and forms.

It is much easier to imagine Gorky as the prophet of dark despair, cursing an ill-starred humanity, than as a saint *a la* Tolstoi, with a saintly halo above his shaggy head and his hand raised in blessing.

_____
* Bitter (Russ.).—*Tr.*

However, Gorky, who spoke to the Russian reader in his deep, muffled voice of the terrible life of the poor, and whose stories were at times unbearable in their intensity, did not strike the reader as being bitter.

Why was this so?

Because Gorky's pockets were full of golden, carmine and azure pictures and fairy tales that were full of a rather naive romanticism, but heroism as well. And even in the magnificent and realistic *Chelkash*, which brought the author great fame, this gold, carmine and pure blue of man's true dignity, of the clear clarion protest of magnificent heroic spirit, illuminate Chelkash's shaggy head, his bronzed chest and rags.

Gorky soon threw off his fairy-tale plumage, but the heroic protest was becoming ever more a part of the truth of life, and thus Gorky's chords, Gorky's harmony and Gorky's symphony were created.

Lev Tolstoi could not draw upon a heroic protest, a call to a struggle enlightened by hope from the lords and ladies of his circle, nor from the peasants of the village of Yasnaya Polyana.

And no one anywhere in the terrible blackness that was Russia, none of its artists could draw upon it. The intellectual novels of the 1860s, grouped around the great *What Is To Be Done?*, appear as a faint promise of the future, but more as monuments of a premonition than true calls to action.

The author of nearly thirty volumes under the general heading of *The Collected Works of Maxim Gorky* is none other than our dear, good friend Alexei Maximovich Peshkov.

But not even in his own heart could he find the fiery ink with which he wrote so many of these pages. He dipped his pen in the fountain of life which had its source in the incoming tide of the revolution.

That is why we see behind the great, vital and dearly beloved figure of Alexei Peshkov a co-author, the monumental figure of the proletariat, whose mighty hand rests gently on the shoulder of the man who became its spokesman.

Tolstoi undoubtedly loved Nature. And very much so, indeed. Much more than the average man, for did he not understand so perfectly the psychology of animals? He loved Nature with every fibre of his soul, with every sense, with every pore. Tolstoi was an inveterate hiker, a horseman until he was eighty, for many years a dedicated hunter, a man who lived mostly in the country; he was, to a very great extent, a man of Nature.

Only such a man could have created a type such as Yeroshka. And can one ever forget the great little old man at the seashore whom Gorky portrayed? One must add a hatred of the city. There is so much of this scornful hatred in the famous beginning of one of Tolstoi's novels which describes the way people choked down the living earth beneath their cobblestones and how it stubbornly sent up green shoots through the stones.

Nevertheless, Tolstoi the writer, Tolstoi the ideologist does not like Nature: he is not only indifferent to it in his own way, but he is afraid of it, he practically hates it.

He is prepared, if the worst comes to the worst, to accept Mother Earth, since it can be ploughed and the ripe ears can then be reaped for man's meagre daily bread, but that is all. For what is Nature? This brightness of day and charm of night? These flowers, sparkling in every hue, their aroma intoxicating? This play of elemental forces which calls upon one to live, to fight, to seek pleasure, to multiply, as the animal world lives, finds pleasure, fights and multiplies, but more wisely, i.e., more forcefully and consciously? What is Nature then? It is temptation! It is a mirage! It is difficult to believe that God could have created this. God has for unknown reasons sown our souls as a myriad of sparks into the luxuriant and evil world and has set these souls a task: not to be tempted, to live a pure life and return to Him, the source of the spiritual fire, cleansed of the filth of contact with Nature.

This is less the peasant than the Asiatic attitude towards Nature, imposed upon the peasantry from Asia, and one which Tolstoi, despite his flaming sensuality and his sensitive genius, tried to adopt and called upon others to adopt.

That is why Tolstoi is so sparing in his descriptions of Nature. If you do come upon a few landscapes in his works, they seem to have been done at random and rather grudgingly.

The few exceptions merely prove the rule.

Now recall Gorky's descriptions of Nature!

Though it weeps and rages and inflicts pain upon man, this is not the impression one carries away. What remains is an elemental grandeur, a great, and, I believe, despite Turgenev, incomparable variety of landscapes unequalled in Russian literature.

Gorky is truly a great landscape painter and, more important, a passionate landscape lover. He finds it difficult to approach a person, to begin a story of a chapter of a novel without first glancing at the sky to see what the sun, the moon, the stars and the ineffable palette of the heavens with the ever-changing magic of the clouds are doing.

In Gorky we find so much of the sea, the mountains, forests and steppes, so many little gardens and hidden nooks of Nature! What unusual words he invents to describe it! He works at it as an objective artist: now as Monet, breaking down its colours for you with his amazing analytical eye and what is probably the most extensive vocabulary in our literature, now, on the contrary, as a syntheticist who produces a general outline and with one hammered phrase can describe an entire panorama. But he is not merely an artist. His approach to Nature is that of a poet. What if we do not actually believe that a sunset can be *sad*, that a forest can whisper *pensively*, that the sea can *laugh!* Indeed, they can do all this; it is only when man will become a dry old stick (and he will never become one) that he will stop seeing in the forces of Nature a magnificently delicate and enlarged version of his own emotions.

In order to create Nature's majestic and beautiful orchestrations for his human dramas, Gorky uses most skilfully the frailest similarities and contrasts between human emotions and Nature, which at times are barely discernible.

Those who will doubt the truth of this and think that I am too lavish in my praise of Gorky, the artist and poet of Nature, should pick up any volume of *The Life of Klim Samgin* and reread the pages which create a background of Nature for the human drama.

But why does Gorky devote so much space to Nature? And does this prove that he is a proletarian writer? How much of Nature does a worker see? Do not the brick factory walls conceal it? Has it not been exiled from the workers' barracks, from the workers' settlement?

Gorky, the proletarian writer, loves Nature for the very reason the old peasant writer Tolstoi does not and is afraid to like it.

We have already said that Nature calls upon man to live, struggle, enjoy life and multiply, but more wisely, i.e., more forcefully and consciously than the animal world.

According to Tolstoi and Christianity, this is temptation, it is Satan's trap. And both the feudal landowning and capitalist systems of the world have proven that, indeed, this principle of life and struggle, no matter what creative force it develops, what sciences it calls to its aid, what arts it adorns itself with, can lead only to sin and filth, to moral death of some as the oppressors and others as their victims.

But it is at this point that the proletariat disagrees with history, it is at this point that it wants to change the course of humanity.

The proletariat says: Yes, Mother Nature, our great, wonderful, merciless and blind Mother, you are right; your world and your way of life is good. They will become a supreme good, surpassing all our hopes in the hands of a wise, united mankind, in the hands of the universal commune which we shall achieve, which we shall build, sparing no effort at all. And we know how to win it, how to build it. And then, what a true paradise you will be, Nature, for the new and wonderful man the future will produce. That is why we love you, Nature.

"And that is why I love it," says Gorky.

V

The very same difference exists in Gorky's and Tolstoi's attitudes towards man. Certainly, Tolstoi loves his fellow man. This love for his fellow man may be considered the chief commandment of his teaching. But this is a strained sort of love. According to it, one must not love man as a whole, but only "God's spark" that lies hidden within him. And one must love only this "spark" within oneself as well, only one's own power to believe and to love. In this respect Tolstoi is a true proponent of the teachings of some Asiatic gnostic, philotheistic, etc., theories.

Tolstoi's man is made of two men: one born of God, the other of Satan. He who perhaps is often endowed with a beautiful body immortalised by sculpture, he whose breast harbours the gentlest emotions and fiery passions, which find expression in music; he whose head contains that most amazing apparatus, a brain, which has created such miracles of science; he who wants happiness for himself and for others, implying by happiness the fulfilment of the ever-growing demands of the rich human body and the human collective—that man is born of Satan, Tolstoi does not love him, he is afraid of him; he has cast him aside, because he sees him as the victim of a terrible social system and, at the same time, as the one responsible for this system; because in the future he sees no happiness for this man, but only an increase in the greedy oppression of capitalism, the state and the Church, and the useless bloody revolutions.

That is why Tolstoi's love went to the other man: the quiet, meek little angel, the passionless, incorporeal and kind one with ever-tearful eyes, ever-thankful to dear God.

While still living on earth this man, this Abel, can cast off all of Cain's magnificence, all of culture, and divide the land up into tiny gardens, he can grow cabbages there, eat them, fertilise his garden and plant some more cabbage, and thus, sustaining himself self-sufficiently and ever so sweetly, he will have no need for his neighbour, except for soul-saving talks or mutual prayer. Gradually, according to Tolstoi, marriages will cease between these little fools (that is how he fondly though seriously calls them, *viz.*, the tale of their kingdom); the human race will blissfully die out, having fulfilled its mission and, washed clean of all the passions of terrible matter, it will return to the source of the spirit.

Such a love for man is more terrifying than any hatred, and we Communists consider Tolstoi's teachings to be but another variety of the old Asiatic poison which crippled man's will.

Goethe confessed that he hated the sign of the Cross. Many of the best representatives of the young bourgeoisie shared this view. With even greater vehemence we hate and reject Christianity and all the teachings which paved the way for it, and any of its distillations which the decadents of all colours are busy with to this day.

Gorky, on the other hand, loves man in his entirety. It is Gorky speaking when Satin says: "How proud the word rings—MAN!"

Gorky knows that people can be mean and foul and these are the people he hates. But he knows that these are ignoramuses, that these are freaks, that these are mere scabs on the beautiful tree of human life.

Moreover, he knows that there are still very few really great men, pure of heart, courageous and wise, that there are practically no perfectly wonderful people.

But this does not keep him from loving his fellow man with a feeling that is true love and to have real faith in him, a faith born of knowledge.

VI

And now we come to the question of Tolstoi's and Gorky's attitudes towards progress.

Here the two writers have much in common. Tolstoi came through his sufferings to despise patriotism, royalty, the nobility, the feudal past and all its remnants.

Gorky can be said to have been born with this burning disgust.

Tolstoi came to hate capital with a truly great hatred and would not be bribed by the glitter of European culture, but, after visiting Europe, he returned full of rage, having seen quite clearly all the black lies that lay beneath the surface of life with its marble and tapestry drapes.

Gorky, too, became a sworn enemy of capital from his earliest youth. And neither was he fooled by America's *Yellow Devil*, and he spat gall and blood into the face of the bourgeois *la belle France*.

Tolstoi saw every manifestation of cowardice, gross drunkenness, petty chicanery, the spider-like cruelty of the petty townsfolk—and of the peasantry to a very great extent as well.

And Gorky, too, driven by horrified curiosity, likes to dig up the Okurov dens and bring their filth to light.

Nevertheless, Tolstoi drew the line here: having washed all that he considered to be a superfluous accumulation from the visage of the old peasantry, he restored the saintliness of the forefathers, the saintly Akims, with their eloquent ineloquence, the fairy-tale-like patriarchs who would give to poor mankind "grain as large as hen's eggs".

Tolstoi built his mystical cabbage heaven for mankind on the myth of the saintly peasantry, on the myth that hidden in each *muzhik* was a saint that could not wait to pop out of him.

Gorky, too, nearly drew the line at the little man, but he searched among them for large and proud specimens, for the nuggets in the gold ore. He felt they were to be found where life's waters washed ashore all that seemed most unsuitable to it, there on the bottom, among the outcasts, among the wolf-men, the unruly protestants, individuals who were not shackled by property and morals, giants of anti-social behaviour, instinctive anarchists.

But Gorky did not stop for long at this extremely anti-Tolstoian stage of development.

There followed Gorky's natural merger with the proletariat and its vanguard, the Bolsheviks.

This great event was marked in literature by many magnificent works, among which *Enemies, Mother* and *The Life of Klim Samgin* are most notable.

Herein, naturally, lay the reason for the great difference in Tolstoi's and Gorky's attitudes towards mankind's cultural treasures.

There is undoubtedly much truth in Tolstoi's invective against bourgeois science and bourgeois art, but he has cast out the child with the bath water. And the child, no matter how badly brought up by the ruling classes, is nevertheless hardy and viable.

If people of the old tenor of life, whom Tolstoi joined, regard science and art suspiciously and have no use for technical progress, the proletariat, on the other hand, accepts them enthusiastically and takes them for its own. It knows that only under socialism can science develop and culture flourish.

Gorky knows this, too. I believe there are very few people on earth who are so inspired by the achievements of science and art and who await new miracles with such anticipation.

VII

The proletarian writer rises to his full height in Gorky the publicist.

We will not analyse this aspect of Gorky here. It is a significant part of the writer's work, an integral part of his forty years of writing.

It rises as a watchtower and bastion against the background of his mountain range.

Even writing from Western Europe, Gorky the publicist has taken it chiefly upon himself to ward off the treacherous blows against the communist cause, inflicted by fear and hatred.

Gorky often disregards a public or even official blow, or snap of one of his many poison-pen correspondents; they circle like a cloud of gnats above his head.

His replies usually deal a moral mortal blow to the inquirer.

On the whole the greater part of Gorky's journalism can be collected and issued as an impressive and forceful well-argumented volume entitled *On Guard of the U.S.S.R.*

VIII

However, there is more than "gnats" buzzing about Gorky's head.

Thousands upon thousands of news items reach the writer's sensitive ears. He keenly absorbs books, magazines and newspapers, he listens to people and has at his disposal an amazing store of knowledge about what is going on in the Soviet Union and in the hostile world that surrounds it.

There is not much he can do for the rest of the world, though he cannot lose sight of it for a moment. However, the news that reaches him from the Soviet Union is not stored away in the vast chambers of Gorky's erudition. It must all serve the cause.

Here Gorky can lend a helping hand.

His aid is undoubtedly valuable as a collector of the achievements of our vast building programme, for instance the magazine *Nashi dostizhenia* (*Our Achievements*).

But this is not his true calling.

And he knows it.

What we need are major literary works. What we actually need is great literature. We do not have it.

And he knows it.

It would be a great undertaking to win over the old writers, among whom there are many talented men and skilled craftsmen, to throw bridges over to them and help them overcome the various inner barriers which prevent them from understanding and accepting our great times. And Gorky can undoubtedly play a tremendous role in this respect.

But our power does not lie in this.

Our power is not to be found in the yesterday, but in the future. Our basic strength lies in the young growth. Without for a moment forgetting our daily tasks and our own work, we must give very much of our attention to our wonderful youth.

The Party delves deep into it to find its cadres.

It is just as understandable that we must delve into it to find our artistic cadres and our writers as well. It is quite understandable that this is a vital detachment of our Soviet creative army.

Ever since the now deceased Valery Bryusov noted so correctly that an artist of the written word, just as any other artist, must possess beside his talent both skill and a cultural background, something is constantly being done to promote such study. But what is being done is done timidly, lacking generosity and vitality.

There are many amateur literary circles, but things are apparently moving too slowly there.

And especially disappointing was the insufficient attention the young leaders of proletarian literature paid to Lenin's great behests on learning from the vast culture of the past.

The dialectics here are very refined: since one must study critically, it means one must study and criticise! If you begin to study without a critical approach or with an insufficiently critical approach, you will find yourself among the epigoni. If you begin to criticise without sufficient learning to back you up, you will not become a one hundred per cent proletarian *Wunderkind*, but Saltykov-Shchedrin's "Neuvazhai Koryto".

Many were the times that, in my capacity as editor of encyclopaedias, magazines and collected works, I came upon such dim-witted criticism. And when you attempt to arouse in such a young, and at times very sincere and sympathetic "critic", a feeling of respect for some great writer of the past, he will drop a rather heavy hint about the mistakes of some "venerable old" Bolsheviks.

It is time to put an end to such things.

We must be able to understand, finally, how we must learn the old skill, how we must analyse the old cultural treasures with true understanding and respect, which in no way precludes but merely presupposes criticism.

In no way is this limited to the literary and other artistic models of the past; this has bearing on the great philosophy of the past, this is especially relevant to science. A young writer should not shun anything, he should strive to achieve the greatest amount of learning, he should not be limited by ignorance when he undertakes to portray life in a new way for hundreds and thousands of readers.

In a recent letter to Romain Rolland Gorky referred to the young writers by saying, "What they lack is culture."

The reader of this article might say, "The author's last statement is probably right, but it has no direct bearing on the subject."

He will be wrong.

In the first place, all that I have written of the necessity of our young writers to acquire a cultural background are things I have read in Gorky's works or heard Gorky say.

Secondly, we can expect real help from Gorky as an organiser in this respect. He can not only convince our young people of the necessity of acquiring a cultural background. They already agree to this and indeed wish to acquire such a background, but do not quite know how to go about it.

No single man, however, is equal to the task.

Even Gorky cannot do it alone. But he can head a group of people who are well suited for the job, who will be entrusted with developing a plan for the tremendous cultural advance of the young writers towards that great socialist literature we all strive for.

IX

We hope Gorky will give us the promised volumes of *Klim Samgin* and other brilliant works of fiction.

We hope he will raise high his sword and shield as a publicist many times over, defending our cause.

Such are our wishes on the fortieth anniversary of the great writer's literary career.

1932

VLADIMIR MAYAKOVSKY, INNOVATOR

IT has been said many times that Mayakovsky's espousal of the proletarian cause was not a chance occurrence. This means that the prerequisites necessary for taking him in this direction existed within him, for in our times there are many people and not a few poets, but not all people, not all poets follow this road. However, this inner voice would never have led him as it did, if not for our times, for no one determines his own way, but the way of any man is determined, to a great extent, by his times and surroundings. In speaking of Mayakovsky's work and life, we speak of his encounter as an individual with the proletarian revolution as a gigantic social event.

The proletariat and its revolution existed in a latent form long before the October Revolution, and even before 1905. Mayakovsky knew of the existence of this great force and at times he came quite close to it in his everyday life, yet, during his early period, he was still quite removed from it. One can say that when Mayakovsky embarked upon his career, he was still beyond the sphere of influence of this gigantic social body, the revolutionary proletariat. The first step Mayakovsky took on the road to revolution, in the broad sense of the word, was renouncing and attempting to destroy that which existed and trying to substitute instead something that was better and nobler.

Mayakovsky often provides definitions and self-portraits in which he says that he, Mayakovsky, is too big for the surroundings in which he must live. He puts a double meaning into the word "big". On the one hand, he is simply stating the fact that he, Mayakovsky, is a very tall, big man; on the other hand, there is a corresponding bigness of spirit, the scope of his ideas, his passions, his demands upon life, his creative powers; they, too, are out of proportion with his surroundings.

It is characteristic that in this respect the words "greatness" and "bigness" merge. As far as he is concerned, these passions, these thoughts, this dissatisfaction, these hopes and this despair of his are not something born of his mind, they do not revolve in some "empyrean consciousness"; all this is of his body, it is all taking place within his Herculean frame. Mayakovsky was a materialist (I will later discuss whether or not he became a dialectician): he experienced intensely everything that was of the earth, of the flesh, washed with hot blood, and he experienced it as Mayakovsky, the corporeal being and as Mayakovsky, the corresponding psyche.

Well, such a Mayakovsky found that he was cramped in the world. This does not mean he was cramped in the Universe. He liked the Universe, the Universe was very big, and he wanted to be on very close terms with it: he invited the Sun to come down and visit him and the Sun came down and talked to him. But the Sun came to him in his dreams, whereas those who were truly close to him and those with whom he tried to come in close contact were none of them as big as he. This is why Mayakovsky felt so melancholy and so terribly lonely. He found it difficult to find true friends. And only towards the end of his life did he begin finding them in a cross between the great vastness of the forces of Nature and individual persons, among whom he still found very few true friends. He never succeeded in closely approaching the greatest men of our epoch, men concerned with other matters in another sphere, the political leaders of our revolution. And yet, he finally found the entities, towards which he lunged with the great force of his desire to end his loneliness.

234

These were social entities: the proletariat and the revolution.

The proletariat and the revolution were close to his heart, firstly, in their Herculean, vast scope, the great battles which they unleashed in the spheres of direct political struggle and labour and, secondly, because they were the key to the future. He obviously did not have a very clear concept of *what* the future would be like. But he knew that it would be a future in which he, a big man, would finally be able to breathe freely, in which he would be able to draw himself up to his full height, in which his heart would find its heaven. That is why, while all but foreseeing his fateful end, he says, in the introduction to his poem *At the Top of My Voice*, that, the big man that he is, he should be revived in the future.

> *Hi, listen!*
>   *comrade heirs and descendants,*
> *to an agitator,*
>   *loud-speaker-in-chief!*
> *Deafening*
>   *poetic deluge,*
> *I stride to you*
>   *through lyrical volumes,*
> *as the live*
>   *with the living speaks.*

When freedom was won, when great, erect people came to live on earth, then one could love, could sing as one wishes. But now—

> *Descendants,*
>   *in our lexicons,*
>   *look up the flotsam*
> *that floats down from Lethe,*
>   *odd remnant words*

> *like "prostitution"*
> > *"tuberculosis"*
> > > *"blockades".*
>
> *For you,*
> > *who're so healthy and nimble,*
> *a poet*
> > *licked up*
> > > *consumptive spittle*
> *with the crude rough tongue of placards.*

Mayakovsky did all he could to pave the way for the man of the future.

This was the starting point from which Mayakovsky began his fight for the big man in pre-revolutionary times. There was no road to the future in the bourgeois world, there were no entities of social order, of the collective which he could come to love, there was only a petty-bourgeois void, and it was against this petty-bourgeois void that he protested.

There were some social notes in Mayakovsky's protest from the very start. However, the essence of this protest was: the world is too shallow to accept a great individual, and the great individual rejects with indignation and disgust this shallow world, this mercenary world, pulverised as it is to a bourgeois level. This was Mayakovsky's first revolt.

Mayakovsky's second revolt resulted from his youth. It was not a matter of a man being young and, therefore, loving to behave defiantly, like a cock-of-the-rock, towards others. No, youth meant something else to Mayakovsky: he felt that the world he had been born into, and of which he had become an integral part, was old and decrepit. It had its own famous personages and museums, revered by all, but these famous personages and museums served only to sanctify and bless the worthless, decrepit world in which he lived.

Mayakovsky realised full well that there were priceless treasures in mankind's past, but he feared that if these treasures were acknowledged, all the rest must, therefore, be acknowledged, too. Therefore, it was better to revolt against everything and say: We are our own ancestors! May our youth proclaim its own young words, such as will make it possible to rejuvenate society and the world!

Youth usually wants to stress the fact that it will say things that have never been said before. This desire produces in Mayakovsky's revolutionary writings the contrasts which many critics have noted and which, undoubtedly, are often paradoxical, are often an unexpected trick, are often rudeness, are often a young boy's prank. And those who, like Shengeli and all the other "old maids", said: "Oh, dear! This is terrible! This is hooliganism!" were horrified because they had no youth left in their blood. One can even be young at an advanced age or be dog-old at an early age, it is not a matter of years, but of creative power. And those who lack it could not understand how the wine fermented in Mayakovsky, how it blew out the cork and even blasted the bottle, how a young talent was forming. These pranks of the young Mayakovsky were signs of his future growth, just as a pure-bred puppy has large and clumsy paws, true signs of his future great size.

His third revolutionary step was born of his skill and, first and foremost, of his skill in the formal sense of the word. He felt in himself a great love for words, he felt that words obeyed him, that they formed into battalions at his command. He was carried away by this power he had over words. He felt that if a person did not know how to command words, but merely repeated what others had done before, he was like a conductor who comes to a well-rehearsed orchestra and waves his baton after the musicians have already played a particular phrase, while the listeners think he is conducting. Such a state of affairs is similar to one in which an epigonus thinks he is writing new poems, while he is actually possessed by old words and thoughts. Mayakovsky was always exasperated by formal impotency, and he said that one should write in an entirely new way. He did not yet know what this new way would be, in form and content, but, above all, it had to be new. And he who would write according to the old tenets should be castigated as a servant of the decrepit world.

Mayakovsky's next revolt (similar to his castigation of his surroundings which was born of his skill) was a revolt of production. Here, to a great extent, we have approached the very essence of his works. Who, Mayakovsky asked himself, are those poets whom I renounce for being imitators, for continuing the process of further ageing the world, regurgitating, as they do, songs that have already been sung? What is the content of their songs? Is there any usefulness in what these poets are producing? Perhaps, then, poets cannot produce anything of use at all?

Mayakovsky was incensed by poets who proudly stated: "A poet does not produce useful things, a poet produces useless things. Herein lies my charm as a poet, this is the exalted nature of things poetic." If one were to listen attentively to the useless things these poets sing about, one would discover they were nothing more than a soulful rigmarole. Historical themes, genres, and what-have-you are put through the so-called subjective, pulled through the stomach and intestines, and then only are they presented to you. If a person is a poet, he must be a "lyricist" first, he must know how to be very musically nauseous in front of the whole world.

Mayakovsky himself was revolted by all this lyricism, by all this musical chirping, by all saccharine melodies, and by the desire to adorn life with artificial flowers. Mayakovsky did not want life to be adorned, because, in his opinion, adorning life, and such a horrible one at that, was a treacherous undertaking; they would camouflage reality's hideous mug with cheap artificial flowers instead of changing it. This, undoubtedly, was the influence of his dormant Marxist feelings, although it was only gradually (as Jourdain only in his maturity discovered that he spoke in prose) that Mayakovsky realised he was a revolutionary in mind, that he realised whose ally he was.

Thus, Mayakovsky asserted quite definitely that one must produce useful things: Poet, prove that your songs are useful!

But in what case can they be useful?

Mayakovsky jested: What does "poetry must light the way" mean? After all, it's not a lamp! Or, "poetry must warm us"? But it's not a stove!

Naturally, this does not mean that Mayakovsky thought poetry could neither light the way nor warm one, for did not the Sun itself advise him to "Shine on—for all your blooming worth"? But he knew that poetry shone and warmed one somehow differently. The question was: how? Not to light the way for a nearsighted person returning home from an unpleasant, unsuccessful rendezvous, or to warm a person in his cozy home. The light and warmth which a poet must disperse should be the rays, the energy which can be transformed into a living cause. He must take part in the production of new things, i.e., though his works are not in themselves utilitarian, they should provide the stimuli or methods or instructions for producing these useful things. All this will bring about a change in environment and, therefore, a change in society itself.

This then is the origin of Mayakovsky's great passion for the slogan "productional" or productive and producing poems which are "a product of production", but in no way born "of the soul" as a pale flower.

Mayakovsky became a revolutionary *per se* at a very early age. He often visualised the revolution as a desired but vague, tremendous blessing. He could as yet not define it more clearly, but he knew that it was a gigantic process of the destruction of the hated present and the creative birth of the magnificent and desired future. And the faster, the more turbulently and more mercilessly this process progressed, the happier the big man Mayakovsky would be. And then he came face to face with the proletariat, the October Revolution and Lenin; he came upon these tremendous phenomena on his life's road and, taking a close look at them, though keeping aloof at first, he saw that this was his place in life, that this was what he had been yearning for, a direct realisation of the gigantic process of reconstruction! And he advanced, as well as he could, to meet this movement; he decided to become, as far as possible, a true proletarian poet. And all that was best in him, all that was great in him, all that was social, all that produced three-quarters of his poetry and which constituted the essence of his work, all this was truly heading towards the proletariat and would have completely won over all the other elements of his nature and would have perhaps given us, as a result, a true proletarian poet.

Mayakovsky felt that everything about the old poetry was flabby, was made of cotton wool, and he yearned for the heavy sledge-hammer which "crushing glass, forges swords". One finds this striving for courage, skill, ringing sounds and pure metal in all of Mayakovsky's works. Symbolically speaking his call was for metallic art.

What method did he follow? Some say: "His method was that of 'lowering poetry'." In other words, they contend that poetry was elevated, that it could at least fly as high as a paper kite on its not-too-strong wings, but now this man had suddenly made poetry heavy and had pulled it down completely.

But if we take a closer look at what Mayakovsky's "pulling down" meant, we shall see that actually he raised it higher, because Mayakovsky pulled poetry down from the point of view of idealism, which is a thoroughly inaccurate evaluation of things and an inaccurate measure of these heights, but he raised it from the point of view of materialism, which is a correct evaluation of things and their proper correlation.

First of all, as to lowering the theme. They say that Mayakovsky chose themes that were vulgar, too common, shallow, light in style, etc.

True, he did not always choose shallow, common themes, sometimes (quite often, in fact) he chose monumental themes. But even his monumental themes are original, they make you feel that they still are in contact with the earth and that their great iron feet are marching to the rhythm of: "Left! Left! Left!" And all his abstractions are the same, all march on heavy feet: "Left!" Why is this so? Because he considered it a poet's goal to change the world and he wanted to tackle only these themes which were part of the very core of this change. He considered it to be beneath a poet's dignity to fly about the heavens in a dream, gazing upon eternity, infinity and similar haziness. That would have meant being a sybarite, a parasite, a superficial skimmer, but Mayakovsky wanted to be a construction worker. That is why he chose themes pertaining to work, to construction—truly earthly themes.

Lowering lexicon. They say he used a great many vulgar words and feared words which had been worn smooth with time, which were covered with this interesting slime accumulated through the ages.

Some say: "Oh, what a lovely word! The poet so-and-so used it!" Thus thought Lomonosov: the more Slavic words used, the higher the style; if there were no Slavic words, it was a "low style". Well, Mayakovsky did not want to write in "high style", he wanted to write in "low style". "High style" has been overhandled. The first poets had formed these words with gentle, inspired hands, there followed others with rougher hands who smudged them, so to speak, and then came those with heavy paws who, perhaps had never thought of any words themselves, nor ever moulded any, but, using the old available words, could even pass for musicians with their heavy paws. Mayakovsky unearthed an entirely new lexicon, words which either lay deep in the earth but which had not yet been turned up as virgin soil by the poetic plough, or those which were just being born, which, like a coral reef, were being covered with live polyps, they had yet to be formed by the language of poetry. And Mayakovsky did this. And yet, there were those who said this was "pulling down" poetry. Why? Because those were words carters used or that was how people spoke at meetings. Indeed, this is how they speak, because these are living words! Mayakovsky never uses dead words.

Sentence construction. They say that his constructions are often vulgar and common, and that they are sometimes quite unexpected, not at all according to the rules of syntax, and thus create an impression of phraseological tricks.

That was done because Mayakovsky captured living phrases. Undoubtedly, it is more difficult to create new words than to use accepted ones, but Mayakovsky created a great many new words, he had the gift of creating words which had never been voiced before, yet after he had set them down they were accepted by all. But sentence construction is a different matter. Here each person is a virtuoso and creator. A person who creates forms of speech which had never been used before and which are extremely convincing is, naturally, a person who is truly creating in the sphere of language. And one cannot but mention that hardly anyone—except perhaps such a poet as Pushkin or, at another stage, Nekrasov, and between them at still another stage, Lermontov—who wrote poetry or even prose has gained such creative victories in rejuvenating and enriching the Russian language as Mayakovsky. This is undeniable.

Lowering rhythm. The question is the rhythm of song, understood as "harmonious melody", "jangling strings", or "the singing of a golden harp", as limp romanticism in which the poet describes his weariness, his exquisite grief for the world, his uncommonly gentle love, or some such thing. But why does this rhythm, so homely and ordinary, appear to be so exalted? Because these people think that they have a soul, that it is immortal, that it is kindred to all the Seraphims and Cherubims, and, through the Cherubims, to God Himself and, therefore, everything that goes on in this soul is sacred and majestic. Actually, as Saltykov-Shchedrin said, one finds in place of this soul "something small and uncomely", and this "something small and uncomely", this crusted essence of such an individual, is not kindred to anything except the selfsame petty individuals around it. And this exaltation is again an exalted state only in the eyes of the idealist; in the eyes of a materialist it is simply "decay and ashes".

What are Mayakovsky's rhythms? Mayakovsky's rhythm is the rhythm of argument, the rhythm of an orator's appeal, the rhythm of industrial sounds, industrial production metres, and the rhythm of a march.

Obviously, from the point of view of an exalted individual who imagines that he lives in a divine world (but who actually never leaves his W.C.) such rhythms seem to destroy the feeling of intimacy, aloofness, warmth and concentration. "What is this? Where have they taken us? Why, this is a market place!" he says and does not understand that this is no market place at all, but a magnificent human, creative world, a true and active society, that this is the revolution, that these are its sounds. One can hear them in these new rhythms, in this new roll of drums.

Lowering rhythm. They say, "What is this, what sort of rhythm is this? It's just a joke. He sets two words in opposition to a third, he commits fantastic violence upon a word, there are too many absurdities there."

Certainly, as Mayakovsky himself said, "dears, fears and tears" cause much less panic than Mayakovsky's rhymes. But Mayakovsky used the rhymes he did, because it made his poems easier to remember. It is a well-known mnemonic formula: in order that a poem be remembered, it is important to have not only a rhyme in general, but a new rhyme, not one that makes you older than you are, for as it is you have already swallowed several centuries and carry them about within you, but one that would complement you, a truly new exchange of words, so original and amazing as to make it memorable. Actually, every part of a poem by Mayakovsky is an aphorism, a saying which should be remembered. He knew most of his own poetry by heart. Valery Bryusov once said to me: "A poet who has forgotten his own poems is either a poor poet or else he has written poor poetry. A good poet remembers all his good poetry." I believe Bryusov was quite right. Mayakovsky remembered his own poems.

They say that Mayakovsky kept pushing everything farther and farther down in poetry, while Mayakovsky's poetry is refined.

But in what sense is it "refined"? There is refinement in the various salons; if one's trousers have been made by the best-known tailor it is considered to be *comme il faut*. And yet, refinement and *comme il faut* are in opposition to each other. *Comme il faut* is the proper way, as accepted by others, while refinement is something expressed in a new way, something that has been found individually, as a pioneer blazing a new trail.

See what Mayakovsky himself said of his method of writing poetry. He recalls where and when he found each rhyme: "I was passing Arbat Gates and recalled this rhyme; spent 7-8 days thinking of a way to say it in a few words." Mayakovsky was a hard worker; no improviser he, but a determined, conscientious searcher. Indeed, he has no empty, blank lines, and not only during the years when Shengeli recognised his talent, but during the years when Shengeli ceased to recognise his talent as well. Each line is worth its weight in gold, because each has been discovered, each has been created. Mayakovsky said he was ashamed of those lines which added nothing new. Mayakovsky is poetry's labourer. Obviously, in the simple production process or in industry one can design models and then go on to make innumerable copies. The question here may be of typographical reproduction: when each line has been found, when an article has been written it can be printed in millions of copies, and this is industrial reproduction. But that which the poet creates is always a new model, is always a new sample. Thus did Mayakovsky work.

We can rightfully state that Mayakovsky's coming to the revolution was an extremely organic arrival, an extremely remarkable arrival. The successes which resulted from Mayakovsky's joining our forces were extremely important to us.

But Mayakovsky had a double, and this was his misfortune. Why, in Mayakovsky's metallic lines and social poems, do we notice a seeming lack of concreteness, as if he is afraid of the concrete, afraid of the individual and is seeking very great and resounding symbols?

In a way, this can be explained by the fact that Mayakovsky did not approach all this closely enough in general. Just as a city seen from afar appears as a colossus in a blue haze or a great electric glow, but you cannot make out the streets, the houses or, especially, the people, so did Mayakovsky approach the city of socialism, the city of revolution in his own way, seeing it, welcoming it and describing it, but never walking its streets.

This is one of the correct explanations.

Besides, Mayakovsky was more afraid of letting his double, who followed him everywhere, into this city, than of anything else in the world. Mayakovsky sensed its presence, he was afraid of him, he disliked him, but he could not get rid of him. The worst part of it all was that his was a rather charming double and its charm was what frightened Mayakovsky most, since, if you ever had a repugnant double, it would be easy enough to get rid of him. The fact that it is charming only proves that it is real and that it has absorbed some of your own traits: you banish them from your consciousness, but the very fact that you banish them from your conscious being makes them condense nearby into another, phantom-like personality, which does not actually follow you about, but lives within you in your subconscious, semi-conscious, supplementary personality.

What was this double made of? It was made of everything petty that still lived in Mayakovsky. However, Mayakovsky's petty-bourgeois traits were not disgusting. If this had been a greed for money, if this had been intriguing, if this had been slander, gloating, or pettiness in relations with others, in a word, everything that comprises the usual background of a trivial individual's life, Mayakovsky would simply have carted all this off to the nearest dump. But this was a great desire for love and gentleness, a great desire for truly intimate sympathy, a great compassion for all living creatures, such overwhelming compassion that Mayakovsky was ready to throw his arms around the neck of a tired old hag.

> I came, glimpsed in the horse's eye:
> the street, up-turned,
> swam in all its reality.
> I came and saw
> huge drop after drop
> roll down the nostrils,
> hide in the growth. . . .
> And an animal anguish
> I couldn't stop
> spilled out of me, rippling,
> and flooded us both.
> "Now, don't, please, horsie!
> You know what remorse is?
> They're human,
> but why do you suppose you're worse?
> Child,
> we're all of us a little bit horses,
> each of us in his own way's a horse."

He was just as ready to embrace a violin, for it sang to him of suffering, and he saw in it a symbol of life's burdens.

I rose,
Staggered over the notes,
The stands bending under me, aghast
           with the violence.
"Goodness!" burst from my throat
As I hugged the wooden neck.
           "Listen, violin,
Don't you think we're alike?
I too, keep wailing, yet nothing doing!"
The musicians yelled,
           "By the love of Mike,
Who does he think he's wooing?"
But I—the devil I care
           what they say!
"You know what, violin,
Let's live together,
Eh?"

Was this good or bad, likeable or not? How could it not be likeable, if a person yearned for love, "at least a tiny bit of love", if a person wanted sympathy, if he wanted to be surrounded by people who loved him? All this, which Mayakovsky had not entirely killed within himself, appeared in the best light, as his ability to really understand people and his terrible need to be understood, sometimes consoled and caressed. And is it not commendable that Mayakovsky felt there was such grief everywhere?

Shengeli says: See how often he uses the word "nerves", he himself says he is not well. Why, certainly, Shengeli thinks that since Mayakovsky said: "I am made of metal", it means he must have a cast-iron head. But this is not at all one and the same thing. Beneath this metal armour in which the whole world was reflected there beat a heart that was not only passionate, not only gentle, but fragile and very sensitive to pain. And perhaps if Mayakovsky was not possessed of such great sensitivity, of shy compassion, his monumental works would not have the warmth they do.

This tenderness sometimes made its way quite successfully into the cast iron of Mayakovsky's bell which later rang out his triumph. It is all for the good when a bell is cast and a little soft metal such as tin is added. But no good is to be gained if there is too much tin, too much of this soft substance in a person, for then it turns into a lump, into a double.

In his poetry Mayakovsky was afraid of this double, this soft, exceedingly intimate and unusually sensitive, painfully sensitive Mayakovsky. He felt that he was living in an age of iron, that a great time had come—and I myself as much a one, I have powerful muscles, my heart beats as a great hammer, and truly I am capable of speaking to great crowds in my great voice. And I want to do this. Why is this ulcer inside me, this deep, bleeding ulcer? Mayakovsky tried his best to rid his poetry of this softness, but he did not always succeed, and his double would sometimes chime in, interrupting him, singing *Of This,* of that—at any rate, of that which the true Mayakovsky, the forceful Mayakovsky, did not wish to sing. This broke through in the sentimental, heart-rending love songs that Mayakovsky would sing on various pretexts and in his laments from time to time, speaking of how discontented he was, of how he had never found understanding or compassion, of how everyone was so terribly stern, perhaps even his closest friends with whom he shared his meals in the same battle-scarred pot, with whom he was fighting on the same common front.

Not all of us are like Marx, who said that poets experience a great need for kindness. Not all of us understand this, and not all of us understood that Mayakovsky was in need of great gentleness, that often he needed nothing as much as a kind word, perhaps even the simplest of words; it would have reached the heart of this double, it would have balanced the deep sadness of this double.

By breaking into the song, this double created Mayakovsky's second melody; Mayakovsky would grab this double by the neck most forcefully, passionately and triumphantly and bend it in two, saying: "You do not dare speak in the name of Mayakovsky!" and then go on in that magnificent, booming voice of his. But from time to time he would let this double go and the double would begin to sing like a violin, it would sing melancholy songs, and then one could no longer distinguish one Mayakovsky from the other.

This divided personality means that Mayakovsky is amazingly characteristic of our transitional times. It would have really been a miracle if he had not advanced battling on the way, if he would have been able to kill this inner soft petty bourgeois, this sentimental lyric without any difficulty at all and immediately become a poet-tribune. Perhaps a true proletarian poet, coming from the ranks of the proletariat, a true social revolutionary of the Leninist type, a Lenin in poetry, will follow this road. But Mayakovsky was not such a poet. That is why the battles he fought, the obstacles he overcame, the struggle he waged to overcome himself were so significant.

Did he succeed? Yes, in poetry he did, and he stepped on his double's throat. When he said that he stepped "on the throat of my own song", he had stepped on the throat of the songs which his double wanted to sing. Mayakovsky felt the urgent need to do so especially after joining the Russian Association of Proletarian Writers.

Despite the fact that he liked his double, despite the fact that Mayakovsky at times wondered: Am I not the double?—despite all this he stepped on its throat. And his double killed him for this. It succeeded in killing him because, though it had only managed to mix in a certain amount of slag in Mayakovsky's works, in his private life it was apparently much more powerful.

Many people ask: "Why did Mayakovsky take his life?" I won't explain, for I do not know. Mayakovsky said: "I would ask you not to rummage about in my life." (The late poet did not like gossip.)

We can approach this death in a very general way only. We do not know the circumstances. All we know is that Mayakovsky said: "I did not fear this double in politics, nor in poetry, nor out there on the high seas, where I spoke, megaphone in hand, to the ship *Nette,* but at a little sentimental lake where the nightingale sings, the moon shines down and the boat of love sails, that is where I was shipwrecked. Do not ask me anything else about it. There my double was stronger than I, there he overcame me and did me in, and I felt that if I did not kill the metal Mayakovsky he would probably go on living as a broken man." His double had chewed a chunk out of him, it had made big dents in him and he did not want to sail the oceans full of holes, it was better to end his life in his prime.

This explanation should suffice, for it is correct, and there is no reason to seek further, nor would it be proper.

We consider the following to be important. The philistines who surrounded Mayakovsky made a pact with his double. They wanted to prove that the double had conquered Mayakovsky, not the fragile boat of his emotions, but that it had won in open battle, that Mayakovsky the politician had been vanquished, that Mayakovsky the poetic innovator had been vanquished. Now Trotsky is the comrade of these philistines. He is no longer the comrade, as we are, of the metal Mayakovsky, but is the comrade of Mayakovsky's double. Trotsky writes that

Mayakovsky's drama lies in the fact that he came to love the revolution as best he could and advanced towards it as best he could, but since the revolution was not a true one, his love was not true, and the road he traversed was not a true road either.

Naturally, how could the revolution be a true one if Trotsky had no part in it! This alone is enough to prove it is a "false" revolution! Trotsky says that Mayakovsky took his life because the revolution did not proceed according to Trotsky; now, had it gone according to Trotsky, it would have blossomed out in such dazzling fireworks that Mayakovsky would never have dreamed of grieving.

So you see that in the interests of his little political shop, so squalid and bankrupt, Trotsky embraces everything that is hostile to the progressive elements of the socialist world we are creating.

But the immortal Mayakovsky lives on. The immortal Mayakovsky is not afraid of his double. The double died, because it was of such a very personal nature. And even if the best works written by the double will sometimes be read with interest, they will be of historical interest, while those which were written by "metal" Mayakovsky, by Mayakovsky the revolutionary, will mark the greatest era in human history.

Long after the revolution has done its work, when there is full socialism and full communism, people will speak of the era in which we live as a most amazing era.

That is why all of us who are living in this era should remember that we cannot disgrace this era by weakness, for it is truly an amazing era and one must work very hard towards self-improvement to have the right to say that one is, in a small way, its worthy contemporary. In his main writings and social work Mayakovsky can be just such a worthy contemporary, and he has many allies. First, these allies are his books, his works. They sing loudly, they shine and warm us, and their light is so strong that all the various owls and bats must hide in far corners, as from the rising sun, until the light picks them out there as well. Secondly, we are his allies. When I say "we" I do not mean myself and my friends, not the Communist Academy or the Russian Association of Proletarian Writers, but the "we" which now comprises the creative revolutionary vanguard of humanity, becoming ever more its numerically superior basis. This is the "we", the "we" of our times, of the 1910s, 20s, 30s and 40s of our century, this is the "we" that is now fighting, creating, living, here in the U.S.S.R. and spreading to all the world. It proclaims itself to be an ally of Mayakovsky, not an ally of Mayakovsky's double, but an ally of the Mayakovsky in whom his socio-political personality became crystallised. Perhaps it did not bring to perfection the poet we dream of, but it has covered a tremendous distance towards such a one. That is why we consider ourselves to be his allies and have the right to say so without shame, as perhaps we could not have done if we had forced our brotherhood and union upon a great person individually, and not on behalf of this collective, this creative "we", since, as concerns each individual, no matter how great, the warmth of comradeship is a great happiness when it is the lot of the living, and even when it is the lot of the deceased.

1931

III

HEROES OF ACTION IN MEDITATION

THE greatest of all great heroes of action was the Greek Hercules, who might almost be regarded as idolised toil. The adoration of this semi-god actually exceeded the reverence accorded to many of the twelve gods of the Greek and Roman Olympus. This adoration constantly increased, reaching its acme, probably, at the beginning of our era. Many highly cultured people of the time even believed that the senile Jupiter would hand over the reins of government, which were quite obviously falling from his dying hands, and the thunderbolts of heavenly justice which no longer frightened the criminally arrogant and godless ones, to his favourite son, the great toiler, fighter and sufferer, who twice triumphed over death itself.

All the great feats the human mind could conceive of clustered about Hercules in a glittering halo which derived its colours both from everyday reality, so full of man's great struggle with the elements, and from the heavenly phenomena which for ever astonished the tiller of antiquity—the drama of the Sun's daily and yearly journeys. The magnificent struggle of that heavenly body with darkness, clouds and autumn, its defeat and death, its victory and resurrection was all verbally clothed in earthly vestments, in the heroic vestments of the tragic sufferings of mankind's toilers and fighters. But the Sun, transformed into a giant and seen as a living being, in payment for its earthly vestments, endows the images and likenesses bound to it and imbued with true reality a superhuman, unearthly scope, its mighty and unconquerable rhythm and unfailing light, the light of faith in eternal victory.

The story of Hercules is well known. His mother was a mortal, but his father was a god, the symbol of royal order. Despite the fact that this man-hero is very dear to his father's heart, wrathful fate pursues him everywhere, in the guise of both super-human and social forces. Even his own ungovernable powers are his enemies.

His labours and the danger that always threatened him began when he was still a babe in his cradle and he strangled the two serpents that were meant to kill him, as the morning sun disperses the creeping mists.

If Zeus-Order had ruled the world, the right of the first-born and royal freedom for the hero, so generously endowed with strength, would have been incontestable. But silly chance—a woman's wiles, the evil duplicity, as Pythagoras called it—upset and confused everything most horribly. Thus, Eurystheus, not Hercules, was born first, a weakling both in body and in spirit, and the great Hercules was fated to serve him for many and many a year. Thus, the myth, still holding true to the Sun—for the Sun is the great toiler, carrying on its work relentlessly through suffering and temporary eclipse—explains the subservience of the great labouring forces to pitiful individuals crowned simply by the chance of birth, as the madness of chance, as a stupid plot, hostile to the natural course of events.

No less significant is another aspect of the hero's slavery, the slavery of love. Queen Omphale made him dress in a woman's clothing and spin. The spinning queens of Aryan myth are the original "cloud maidens" who swiftly and silently spin the clouds. The winter Sun, devoid of its glittering vestments of rays, seems to be spinning its own cloaks of cloud. This poetic metaphor is revealed in the myth of Hercules and Queen Omphale. But, with the skill inherent in the popular genius which has created our myths, the solar metaphor has a deep socio-psychological meaning as well, being, as is the myth of Circe, an indication of the power of a woman's charms.

The hero's strong passions are often his own terrible foes. At times he cannot repress the flaming passions of his mighty body, he runs amuck, he bursts forth from his normal self and becomes a menace, both to himself and others. Aflame with insane rage, he kills his own children to his great and ever-lasting sorrow. Thus does the Sun with its scorching rays kill its own children, the living things it has nurtured into being.

Hercules's life is a series of great labours and toil: he kills the Nemean lion, the Learnean hydra, he is debased to such an extent that he must clean the Augean stables which had not been cleaned for years and, as the Sun, he descends to the kingdom of darkness and returns, having conquered death.

It is impossible to enumerate all the moving and significant myths woven about Hercules, the deliverer of Prometheus, the hero who died a terrible death for the love of his devoted and faithful wife Deianira, who set fire to himself voluntarily and burned to death in a great fire, as the Sun burns in the bloody fire of sunset in order to become resurrected and transfigured for a new existence, for a triumphant marriage with eternal youth—Hebe.

This mighty image fired the imagination of Polycletus, one of the world's greatest sculptors and friend of Alexander the Great.

History has not preserved his bronzes, which so awed and fascinated his contemporaries. But in the National Museum at Naples there is a revered, amazing marble copy by Glycon of Athens, known as the *Farnese Hercules*.

Glycon has been accused of inaccurate proportions. His was a true copy, but the exaggerated form of the terrifying, colossal, hyperbolically bloated muscles was formerly mitigated by the dark bronze, while in clear, white marble they appeared, according to the experts, in all but obnoxious relief. Perhaps. It is certainly a paradoxical sculpture. The first impression one has upon viewing the Farnese Hercules is one of incredulity, and a rather unpleasant incredulity at that. The plastic beauty of the calm pose penetrates your consciousness later; the exaggerated muscles are too astounding.

But it is not a question of muscles, no matter how remarkable the fantastic realism of the anatomy, nor is it a question of the serenity which favourably distinguishes this statue from the alarming pseudo-plasticity of our contemporaries, something which holds true for any masterpiece of antiquity. It is a question of the astonishing concept of its creator. The Farnese Hercules's greatest value is its significance as a philosophical poem in marble.

You see this giant and realise with mingled feelings of horror and delight that you sense a reflection of his great strength in your own body; you feel that the earth should sink under his fleet yet mighty soles, you have a vague sensation of the crushing power of his fist, his biceps, his titanic shoulder. The massive club and the skin of the monstrous lion he has killed complement the towering figure. If you walk around the statue and timidly view the back of the colossus, so alive, so full of resilient strength, you will see that in the hand he holds behind him are the three golden apples of the Hesperides, the apples of happiness and immortality.

But is the conquering hero content? Is the greatest of all toilers content? Is the symbolic representative of mighty action, of tireless labour content?

The reader may recall Lev Tolstoi's appeal to the practical world of our time. Its meaning is: people are always preoccupied with their own affairs, which seem so very important to them; but do they not imbue them with such importance and such alleged significance because the very commotion, which accompanies these affairs, never gives them a chance to come to their senses, a chance to stand aloof and take a good look at themselves? Would this all seem as unquestionably important if they could only stop and think, step aside for a moment from the clatter and noise of everyday life and gaze deep into their hearts, life and nature? Tolstoi believes it would not.

Polycletus apparently shared this view. He transformed the symbol of lifelong heroism and toil triumphant into a symbol of the great hero's moment of idleness, an image of disenchanted meditation.

He had killed the Nemean lion, this Hercules had, he had obtained the golden apples of the Hesperides and had brought Cerberus, the three-headed dog, up from Hades. But what of it? The triumphant toiler has lowered his head, he is reflecting sadly on his great labours and finding no consolation. What is it all for? What is this endless, onerous servitude for? Does a man who has murdered his own children need immortality? Is not happiness a doubtful boon when there is such bitterness weighing upon one's soul? The heroic toiler feels the icy, poisonous fingers of doubt gripping his heart.

Was not the Hellenic world lost in just such meditation, faced as it was with the inevitable destruction of all the cultural structures it had erected? Was it not this sorrow that overcame the Greek, culture's great toiler, when he heard Demosthenes's bitter reproaches?

And did not Polycletus, the court sculptor of Alexander the Great, sense the fragility of this vast monarchy his great master was building, cementing with blood his doomed fortress? And did not Polycletus want to tell Alexander and all the "men of action" of his century how amazed he was at the breadth of their chests and shoulders, the endurance of their legs and feet and the strength of their ever-victorious hands, and how surprised he was at the same time at the unusually small size of their heads?

Did not Polycletus want to cry out, as did Tolstoi: "Oh, Mankind, so richly endowed with power, determination and diligence, rest your tiny head on your mighty chest and reflect, are not your efforts in vain, are you not striving for the non-existent, are you not following the wrong path?" There is a tragic scepticism about Hercules, the ultimate scepticism and doubt in the fruitfulness of all effort.

And perhaps the meditation of the small head on the mighty toiler's body is capable of producing such results. There is a story by Gleb Uspensky entitled *Lost in Thought* in which, laughing through his tears, our most sensitive and honest writer speaks of the disastrous effect a moment of idleness, a moment of do-nothingness, a moment of reflection has on the peasant.

But if Hercules's head had been proportionate to his body, if his mental powers had been equal to his physical powers, would meditation have been as dangerous to his life and to the future of his creative labours?

This question brings to mind a natural analogy.

There is a statue by one of the later descendants of Michelangelo, Rodin's *Thinker* on the square opposite the Pantheon in Paris, erected at democracy's will by popular subscription.

Here we see a body almost as mighty as Hercules's, in a seated position, bent forward, crushed by the weight of unusual thought. The head is just as disproportionately small and the forehead just as narrow.

"Is this a thinker?" a Russian sculptor living in Paris shouted, pointing his cane at the small head and the wildly gloomy, distorted face. *"Mais c'est un brute tout simplement."*

I know: a thinker is a weak-chested, thin-legged and big-headed creature. Is that not so? However, my sculptor friend forgot that the most interesting thinker of our time is not a professor, dreaming up a new metaphysical apology for the existing system, not a researcher covered with library dust, nor even a naturalist in his laboratory, but none other than a toiler, intensely thinking, a man not used to thinking, pondering over his terrible fate, comparing his strength with his wretched lot, preparing for new exploits in the name of new ideals. Should this thinker rise, the very heavens will crack under the pressure of his shoulders and come crashing down on the heads of the Eurysthei.

They do not fear the most terrible flexing of the muscles of this gigantic back, but this tiny little flexing of the muscles of the forehead which makes a deep ridge between the brows is truly terrifying to them.

Let us pass now from the bitter meditation of a heroic toiler to the magnificent portrayal of a tragic moment of idleness in the life of a hero of action, of energy that would seem totally spiritual in nature. Titian has left us such a portrayal in his famous portraits of Pope Paul III.

II

Pope Paul III of the Farnese family was one of the most outstanding men of ceaseless, concerted thinking known to history.

The epoch during which he ruled the Church was one of the most turbulent ones. The Reformation was fast gaining momentum, and this wave of heresy, shattering the very foundations of the Church and wrenching entire nations away from it was enough to fully consume the spiritual energies of a man destined to stand guard over the interests of Catholicism. As if this were not enough, two outstanding monarchs, Francis I of France and Charles V of Spain, who was both King and Emperor, men of insatiable ambition supported by tremendous forces, were waging a struggle for everything and against everyone, constantly threatening the selfsame shaken Church.

It was here that Pope Paul III developed a grandiose, most cunning plan of action. He reconciled and provoked enmity between Francis and Charles in turn; when necessary, he even took the Protestants' side against the Emperor whose constant victories were causing him too great concern. Everything served his politics, especially the marriages of his sons and grandsons; each and every marriage contract was a carefully planned diplomatic move.

A true faith did not provide the support needed for the Pope's soul in his titanic struggle to strengthen "St. Peter's throne". He is a humanist and astrologer, a pupil of Julius Pomponius Laetus and the Florentine Academy; he corresponded with the all-but godless Erasmus and compiled horoscopes with fervour.

His paramount goal was the secular might of the papacy. The interests of the Church *per se* were secondary. England's breaking away was a terrible blow to Catholicism, but though the pope interdicted Henry VIII, he helped the establishment of the Reformation in England under Edward VI for purely diplomatic reasons.

But when the need arose, the Pope, who was never a great believer, was ruthless in his cruelty. It was he who confirmed the Jesuit Order and founded the Congregation of the Inquisition.

However, great political aims and anxieties did not exhaust the indefatigable Pope's field of action. A more petty goal, but one apparently closest to the Pope's heart, was the enrichment and ascendancy of his illegitimate family. He married his grandson Ottavio to Margaret of Austria, Orazio to the daughter of Henry II, he made his son Pier Luigi Prince Nepi, and did his best to present Milan to Ottavio. Contrary to the will of the cardinals, he transferred the Church cities of Parma and Piacenza to his family.

Undoubtedly, not a day passed that swarms of thoughts, the most diverse, worrisome and of varying importance—from a general evaluation of the world situation to a counter-intrigue against a treacherous plot hatched by petty courtiers—did not crowd the Pope's small head, making deep furrows on his sharp, crafty face with its mobile goatee. Messengers and letters arrived and were dispatched, reports followed one another, the threads of great worldly dramas and petty court farces were all joined in the thin restless fingers. And these fingers were for ever weaving endless webs for great and small human flies, while the small cropped grey head kept plotting feverishly, putting everything in order, and the beady little eyes searched the souls of friend and foe.

The Pope found time for fine arts. While still a cardinal he had built a magnificent palace in Rome and a famous villa in Bolsena. And he had a large art collection. He summoned the great Titian to produce various works, but chiefly to immortalise his features with his magic brush.

And the great Venetian really worked hard to portray the tireless Pope. He took up his brush many times, and there are many portraits by Titian of Pope Paul III. The best of these are the two in the Naples Museum.

These two portaits are a great human document.

If you read about Titian in any history of art or in any of the numerous monographs dealing with his works you will certainly find the greatest admiration and sometimes worship on the part of the authors. You will read of the unexcelled splendour and harmony of Titian's palette, of the charm and beauty of his nudes and semi-nudes, of the almost sublime sensuousness, more passionate and languid but no less pure than the voluptuousness of the ancient Greeks. You will probably discover that Titian was one of the greatest romantic landscape painters, that he created his landscapes from memory, endowing them with velvety colours and the munificence of an August day. And you will certainly read of Titian the portraitist. There was good reason why all the great men and women of the 16th century had their portraits done by him. And this was the age of Shakespeare, the age of the blossoming individual, the age which had weathered the storms of the early Renaissance and amidst the storms of the Reformation, had carried to the surface of the worldly sea individuals unmatched in the greatness of their passions, the sweep of their terrible ambition, the scope of their activities, the complexity of their spirit. And it must also be said that kings, noblemen, popes, cardinals and senators, generals, scientists and artists of the 16th century, no longer possessing the touching simplicity or expansive frankness of the *quattrocento*, concealed their troubled souls beneath a mask of pomposity, *signorilità*, as they concealed their bodies beneath the folds of their heavy, magnificent dark robes.

The individual blossomed forth—at least at the top of the social ladder; he knew his own worth and felt that by creating history he would go on living after death. That is why any man or woman of even modest means and power considered a portrait to be a very serious business, a thing of paramount importance. That is why the 16th century has given us Holbein and Dürer, Titian and Morone. That is why the very same century gave us Shakespeare.

But this is where the confusion usually begins. No one will deny that Titian is a portrait painter of great force. His drawing, at times vague in his paintings, in his portraits becomes sharp and definite, conceived on a grand scale, yet concise and expressive. There is the same feeling of reserve in the use of colour, so lavish in some of his paintings, but always in the highest aristocratic taste and noble beauty in his portraits.

But what about the soul? It is a synthetic soul that gives us the whole of Charles, the whole of Philip, Maximillian, Henry, Paul, and nearly a hundred—just think, nearly a hundred!—other remarkable personages, each captured in a single moment, a single pose, a single expression of the face and eyes.

Titian's portraits are like magic books. As you stand before them, you feel that their pages, so full of mysterious characters, begin to turn slowly, revealing ever-new mysteries. So much has already been said and revealed, yet so much remains unsolved, and you can delve deeper and deeper and always find the pure gold of the deepest psychology.

How could Titian achieve this? Will you find anywhere in the thousands of pages written about him the fact that he was a great sage and connoisseur of the human heart, a man of great powers of concentration and contemplation? Not at all. He was a vivacious and even superficial *galantuomo* who loved splendour, wine, women and his paints until old age.

Faced with this mystery, we hear the all-encompassing word: intuition. But does this word actually explain anything?

We have heard of great musicians who seemed able to fathom the faintest emotional stirrings and yet were unbelievable dolts. There are also quite a few numskull artists who have won great fame as sensitive landscape painters.

Let us assume that this is all intuition. But then there must be so many limitations. First of all, not a single *great composer* was ever a stupid man; he might often have been a most unpractical person, a man who lacked a definite outlook or the ability to act logically, but he was always a sensitive and capable person, who could, if necessary, express his feelings and observations magnificently, in words as well as music.

The letters of Beethoven, Schumann, Berlioz, Wagner and Mussorgsky amaze one by their clarity and beauty of expression. And if these titans were truly men of outstanding intellect or, so to speak, had a very sensitive and intensely developed nervous system, then, I repeat, *none* of the great composers was ever a man of average intellect. Outstanding virtuosi are more often men of average or below-average intellect, but a virtuoso is, primarily, an impressionable individual who easily falls under hypnotic-like influence, one who may be likened to a magnificent instrument, and naturally, you would never demand that a wonderful violin have an intellect as well.

Thus does the case stand, more or less, as concerns intuition in landscape painting. Some impressionists, famed for their poetic landscapes and, at the same time, the virgin sterility of their intellect, are not at all poets or creators, but simply men with extremely keen powers of observation who are able to copy nature faithfully; the mood, i.e., all that is subjective that they have introduced in their landscapes, is nearly always imitative and stolen from the true, intelligent masters.

When a true virtuoso or a sharp-sighted artist tries to create something original, i.e., something fantastic, for instance, something that has not been dictated by Nature or a great master, the result will inevitably be shabby.

Intellect, as reflected in sensitivity, a keenness of observation, the ability to synthesise, to stress that which is typical and characteristic and, at the same time, to freely combine in harmony elements provided by the environment, is the condition, lacking which there can be no great artist. The greatness of an artist is usually in direct proportion to such intellect. However, it should neither be confused with the German *Klugheit* (practical reasonableness) nor with theoretical talents.

Corot, like Turner, one of the greatest landscape painters of the past century, was, as is known, a super-naive man whom everyone considered to be rather foolish. However, one needs read but two or three letters written by the dean of the Fontaine-bleau School, in which he describes Nature, to realise what a sensitive poet and sage of Nature we are dealing with.

Now let us return to Titian. His nature obviously was not limited to voluptuous colour and an aesthetic love of women. And how could it possibly have been limited thus? Did not the giants Giorgione and Tintoretto grow up beside him by the same Venetian lagoons?

Giorgione is also in love with colour, but his passionate sensuality carried him off in his prime. Look at his *Concerto*, his portrait of a knight of Malta, or the *Uomo ammalato*—is this not the same psychology we find in Shakespeare? Tintoretto's paintings are both tragic and deeply psychological. He is less epicurean and less of a colourist than the two other giants of Venetian art, and his works reflect, as it were, the pure essence of the elemental tragedy of the spirit which in Titian and Giorgione is combined with the luxuriant colours of sensuality and is sometimes concealed by it.

This tragedy was born of the deep struggle of all against all which raged continuously in Venice under the bright covers of its oriental splendour. Feasting and love-making were often cut short by the blow of a dagger, the cloudless life that resembled a brimmer of untold pleasures more often than not ended in the lead mines. One had always to be on guard; cruel cunning served as a sword, while virtuoso shrewdness was a shield. Only the most superficial of observers would find the atmosphere of Venice to be sunny and cloudless; actually it was an arena of offensive and defensive treachery. A century later this treachery would degenerate into the endless knavery of malevolent spoilers. But in the 16th century the Venetian aristocracy still possessed true statesmanship, its political plans encompassed the world. Scholarship, courage and unconquerable pride walked hand in hand with treachery.

Such was Titian's background when he undertook to do a portrait of the great Pope.

He studied him as a psychologist would, he did several portraits, coming ever closer to the man's heart. Finally, he captured the very essence of Pope Paul III, not only that which was most characteristic of the individual, but that which was characteristic of his environment, of his century, as well.

Titian presented in two canvases the tragedy of one of the greatest men of action in all history.

The first is a large unfinished group: Pope Paul III is shown closeted in his study with his two grandsons, Cardinal Alessandro and the duke Ottavio, with whom he is consulting on the affairs of the Farnese family.

Cardinal Alessandro seems rather indifferent. The attractive eyes in his serene face are straightforward, intelligent and confident. Why should he worry? With such a grandfather he need not fear anything. Besides, the old man would never let any one play an active part, he must do everything himself, everything himself!

Young Ottavio, in magnificent court attire, bends low over his grandfather's chair, listening attentively to what he is saying. There is both malice and pleasure in his eyes, for the intrigue the old man has thought up will apparently strike some enemy right in the heart. His bent back is ready to straighten up like a steel spring and his feet seem impatient to be off, running to carry out the cunning orders.

The Pope, dressed haphazardly, fidgeting in his chair, is completely carried away by his game, his fingers are alive, they illustrate his words with an expressive gesture. His neck is stretched forward, his piercing eyes burn with the rapture of creative effort; every nerve in his body is taut, he is aflame with the sport, he is in his element and, apparently, the more difficult the problem, the greater his delight.

But now his kinsmen have gone. The Pope is alone for a few moments. His head cools. One problem has been dealt with, another will soon demand his attention. This is a short pause, a moment of idleness.

Just as a wheel falls when it stops rolling, so does the Pope feel tired when the heat of the affair at hand no longer supports him. Weariness brings doubt and hesitation.

These were not the doubts and hesitation that belonged to the range of ordinary intrigue and calculations, but were quite different, of the kind that are usually hidden far away in the innermost reaches of the soul, shut away in its vaults behind a heavy door. But when the noisy voices of everyday affairs die down in the upper stories and a short pause sets in, they creep out like snakes to eat at the heart of Pope Paul III.

"What's the use of it all?" Everything that has seemed of value in the feverish atmosphere of sport has suddenly lost its value. The great goals seem so alien, one's kinsmen so indifferent and one's own body so frail. And death so imminent.

The Pope leans against the back of his armchair, his bones ache, his back is bent, his head has dropped, he seems to have lost heart. His dull eyes stare vacantly at the floor. But this is not a state of light slumber, a moment of forgetfulness: look, the nervous hand on the arm of the chair is moving restlessly, revealing the inner tension, a new struggle against a new and unconquerable enemy.

Poor Pope Paul III! Despite all his efforts, the secular might of the popes, far from growing, had been steadily declining, until it was finally snuffed out altogether. The most active of Popes died in sorrow and bewilderment, having gained nothing!

In the two great portraits described here Titian presented the tragedy of any undertaking, no matter how great it might seem, if it is more an ambitious sport and fascinating gambling than true service to a genuine and deep ideal.

How many ministers, bankers and all other sorts of dealers there are who repeat: "Business before pleasure. *Les affaires sont les affaires*", but in time of truthful contemplation suddenly realise with horror that the "business" which has consumed their life and soul is in itself both empty and as cold as ice!

And thus arise these strange parallels between the two thinkers, Polycletus's *Hercules* and Titian's *Paul*.

1909

BACON AND THE CHARACTERS
OF SHAKESPEARE'S PLAYS

WITH astonishing, still unsurpassed genius, Shakespeare perceived and described that in some ways terrifying yet, at the same time, bright and splendid phenomenon—the mighty upsurge of reason in the society of his time. Our intention is to use Shakespeare's images in order more exactly to define the characteristics and tendencies of reason in one of its most brilliant representatives of that period—of the hero of this article, Francis Bacon.

Conflict plays a great part in all Shakespeare's plays, and, perhaps, the decisive part in the so-called Histories.

The end of the Middle Ages and the beginning of the Renaissance, of which Shakespeare was a witness, was a time of tempestuous individualism; the disintegration of a still fairly firmly established social structure was making itself felt everywhere. Jacob Burckhardt, in his profound studies of the Renaissance, notes as one of the basic characteristics of this epoch this emancipation of the individual and his active endeavour to discover in himself his own self-determination and independently to determine his road through life.

The emancipated individual is the constant object of Shakespeare's concern. The fate of this individual is a matter of profound interest to him. What lies before him: a success to crown his ever-increasing desires, or premature destruction? Either is possible in this wide, chaotic world, in which individual wills are so mercilessly pitted one against the other. Shakespeare's characters (and still more, perhaps, the heroes of Shakespeare's immediate predecessors, the Elizabethan dramatists) ask themselves: are not all things permitted? The authority of the Church had gone down badly, belief in God had become very feeble, and, in place of that Divine Will which had been quite precisely set out in the teachings collated by the churches, men began to suspect the existence of some other divinity—Pan, perhaps, or some dark Fate, unlikely, it was felt, to be either benevolent or just, possibly even simply cruel, more likely to enjoy the sufferings of mortals than to feel compassion for them.

If all things are permitted, then the following question remains: of all that is permitted, what is actually accomplishable?

Every form of retribution, whether it be the result of a confluence of circumstances or the cruel reaction of government, society, or enemies, can, in the last analysis, be defined as failure. If a man succumbs to the buffeting of such retribution, it means merely that he has failed to calculate his actions, that, having accepted the more or less (morally, in the eyes of the Renaissance man) justifiable thesis that "all is permitted", he has left out of account that this does not mean that everything is simply there for the taking, or that it is possible to live selfishly like a beast of prey in a world where the prize goes to the strong, or that he has forgotten the existence of society, of the forces of state and of other, perhaps better-armed predators.

It is better not to be moral—in battle, morality is nothing but an encumbrance; true, morality can very often be useful, but only as a mask behind which to hide cynicism and cruelty. But it is essential to be clever; to be very, very clever. It is essential to be able to play various parts according to the demands of the situation. It is essential to know how to impress other people. It is essential to be able to subjugate them by force. It is essential to calculate in good time what forces you are about to set in motion, and to base your calculations on their maximum prospective strength. To be clever means to leave out of account all religious and moral nonsense, all preconceived opinions, all false values, and to look life straight between the eyes. But this also means taking in the very real dangers of life with the same sober glance.

No genius in the cultural history of the world has made concentrated and intuitively brilliant an analysis as did Shakespeare of the appearance of reason, of the appearance of intellect, of mind as such, of mind unfettered and enthroned.

Mind has been declared a safe pilot. Yet, in Shakespeare, this power awakes the greatest doubts. He is far from convinced that this pilot does not almost always steer to ruin. Be that as it may, the arrogance and the new pre-eminence of intellect is a theme which not only interests Shakespeare but torments him. He is imbued with the most profound respect for intellect. He is far from despising, far from detesting even the most cynical "chevaliers of intellect". He understands their peculiar freedom, their predatory grace, their incomparable human value which rests in their very contempt for all preconceived opinions. But, at the same time, he realises that their lot is a perilous one; he who abandons the trodden path, he who sets out to seek happiness and success in the ocean, trusting himself to the will of the winds, with only one captain on board—Reason—is taking too great a risk.

Reason as a weapon in the struggle for success—this is one aspect of Shakespeare's attitude to intellect, which had become such a great force in the world of his time.

The other aspect was contained in the thought that, to the man of intellect, who uses his reason as a brilliant torch, many things become clear which, for ordinary people, are still dark.

Suddenly, with extraordinary lucidity and distinctness, he sees himself and all that surrounds him in this strange and terrible world. Illuminated by the search-light of reason, it appears that the world is not only strange and terrible, but mean and stupid as well, that, possibly, it is not worth while living in it at all, and that even the greatest successes and victories which it has to offer do not justify this absurd existence, not to mention the fact that such victories are rare and ephemeral and that, come what may, old age and death reign over all, the inescapable lot of all living things.

Here reason, precociously wide awake, becomes the direct cause of the sufferings of the person whom it informs. Here we have to do with one of the most vivid instances of that vast phenomenon which was so correctly and precisely formulated in the title of Griboyedov's comedy *Woe from Wit*.

Francis Bacon, a man of intellect, possessed of a mind of huge daring, emancipated by the whole set-up of the Renaissance, had something in common with both types of Shakespeare's heroes-of-the-intellect. As we become more closely acquainted with his common-sense morality, with the maxims he professed for behaviour in everyday life, we will see his kinship with the followers of Machiavelli.

At the same time, it must be emphasised right from the beginning that, although Bacon feels absolutely no shadow of reverence for what is called morality, he perfectly understands all the importance of the moral mask, all the importance of not provoking his entourage by over-frank revelations, all the importance of veiling the audacity of the independent intellect behind verbal concessions to generally acceptable views. And where should Bacon do this more effectively than in his openly published works which he dedicated to various high-born patrons! This transparent moral mask, however, for anyone gifted with the least perspicacity, represents no barrier to the understanding of Bacon's extremely far-reaching intellectualising amorality.

Only from this point of view can we explain Bacon's behaviour at certain moments of his life when his cynicism overleapt all bounds and, even in the emancipated society of the Renaissance, provoked a reaction of hostility towards Bacon himself. Again, it also explains the seeming "thoughtlessness" which led Bacon to ruin his brilliant career by taking bribes in a manner which, even for that time, was not sufficiently discreet, not sufficiently adroit.

But, if all these sides of Bacon's character—his common-sense, his cunning, his lack of principle—lend themselves to comparison with Shakespeare's heroes of the emancipated intellect, then there can also be no doubt that Bacon is very close to Shakespeare's more sombre and, at the same time, nobler types—to his Hamlet-types, of which we shall single out three for close analysis: the melancholic Jaques, that Hamlet in embrio, Hamlet himself, and Prospero who is, as it were, the final solemn chord of the whole theme of doubt and thought associated with the name of Hamlet.

But first, let us take a look at Shakespeare's cynics. There are a good many of them. The first, most grandiose place in their ranks is occupied by King Richard III.

As I have already said, in Shakespeare the conflict between individuals (usually a struggle for power) plays a major part, especially in the Histories. *Richard III* is the culminating point of the Histories. In the person of Richard himself, Shakespeare gives the most finished product of this time—of an age of ruthless mutual extermination among the ambitious nobility.

The historical Richard III may not, perhaps, have been as black as Shakespeare painted him. He was a warlike, ambitious king, unscrupulous enough in the pursuit of his policies but probably little worse or better than the others. However, the fact remains that the masses of the people took a particularly strong dislike to Richard III. His general reputation was that of a man of extreme cunning and bestial ruthlessness; people were ready and willing to believe in all the long series of crimes thanks to which he is supposed to have achieved and maintained himself in power. It is very likely that those critics, who hold that Shakespeare's characterisation of Richard III was such a tremendous success with the London public because the image which Shakespeare gave them corresponded to the image which this same public expected, are not far from the truth. Nevertheless, one has only to run to Helinshed (i.e., to Shakespeare's immediate source) to be able to say that, this time, Shakespeare was not entirely faithful to this basic source; he was also considerably indebted to the well-known book on Richard III written by one of the greatest intellectuals of the Renaissance—Thomas More, the greatest figure of Henry VIII's reign and, one might even say, in his own way, the precursor, of both Bacon and Shakespeare.

Chancellor Thomas More, having undertaken the task of compiling a biography of Richard III, wrote what was in fact a profoundly polemical and political work. Thomas More's aim was not so much to curry favour with the house of Tudor by servile praise as to exult it at the expense of its predecessors—not, of course, as a flatterer, but in as much as he was, in a general way, trying to get his own humanitarian and, for the times, profoundly progressive bourgeois politics implemented under the protection of the Tudors (true, this rather failed to come off and Thomas More himself, eventually, fell victim to the monstrous despotism of Henry VIII).

Henry VII, Duke of Richmond, the actual conqueror of Richard III and the first Tudor to ascend the throne was, in fact, repulsive miser and a most ungifted man. This did not prevent Thomas More from all kinds of hints to the effect that the Duke of Richmond was a virtuous knight whose advent entailed the triumph of justice and the punishment of vice, whereas Richard III was a fiend incarnate, the worst conceivable product of medieval civil strife.

This idea of Richard III's profound viciousness Shakespeare took from More. However, we are immediately brought face to face with a tremendous difference. For More, Richard III was merely a politically negative figure, a bad king who had fortunately been deposed by a good king from a dynasty in whose service More himself happened to stand; for Shakespeare, the interest lies in the personality of the individual, the grandiose figure in its historico-cultural setting, the unique titanic character.

It never enters Shakespeare's head to try to rehabilitate Richard III, to deny one single crime—on the contrary, he ascribes to him such crimes as even More does not mention; but from all this he draws no poetic or ethical conclusions. Shakespeare's Richard III is a monster, but such a splendid monster, so talented, so successful, so sure of himself, so bold, that Shakespeare admires him.

Like the subtle psychologist he is, Shakespeare tries to distinguish various features of Richard's character and to show them at various turning points in his spiritual life. Although Shakespeare is bound always to condemn Richard politically as a usurper, in spite of the fact that he piles horror upon horror, that he is constantly appealing to the spectator, exciting his anger against the shameless Richard—in spite of all this Shakespeare still respects Richard. I repeat, he admires him. Not for one moment does he desire to discredit the actual principle of the disciples of Machiavelli, the principle, that is, of rationalised ambition, of civic ambition directed to a definite end, prepared to draw on all the resources of scientific analysis and predatory hypocrisy, taken to its logical conclusion.

The History devoted to Henry VI was most probably in the main not written by Shakespeare and it is very difficult to establish the truly Shakespearian passages with any real certainty. However, in view of the fact that *Richard III* was in all essentials written by Shakespeare, it may be safely assumed that those first steps of the ladder which, in this drama devoted to Henry VI, lead up to the chronicle of Richard III, were penned by none other than Shakespeare. In this case, we are presented with a picture of genuine development of character.

Gloucester (the future Richard III) is first and foremost a dashing soldier. He is not afraid of bloody battles, nor does he shrink from letting blood—his own or others'. He is more energetic and active than his relatives. He is a wild, rough lad, and is feared accordingly. At the same time he is a cripple. His physical deformity is emphasised in *Henry VI*, it makes him unlikeable, even repulsive to those about him, sets him apart from them, isolates him, forces him into a kind of basic self-reliance. The psychology which is the natural result of these circumstances is voiced by Gloucester in several monologues, which we shall not quote here since, at the very beginning of the play *Richard III*, we have a brilliant soliloquy which sums them all up (characteristic, by the way, of the artistic device adopted by Shakespeare to show us the inner workings of Richard's mind).

Richard is a cynic, he knows perfectly well what he is about, he despises prejudice and recoils before no crimes. Crime for Richard is not crime at all, but the means to an end. For this reason he can rehearse his plan to himself quite openly and without fear. On the other hand, it is, of course, scarcely possible to imagine Richard having a confidant to whom he might have told this plan in all frankness. To admit the existence of such a confidant would be to ruin the picture we have of Richard's character. He must be reserved enough before others. But here the dramatist is saved by the convention of the soliloquy. Richard III, left alone with himself, ponders his situation and, with a rare brilliance of imagery, exposes his most inward thoughts to the audience (who are presumed absent).

Let us cite the whole monologue which, at the same time, serves as a kind of introduction to the entire play.

> *Now is the winter of our discontent*
> *Made glorious summer by this sun of York;*
> *And all the clouds that lour'd upon our house*
> *In the deep bosom of the ocean buried.*
> *Now are our brows bound with victorious wreaths;*
> *Our bruised arms hung up for monuments;*
> *Our stem alarums changed to merry meetings;*
> *Our dreadful marches to delightful measures.*
> *Grim-visaged war hath smooth'd his wrinkled front;*
> *And now—instead of mounting barbed steeds*
> *To fight the souls of fearful adversaries—*
> *He capers nimbly in a lady's chamber*
> *To the lascivious pleasing of a lute.*
> *But I, that am not shaped for sportive tricks,*
> *Nor made to court an amorous looking-glass;*
> *I, that am rudely stampt, and want love's majesty*
> *To strut before a wanton, ambling nymph;*
> *I, that am curtail'd of this fair proportion,*
> *Cheated of feature by dissembling nature,*
> *Deform'd, unfinisht, sent before my time*
> *Into this breathing world, scarce half made up,*
> *And that so lamely and unfashionable*
> *That dogs bark at me as I halt by them;—*

Why, I, in this weak piping time of peace,
Have no delight to pass away the time,
Unless to spy my shadow in the sun,
And descant on mine own deformity:
And therefore, since I cannot prove a lover,
To entertain these fair well-spoken days,
I am determined to prove a villain,
And hate the idle pleasures of these days.

If we consider this monologue carefully, we are forced to admit that Shakespeare makes the first motive of Richard's "villainy" the fact that he is made "so lamely and unfashionable", and, because of this, is at an exceptional disadvantage in peace-time existence amongst the gallant pursuits of the court.

Nevertheless, it is essential to note from the start that, though Gloucester may use the term "villain" here, he is in fact most indulgently disposed towards villainy and we feel at once that he is not in the least inclined to see himself as a "second-rate" person just because he happens to be physically ugly. On the contrary, we feel that this physical deformity which condemns him to a peculiar isolation will only serve to temper him for the main object, for that in which he finds himself, for that in which he finds the chief pleasure of life, which is in struggle, in conquest, in the achievement of his aims by making others the submissive tools of his will. In the famous scene between Richard III and Anne, Shakespeare hurries to prove this. It is not only that here Richard shows magnificent talent as a man of intrigue, able quickly to put two and two together and to see how he should direct and combine circumstances so as to make his way towards the throne as fast as possible. In exactly the same way, it is equally not that Richard here shows himself such consummate actor, though this is most important, nor is it the tremendous art which he brings to pretence and deception. The specific flavour of this scene is given by the fact that the deformed Richard here speaks of love, of passion, that he wins the hand of the wife of a man whom he has slain, and that in the shortest possible time, he breaks down Anne's hatred and changes it to a certain sympathy. This proves that Richard's crooked shoulders, withered hand and uneven legs are no hindrance to him whatever even when he needs to use erotics as a weapon.

I would like to draw the reader's attention to the conversation between Richard and Buckingham. This conversation shows what an enormous part was played by the ability to act a part and by cunning dissembling in the relationships between the intellects of that time.

Gloucester asks in the course of his conversation with Buckingham:

Richard.
Come, Cousin,
Canst thou quake, and change thy colour,
Murther thy breath in middle of a word,
And then begin again, and stop again,
As if thou wert distraught and mad with terror?

Buckingham.
Tut, I can counterfeit the deep Tragedian,
Speak, and look back, and prie on every side,
Tremble and start at wagging of a straw:
Intending deep suspicion, ghastly looks
Are at my service, like enforced smiles;
And both are ready in their offices,
At any time to grace my stratagems.

A high degree of this particular kind of acting ability is shown by Gloucester in his scene with the people. It is ravishing in its exquisite out-and-out hypocrisy. I can recommend it to anyone who has either not read or forgotten it. Here, I will confine myself to indicating that Gloucester can not only draw in his talons, and hide his predatory essence, his warlike qualities, the corrosive, mocking sarcasm which is so characteristic of him: he can put on the mask of a Christian, of a man of prayer, of an almost holy man with a hatred for all the vanities of life—and all this in order to take the simplest and easiest way of giving substance to a perhaps passing mood of the people which has led them to seek in him a king, an upholder of law and order. Later on, when the forces of history are already beginning to turn against him, with what incredible daring does he approach Queen Elizabeth, suing for her daughter's hand! How much passion, how much urgency, how much disarming tenderness is implicit in the words of Richard! It may seem that even the experienced Elizabeth, who knows him very well indeed, will be deceived. At all events, however hard it must be for him, he again puts up a tremendous stake and, with all the old skill and the old self-possession, sets about building up a whole new system of political relationships, a whole system of alliances with people whom he has mortally offended in order to rebuild a firm foundation beneath his feet.

However, the figure of Richard would remain quite incomplete in our eyes had we not seen how Shakespeare organises his ruin.

Richmond is advancing against him at the head of a great army. One after another, Richard's false friends go over to the enemy. It becomes clearer with every passing hour that the force of this enemy is crushingly superior. At the same time, Richard is troubled in his own mind. After a whole series of crimes he has killed two innocent children. Here, the motif which Pushkin was later to develop in his

Boris Godunov is introduced with tremendous effect. But Richard is no Boris. Although he does indeed suffer pangs of conscience, although he is possessed of a human nature which, in accordance with a thousand-year-old tradition, cannot but reproach him, albeit in dream, with his inhuman cruelty, he nevertheless shakes off all these terrible dreams and reproaches, all this trouble of the mind, as soon as it is morning and the time has come to go into battle.

We can only advise reading this truly superb scene, where every word adds a monumental stroke to the potrayal of this terrible, monstrous man.

Here, it is enough to quote Richard's last rallying speech, which gives an inspired picture of his Machiavellian policy, his ability to choose the only words which could possibly put heart into men who are, in fact, far from being his friends and far from being idealistic "patriots" of his cause. Here, we have a knowledge of mass psychology surpassing even Napoleon's. And, at the same time, what inner resolution, what steadiness of mind, coming, after a troubled night, to illumine the decisive moment of the struggle.

Richard.
> *Go, Gentlemen, every man to his charge,*
> *Let not our babbling dreams affright our souls;*
> *For conscience is a word that cowards use,*
> *Devis'd at first to keep the strong in awe,*
> *Our strong arms be our conscience, swords our law.*
> *March on, join bravely, let us to't pell mell,*
> *If not to heaven, then hand in hand to hell.*
> *What shall I say more than I have inferr'd?*

Enough of Richard III. Of course, this figure is conceived in a far more grandiose mould than the figure of Bacon, but Bacon's amoral moods are in many ways very close to Richard's. It is one and the same school of life, one and the same world.

Perhaps Shakespeare comes closer to Bacon in scale when he creates the illegitimate son of Gloucester—Edmund, in the great tragedy of *King Lear*.

It should be noted from the start that Edmund, also, has his justification. Richard enters into a monstrous struggle for power and explains this by the circumstance of his physical deformity. Edmund enters into a similar plot and explains this by the circumstance that he is a base-born son. Here, we are evidently confronted with a broad generalisation.

Shakespeare asks himself: why has a type of man come into being who is prepared to put his reason at the service of careerism, of ambition, and who makes so dangerous a servant of this reason, so sharp a poisoned dagger of his will? And he answers— why, yes, all men like that are, in a way, baseborn, they are all people to whom fate has not given all that they should like to have. They are people who see themselves as unfairly done out of their rightful place in life, as slighted from the cradle, and who for this reason set about righting what, they are convinced, are oversights of Nature, with the help of superbly thought-out intrigues.

It must be admitted that the Russian translator of *King Lear*, Druzhinin, gives, in his preface to the play, an excellent analysis of Edmund's character— an analysis which is so firmly drafted that we prefer to borrow the whole passage just as he wrote it:

"The basic feature of this type is that brazen insolence and shamelessness which always enables the possessor of such a trait to lie without the least twinge of conscience, to don any mask, acting always under the influence of one dominating desire to make their own way at any cost, even if that way should lie over the dead bodies of father or brother. Edmund is no mere narrow egoist, neither is he a blind villain capable of taking pleasure in his own ill-doing. Edmund is a richly gifted character, but a character who has been cankered at the root and who, because of this, can only use his exceptional talents to the detriment of his fellows. Edmund's genius is evident in his every step, in his every word, for not one step does he take and not one movement does he make which has not been carefully calculated, and these eternal calculations so dry up Edmund's heart and mind that he becomes old before his time and learns to govern even those bursts of youthful passion before whose onslaughts fiery, easily tempted youth is usually so vulnerable. Another undoubted sign of Edmund's genius is the way in which all around him submit to the magic influence of his gaze, of his speech, of the general aura of his personality, which inspires women with uncontrolled passion for him and men with trust, grudging respect, and even something resembling fear."

To this sketch of Edmund's character we are tempted to add only the famous monologue pronounced by Edmund himself, for this monologue in many instances corresponds almost word for word with some of the tenets of "free morality", to which Bacon, in spite of certain reservations, comes so close to subscribing wholeheartedly.

Edmund.
Thou, Nature, art my goddess, to thy law
My services are bound. Wherefore should I
Stand in the plague of custom and permit
The curiosity of nations to deprive me,
For that I am some twelve or fourteen moonshines
Lag of a brother? Why bastard? Wherefore base?
When my dimensions are as well compact,
My mind as generous, and my shape as true,

As honest madam's issue? Why brand they us
With base? With baseness? bastardy? base, base?
Who in the lusty stealth of nature, take
More composition and fierce quality
Than doth, within a dull, stale, tired bed
Go to the creating a whole tribe of fops,
Got 'tween asleep and wake? Well, then,
Legitimate Edgar, I must have your land.
Our father's love is to the bastard Edmund,
As to the legitimate. Fine word, "legitimate."
Well, my legitimate, if this letter speed,
And my invention thrive, Edmund the base
Shall top the legitimate. I grow; I prosper;
Now, gods, stand up for bastards!

Shakespeare's Iago we consider a third type of intellectualist-cynic, one who uses his mind as a weapon against his fellow man. On the whole, he seems the most puzzling of all the series of characters to have been created by Shakespeare in this field. Indeed, it is impossible to say what were Iago's guiding principles as he carried out these supremely artful manoeuvres, dangerous to himself and infinitely cruel to others, by which he intended to encompass the ruin of two beings for whom, at the very worst, he could have felt nothing but indifference.

Shakespeare confines all Iago's motivation to the scene between him and Rodrigo. Here, we are treated to a whole system of strange attempts at self-justification. At first, we see Iago entering into a plot with a crazed man of crazy desires and, quite without rhyme or reason, just like that, as a kind of low joke, agreeing to forward these desires on condition the other fills his purse. But then it turns out that Iago has other motives of his own for wanting to do Desdemona and Othello an ill turn. Here, there is some suspicion that Iago's somewhat

A. V. Lunacharsky with his daughter Irene, 1932

scatter-brained wife, by whom her husband does not elsewhere appear to set much store, has not been sufficiently nice in her dealings with the General. All this is mixed up with various other considerations, all of them trifling, contradictory.

Why such a subtle psychologist as Shakespeare needed all these various motives leaps to the eye immediately. Obviously, they are not needed to provide the real motivation of Iago's behaviour but in order to show that Iago himself does not know his own motives.

In all this long scene, which represents a series of confused attempts to provide some justification for an enormous, criminal plan which is due to be executed with the most exquisite cunning and with iron will, the important thing is not the attempt to suggest motive but the definition given by Iago to the power of human will in general.

This last statement, however, must be modified straight away: *not* "human will in general", but the human will of people such as Iago and, perhaps, such as Richard III, as Edmund, as all these Machiavellians in politics and in private life; and, to a considerable extent, of people such as our Francis Bacon.

Here is this amazing passage:

Iago. Virtue! a fig! 'tis in ourselves that we are thus or thus. Our bodies are gardens; to the which our wills, are gardeners: so that if we will plant nettles, or sow lettuce; set hyssop, and weed-up thyme; supply it with one gender of herbs, or distract it with many; either to have it sterile with idleness, or manured with industry; why, the power and corrigible authority of this lies in our wills. If the balance of our lives had not one scale of reason to poise another of sensuality, the blood and baseness of our natures would conduct us to most preposterous conclusions: but we have reason to cool our raging motions, our carnal stings, our unbitted lusts; whereof I take this that you call love to be a sect or scim.

It is quite evident that Iago is aware of tremendous strength in himself; he understands that he is his own master; he understands that, in this little garden which he has just described to us, he may plant out a remarkable series of most subtle poisons; he understands that he is a man of strong will and clear mind, a man not bound by any prejudices whatsoever, not enslaved by any laws outside himself, by any moral heteronomy, and that such a man is terrifyingly strong. In those times, still grey at dawning, when the vast majority did not know how to use their reason, when almost all men were bound by religious and moral prejudices, such a free strong man must have felt himself akin to the Novgorodian hero of our ballads: he would seize a man by the arm—the arm would come off, he would seize a man by the leg—the leg would come off. He can challenge anyone he likes to a battle of wits and can beat him, can make him look foolish, can deprive him of property, reputation, wife and life, and himself remain unpunished.

If there is a certain element of risk, who does not know after all, how much charm risk lends any game for the real gambler. And Iago is a real gambler. He is a poisonous vernal flower, unfolding his petals in the first warmth of the spring of the mind. He is enjoying the sense of his own newness, he wants to try the power of his youth straight away and is spoiling for action.

But why does Iago fall upon Othello, and not some other? Why does he ruin Desdemona, and not some other? Of course, the reasons which he gives are purely ridiculous. No, he falls upon Othello because Othello is his Commanding Officer, because he is an illustrious general and, very nearly, a great man, because he is covered in the glory of past victories over countless perils and sure of his own courage and might. Surely, it must be pleasant indeed to triumph over a man like that? Incidentally, it is also easy, because he is ingenuous, trustful, inflammable as dry straw; it is very easy to get the mastery of him, to lead him by his black nose. And don't you see what a pleasure that is? Don't you see how delightful it is to see oneself, Lieutenant Iago, a rascally smart-Aleck without the least claim to distinction, in the role of guide, master, Fate, Providence and God in relation to this famous, hot-headed, powerful, dangerous and fiery general?

And Desdemona? She is the daughter of Senator Brabantio, she is the finest flower of Venetian culture, she is all lyrical sensuality and noble devotion, she is a great prize, the highest reward for which a man could hope; and she has surrendered herself to Othello without reserve, has granted him the prize of herself. But she is trusting, she is defenceless, she is honourable. She is incapable of suspecting anyone of double dealing, she does not even know the meaning of the word. It is very easy to lure her into any net. And, surely, you must see how agreeable it is to feel that the fate of such a beauty, such a miracle of nature is in one's hands, to push her in any direction one wishes—to suffering, to ruin, to cause her to change from a blessing and a delight into a torment and a malediction?

All this, Iago savours in advance with his subtle Renaissance sensibility, and he triumphs in advance, in advance he sees himself as the god of these people or, rather, as their ill angel. And to see himself as a devil manipulating the fate of such exalted personages is a sight which fills him with pride.

That is his motive.

It is also a very significant complementary trait in the make-up of the type of the "intriguant". Nowadays things are different, nowadays the "intriguant" has lost his freshness. The genuine, true "intriguants" were running about over the earth's surface in the 17th-18th centuries. This was the age which gave scope to the most amazing combinations in these campaigns of human cunning, this was the heyday of the amorous intrigue such as the one we see so perfectly described by the Frenchman Choderlos de Laclos.

Generally speaking, Francis Bacon was sufficiently far removed from any form of amorous scheming, as we shall see from his biography. Intrigue as such, however, provided an atmosphere in which our philosopher felt rather well at home, as we shall also very soon see for ourselves. I do not know whether he was ever possessed by such arch-diabolic powers of ambition as was Richard III, or by such petty, but uncontrollable and fathomlessly vicious demons as Iago. The intrigues in which he was actually involved were perhaps nearest to Edmund's in type.

Yes, indeed, Francis Bacon really did consider himself not altogether legitimate. He did not choose his parents, but had he been offered a choice, he would have chosen others. He was always having to pull strings through his influential uncles. And after all, in Cook he had a powerful opponent. He cultivated the strangest, most tortuous friendship with the most original figure of his age—with Essex. He was not above playing the part of flatterer to the most despicable people such as King James and his favourite Buckingham. He had to move among shameless courtiers, cunning lawyers and knavish parliamentarians in a world that was dangerous, unprincipled, alert—and, in this world, he managed to carve himself out a great career, almost entirely thanks to intrigue, and clambered his way to such a height that once, in the absence of King James, he even enacted the part of monarch in London. Then— he came unhinged.

To understand all this aspect of Bacon in only possible by taking into account his own moral philosophy, although he himself expressed it but cautiously, and by examining it in the light of that psychology of the shameless chevalier of intellect which we have just been analysing, and which is embodied in the three Shakespeare types we have just been discussing with the reader.

Now let us turn in another direction. Let us examine those Shakespeare characters in whom is reflected the spring-like yet infinitely melancholy "woe from wit" which afflicted the world at that time. In the sense of what might be called scientifically psychological observations about reason, Shakespeare had predecessors and contemporaries. In the field of the *active* intellect he had a splendidly concentrated mentor in Machiavelli.

In the case of the contemplative types, the part of Machiavelli might have been played by Montaigne; it is significant that the appearance of this contemplative and profoundly mournful reason, enjoying as it does the author's unlimited, albeit melancholy sympathy, is bound up in Shakespeare with a tendency to contrast "pastoral" philosophic principles with the hypocrisy of court life—a tendency which is also characteristic of Montaigne. Berthelot, in his work *La sagesse de Shakespeare et de Goethe,* sets out to prove that Shakespeare in general paid a very considerable tribute to the preaching of elegant simplicity of life in contrast to arrogance and vain luxury, but this was the essential significance of all the pastoral moods of the 16th, 17th and, in part, 18th centuries. Be that as it may, Shakespeare's comedy *As You Like It* is, as it were, the central play indisputably dedicated to the philosophy of the pastoral.

It is not, however, this particular Shakespearian trend which interests us. We do not, in fact, even consider that Shakespeare defended the pastoral spirit with any very particular vehemence in this comedy. We are, however, interested in one of the most important, though not most active, characters of the play—in the melancholy Jaques.

Jaques is referred to several times as a melancholic, and this is significant. He himself tries to define the reason for his melancholy and does this in a special, half-jesting way. It is one of his general characteristics that he clothes his high wisdom and the findings of his mind, which differ from the vision of the so-called averagely clever man to the point of paradox, in an ironic, joking form.

Here is how Jaques defines the genus of his melancholy: "I have neither the scholar's melancholy, which is emulation, nor the musician's which is fantastical, nor the courtier's, which is proud, nor the soldier's, which is ambitious, nor the lawyer's, which is politic, nor the lady's, which is nice, nor the lover's, which is all these; but it is a melancholy of mine own, compounded of many simples, extracted from many objects, and indeed the sundry contemplation of my travels, in which my often rumination wraps me in a most humorous sadness."

Jaques does not wish to hide his extraordinarily sad conclusions from other people. But he knows that they will not understand them straight away. And he is visited by the desire to put on the motley and to act like a jester whose privilege it is to speak in paradox. He "can use his folly like a stalking-horse and under the presentation of that he shoots his wit!"

O, that I were a fool!

cries Jaques.

I am ambitious for a motley coat.
                    ...It is my only suit
Provided that you weed your better judgements
Of all opinion that grows rank in them
That I am wise...

. . . .
Invest me in my motley; give me leave
To speak my mind, and I will through and through
Cleanse the foul body of the infected world,
If they will patiently receive my medicine.

From this it is clear that the melancholy Jaques does not consider the world a hopeless invalid. He simply sees that the world is seriously ill, and believes that Reason, having diagnosed the disease, can cure it by speaking the truth—even if Reason must go clothed in jester's garb.

Jaques looks for the most exact parallel to this world, and finds it in the theatre.

We shall not quote in full Jaques' wonderful monologue

> *All the world's a stage,*
> *And all the men and women merely players....*

But only the end:

> *Last scene of all,*
> *That ends this strange, eventful history,*
> *Is second childishness and mere oblivion*
> *Sans teeth, sans eyes, sans taste, sans everything.*

In this way, the basis of Jaques' understanding of the world becomes quite clear. It is a repetition—not a theoretical, but a practical repetition of the famous Eastern saying: "He who increases wisdom increases boredom".

The world is so arranged that it is only possible to play one's part with verve and pleasure, if one does not realise that one is on the stage. Otherwise the transience of all that is, the aimlessness of all that goes on, will poison the whole act for you, and the whole part,

The question remains as to whether, having such a truth to disclose to the world, it is possible to open the eyes of this same world to the fact that it is "a dream", that it is "a play", and to what extent it is possible to put it right.

The cure, evidently, can only consist in people adopting a Buddhistic attitude and ceasing to attach importance to youth, to beauty, to ambition, to honour, to victory, to success. All this should, in their eyes, carry the stamp of mutability.

In the works of our hero Francis Bacon, it is possible to come across bitter aphorisms in the same spirit. He is not out of sympathy with Montaigne, whom he knew. However, such words are not typical of him. The hypothesis that Bacon is the author of *Hamlet* is ridiculous. But that Bacon is a kindred spirit of Hamlet's is undoubtedly true.

In what particular does Hamlet differ from his prototype—Jaques? Why—in so far as Hamlet is not void of Machiavellism, of intellectualism.

He is a prince of talent, a prince of humanity, a soldier-prince. He is not just "a talker"—he is a soldier. This is the side of his nature which seduced Akimov in his paradoxical production in the Vakhtangov Theatre.* The fact that Hamlet is a strong-willed young man has been noted by many.

Why, it is enough to reread Hamlet's famous words at the end of the third act:

> *There's letters sealed, and my two-school-fellows,*
> *Whom I will trust as I will adders fanged,*
> *They bear the mandate; they must sweep my way,*
> *And marshal me to knavery. Let it work;*
> *For'tis the sport to have the enginer*

---

* Nikolai Akimov's paradoxical production: in 1932 the Soviet producer N. Akimov staged *Hamlet* in the Vakhtangov Theatre. This was Akimov's first independent production and was of an experimental nature.—*Ed.*

Hoist with his own petard, and 't shall go hard
But I will delve one yard below their mines,
And blow them at the moon. O, 'tis most sweet,
When in one line two crafts directly meet.

There is no need to point out that these words could have been spoken by Richard III, or by Edmund, or by Iago.

On such a path, Hamlet might not only have survived the struggle, but might well have emerged victorious. But such a prospect would have given him no pleasure, for he knows that the "world's a prison" in which there are many confines, wards and dungeons, "Denmark being one o' the worst".

His acute mind penentrates all the imperfections of the world. But to understand the imperfections of the world implies the possession of high ideals of some sort with which to contrast it. And indeed, Hamlet dreams of a world which has been somehow made straight, a world of honest people, honest relationships, but he does not believe that such a world will ever in fact become reality.

Hamlet respects his friend Horatio most of all for his honesty and firmness of character, that is, for his ability to bear misfortune with dignity. Hamlet is moved by his meeting with the host of Fortinbras.

...Examples gross as earth exhort me:
Witness this army of such mass and charge
Led by a delicate and tender prince,
Whose spirit with divine ambition puffed
Makes mouths at the invisible events,
Exposing what is mortal and unsure!
To all that fortune, death and danger dare,
Even for an egg-shell...

And, dying, Hamlet has not forgotten Fortinbras:

> *O, I die, Horatio;*
> *The potent poison quite o'ercrows my spirit.*
> *I cannot live to hear the news from England;*
> *But I do prophesy the election lights*
> *On Fortinbras. He has my dying voice.*

These are the people whom Hamlet is prepared to respect. They seem to him to be leading the kind of life which would have suited him.

The soliloquy "To be or not to be" is so well known that it seems unnecessary to quote it here in full, but to subject it to some analysis in this particular aspect is absolutely essential.

We will leave aside Hamlet's doubts as to whether a man can risk suicide when he is uncertain what may await him beyond the grave. This is a special question which does not, for the moment, concern us. We are interested in how Hamlet sees *this* life. He asks:

> *Whether 'tis nobler in the mind to suffer*
> *The slings and arrows of outrageous fortune,*
> *Or to take arms against a sea of troubles,*
> *And, by opposing, end them.*

And points out that the lot of the living is "heart-ache" and a "thousand natural shocks":

> *To die—to sleep—*
> *No more; and by a sleep to say we end*
> *The heart-ache and the thousand natural shocks*
> *That flesh is heir to!*

And, further on, he elaborates his thought rather more clearly. He says:

For who would bear the whips and scorns of time,
The oppressor's wrong, the proud man's contumely,
The pangs of despised love, the law's delay,
The insolence of office and the spurns
That patient merit of the unworthy takes,
When he himself might...

And so on.

The first discovery made by Shakespeare's awakening mind is the existence of tyranny, the absence of rights.

This is not the place to go into the question of which social strata it was Shakespeare's intention to show. It is enough to have ascertained that the first and most repulsive aspect of life to be discovered by reason is the profound contradiction between the idea of justice and reality, which is found to be subject to tyranny. What follows are the more abstract moral complaints of Hamlet. Everything can be reduced to one and the same idea: that very bad, despicable, unworthy people do exist and society is so organised that they have power, that they are in a position to oppress others, to spurn others, that the world is so constituted that the best people, the worthy, noble and clever people, are pushed to the wall.

It goes without saying that such an attitude was acceptable not only to some of the "malcontents", that is, to certain representatives of the gilded youth of the old aristocracy, which was feeling the pinch under Elizabeth's middle-class monarchy, but also to a part of that very intelligentsia which represented talent, which represented those devoted to the arts, and which was flesh of Shakespeare's flesh.

For the gilded youth, on the one hand, in so far as their whole class was slipping and sliding across the surface of life and could see ahead of them only something in the nature of ruin, and, on the other hand, for the middle-class intelligentsia which had only recently awakened to life, the world around had suddenly been stript of illusions (and even to these newly awakened people there seemed to be no solution)—and it was at this moment that the thought of suicide obtruded. If, on the other hand, they did consent to go on living, then only clothed in mourning because of the impossibility of calling life good or of making it so.

The real meaning of the monologue becomes apparent to us if we compare it with the LXVI *Sonnet,* written about the same time, in which Shakespeare puts forward Hamlet's basic arguments. But, this time, in his own name:

> *Tired with all these, for restful death I cry,—*
> *As, to behold Desert a beggar born,*
> *And needy Nothing trimm'd in jollity,*
> *And purest Faith unhappily forsworn,*
> *And gilded Honour shamefully misplaced,*
> *And maiden Virtue rudely strumpeted,*
> *And right Perfection wrongfully disgraced,*
> *And Strength by limping sway disabled,*
> *And Art made tongue-tied by Authority,*
> *And Folly, doctor-like, controlling Skill,*
> *And simple Truth miscall'd Simplicity,*
> *And captive Good attending captain Ill.*
> *Tired with all these, from these I would be gone,*
> *Save that, to die, I leave my love alone.*

Here, all the reasons for the sadness of the awakened intelligence are particularly clearly shown.

Everything is topsy-turvy. High places are occupied by hideous masks. True might, true modesty, true sincerity, true talent—all these are set at naught, and there is not the least hope of setting things to rights.

It may be that, at the time of Essex's plot, Shakespeare did nurse some absurd hopes that this particular, impractical plot with its extremely indefinite programme might change something or other for the better; but it is quite certain that the suppression of this plot could have been the cause of that terrible disenchantment which left such a profound imprint on the second period of this great world poet.

Bacon knew Elizabeth's court. He also knew the court of James. Of the injustices of both these courts and of the contemporary world in general he had particularly acute personal experience. He himself, for that matter, was not above committing similar injustices when the opportunity offered. But Bacon was a friend of Essex and was close to the plot, though admittedly in rather a curious position.

When we become better acquainted with Bacon's so-called wordly morality, we shall see in it traces of that disenchantment and of that sadness which was so disturbing society. However, it is safe to state categorically that, although Bacon is related in type to Hamlet (because he is equally intellectual, whether as an active or an analytical intellect), he nevertheless represents quite a different type. And, perhaps, in order to come a little closer to him, it is essential to bring on yet one more figure from Shakespeare's gallery of wise men, the most mature figure and the last, the hero of *The Tempest*—Prospero.

Prospero is a scholar, Prospero is a wizard. Prospero wields a magic book and a magic staff by whose power he can control the forces of nature.

Prospero has much in common with Bacon.

By means of creative invention, by means of scientific investigations, man achieves great power over nature. Bacon is on the look-out for just such a magic book, just such a staff. If he denies the old magic, it is because it is false. At the same time, he is inclined to call the power of technical knowledge which man achieves through applied science a new magic. Through his own peculiar Academy, Bacon passes out into the Utopian Atlantis. Bacon really is a kind of Prospero.

It is almost possible to believe that Shakespeare was familiar with some of Bacon's most subtle arguments. In this way, for instance, it is very easy to explain Ariel as the embodiment of that which Bacon calls "form", a conception to which we will return. Prospero's power over Caliban represents at one and the same time his power over the lower elements of nature, over the common people in general and over the "natives" of colonies in particular.

However, Prospero is not so much unhappy as indifferent to happiness, setting no store by it. He does not even desire to revel in his revenge on his enemies. He does not even desire to see some acceptable order established on the earth. True, he arranges the affairs of those who are to go on living, or at least improves their lot; he takes care of his beloved daughter Miranda. But his first concern is to divest himself of his power as quickly as possible and to seek retirement. The world does not seem to him worth ruling. He does not hate the world, he simply knows its worth. He has had enough of this "fata Morgana".

These our actors,
As I foretold you, were all spirits
And melted into air, into thin air;
And, like the baseless fabric of this vision,
The cloud-called towers, the gorgeous palaces,
The solemn temples, the great globe itself,

Yea, all which it inherit, shall dissolve
And, like the insubstantial pageant faded
Leave not a rack behind. We are such stuff
As dreams are made on, and our little life
Is rounded with a sleep.

This is the message of Shakespeare's idealistic and pessimistic wisdom.

Having passed through a stage of infatuation with the world, having passed through the bitterness of struggle with the world, he has arrived at a certain reconciliation with it, but he is reconciled only in so far as he has realised the full extent of its vanity.

How good it is that life is not eternal. How good that everything passes. How good that death must come. How good that there is an ending. On these conditions it is still possible to keep one's seat for a while in this theatre.

It goes without saying that such a mood is neither the "beginning" nor the "end" of human wisdom. It is the distinctive mood of a class. The great mouthpiece of a déclassé, changing aristocracy in the process of transition into a class of bourgeois magnates and, at the same time, in his own person, the representative of the class of bettered craftsmen who provided the nobility with their cultural distractions, Shakespeare, in that epoch when the middle classes as a whole were developing into the incarnation of avarice, hypocrisy and puritanism, could see no bright rifts in the massing clouds ahead. No such rifts were promised by the monarchy which was being built up from these confused social relationships. There was no way out. The alternatives were to kill oneself, or to grumble on endlessly about the unfortunate way the world had been made, or to be thankful for mutability, instead of discovering therein cause for melancholy.

For our hero, Bacon, things were quite different. In his wisdom there is a special note which we do not hear from Prospero, which is broken in Prospero. Bacon holds fast to one thing: to his magic book and to his magic staff. A great work needs to be done here to sort out all the methods and inventions of science.

Bacon is full of youthful, happy, sparkling, naive faith in science. He knows that the social order is unjust. He knows that it is necessary to come to terms with many things as inevitable. And, in general, he is well aware of various shady aspects of the world, but he makes light going over them. He is not like Prospero, who is prepared to put away the staff of science and the possibility of technical power simply because he feels, or assumes, that "there is nothing but heart-sorrow and a clear life ensuing".

No, Bacon leaves "heart-sorrow" out of it and announces first and foremost: with the right method we will discover the nature of the world, establish our authority over it, and then it will be time to take another look round!

From this point of view, it would be possible to maintain that Bacon, a giant of intelligence, stands lower than the highest giants of intelligence, created by Shakespeare, for he fails to penetrate the last depths of the folly and unsatisfactoriness of the world as it really is in a class society.

In this sense, Shakespeare's pessimisms or the high resignation of Prospero rises like a tower above the head of our far more prosaic and practical chancellor. On the other hand, Marx was not letting fall idle words when he said that matter was still smiling encouragingly at man in the person of Bacon, that, for him, it still appeared full of life, charm and promise. Bacon's strength is in his youth, in his talent: the main thing is not that, armed with reason,

I make my career, like a snake, and crawl up high (but, perhaps, only to fall back again to the depths), nor is it that, with the great, sad eyes of the clever man, I see much that is sad in life; the main thing is, that reason should give the strength and the ability to pass on to another kind of power—to the power of science and technical knowledge, on which we will found new forms of social life. There, before us, open up the most attractive perspectives, almost limitless perspectives, whither I am calling.

And, as, in all the works of Shakespeare, there is not one representative of the intelligence in whom this note dominates or even sounds particularly strongly, this may be taken as one further indication that Bacon had no direct influence on the works of Shakespeare.

It seems to us, however, that we have made this colourful excursion to some purpose, since in it we have met people resembling Bacon among the "chevaliers of intellect" in the great gallery of William Shakespeare's portraits.

1934

I

SATIRE must be jolly ... and wrathful.

But is there not some contradiction in this statement? Is not laughter in itself good-natured? A person laughs when he is happy. If someone wants to make a person laugh, he must be put down among the merry-makers, comforters and entertainers.

This is what Swift wrote about himself: "I do not wish to entertain, but to irritate and insult people."

That's a nice how-do-you do! If you want to insult us, why do you laugh? Why are you witty?

However, everyone knows that there is something else to laughter besides being an indication of "fun".

There is a common saying: to kill with laughter.

How can this be so? How can such a "merry" thing as laughter kill a person?

Laughter does not kill the one it entertains, but the one at whose expense this merriment occurs.

What is laughter from a physiological point of view? Spencer provides a very good explanation of its biological nature. He says that every new idea, every new fact or subject arouses a person's interest. Everything unusual is a problem, it worries us. To reassure ourselves we must reduce the new idea to one that is already familiar, in order that it cease being something mysterious, and, therefore, possibly dangerous. Thus, faced with an unexpected combination of external irritants, the human body prepares for a certain amount of increased activity (speaking in terms of reflexology, the body produces a new conditioned reflex). It suddenly becomes evident that this problem is an imaginary one, that it is merely a flimsy veil behind which we recognise something quite familiar and not at all dangerous. The entire problem, the entire "incident" is "unimportant"; meanwhile, however, you have armed yourself and mobilised your psycho-physiological powers. This mobilisation proved unnecessary. You are not faced with a formidable enemy. You must demobilise. That means the store of energy concentrated in the given thinking and analytical centres of your brain must be used up immediately, i.e., it must be drained off along the channels that prescribe the body's movements. If the resultant irradiation of energy is weak, the movement will be insignificant—a smile touching the lips. If more energy has been stored, there will be a convulsing of the diaphragm, and sometimes even the convulsive laughter of which we say: "howling with laughter", "shrieking with laughter", "splitting one's sides laughing". This is especially true when a whole series of unexpected solutions to seemingly serious problems produce a number of corresponding reactions.

It should also be noted that the convulsing of the diaphragm which, by the way, also produces the sound of laughter, is, at the same time, a convulsive, forced expulsion of air (and, therefore, of oxygen) from our lungs: according to Spencer this is a new "safety valve". This lessens the oxidation of the blood and, therefore, the activity of the various processes in the brain, so that laughter, from this point of view, is once again a peculiar means of demobilisation.

It now becomes quite clear why laughter is a merry and pleasant experience. You were prepared for stress and ... demobilised instead. And then quickly returned to a state of equilibrium. Any good-natured chuckling is proof of the fact that, at the present time, you have no serious enemy. Complacent laughter proves that you consider yourself to have held an easy victory over quite a number of difficulties.

Now a satirist is, first and foremost, a very keen observer. He has noticed several revolting features about society which pose a problem to you. You, his readers, his public, do not yet see these revolting features or are not paying sufficient attention to them. The publicist, in writing in a serious vein and drawing your attention to this evil, views it as an important and serious obstacle to the normal course of affairs. In a way, he uses it to frighten you. A satirist differs from the "serious" publicist in that he wants you to laugh at this evil here and now, that is, to give you to understand that you are the victor, that this evil is miserable, weak and does not merit serious attention, that it is far beneath you, that you can just laugh it off, so morally superior are you to the level of this evil.

Thus, the satirist's method is to launch an attack against an enemy while simultaneously declaring him already vanquished and making a laughing-stock of him.

A person likes such jokes. For if you laugh at someone, it means his ugliness, his peculiarities do not arouse your fear or any other form of positive or negative "acknowledgement". Thus, you sense your own power. By laughing at another you acknowledge yourself to be better than he. Incidentally, this is the terrible power of the source of the method used so successfully by Gogol in his *Inspector-General*: "Whom are you laughing at? You are laughing at yourselves!" This means: all that is best in you, awakened by me, is laughing at your worst traits as at something ugly, but pitiful.

The satirist anticipates victory. He says: "Let us laugh at our enemies. I assure you they are pitiful and we are much stronger than they."

That is why laughter can kill. If a publicist calls upon you to fight the enemy, it does not mean the enemy has already been killed. He might even prove to be stronger than you. But if he calls upon you to ridicule him, it means you have finally and irrevocably passed judgement on him as something you have overcome, as something you can treat with scorn.

Homeric laughter, a truly healthy, victorious tone, is the triumph of an absolute and easily-won victory.

But why should satire be wrathful (and satire which is not wrathful, is bad satire)?

This is precisely the question, for satire only pretends that the enemy is so weak. It only pretends that it is sufficient to make fun of the enemy, that it might as well have been beaten already and disarmed. But satire is not at all convinced that this is so. Moreover, in the majority of cases, the satirist is sadly convinced that the evil he has challenged is very formidable, very dangerous. He is just trying to encourage his allies, his readers. He is merely trying to discredit the enemy beforehand with a peculiar bit of bragging: We'll knock the stuffing out of you, all we can do is laugh at you. Satire strives to kill the enemy with laughter. The less successful it is, the more enraged it becomes. Laughter, instead of being victorious, Homeric, becomes sarcastic, it becomes a series of scathing attacks mixed with extreme rage. Sarcasm is the effort to appear as a victor over that which is far from being vanquished. Sarcasm is the arrow of laughter shot, not like Phoebus' arrow at Python* from above, but from below.

But how can this be possible? Are satirists no more than impudent boys, insolent braggarts,

---

* This myth is of the Greek God of Light, Phoebus Apollo, who shot an arrow at the serpent Python, a frightful monster who symbolised darkness and night.—*Author's note.*

deceivers of the human race, who would convince it of the insignificance of something that is actually important?

No, it is more subtle than that. A satirist is truly the victor over that which he mocks. But he is only a victor in theory. His moral superiority makes him a victor. If a satirist had the necessary physical strength besides his intellect and fine emotions he could truly vanquish his enemy quite easily and laugh triumphantly. But the trouble is that Python did not "fall, writhing, dead", because our Apollo does not yet have a bow that is mighty enough, or an arrow that is sharp enough.

Satire is a moral victory, lacking a material victory.

It is obvious, therefore, that satire will attain its greatest significance at a time when a newly evolving class or social group that has created an ideology which is considerably more advanced than the ruling ideology of the ruling class, has not yet developed to an extent where it can conquer its enemy. Herein lies its truly great ability to triumph, its scorn of its adversary and its hidden fear of it; herein lies its venom, its staggering energy of hate and, quite frequently, the grief which is a black frame around the glittering vivacious images of satire. Herein lies the contradiction of satire, herein lies its dialectics.

II

Swift! There is something satanic in his very name. Something hissing, whistling. Swift. Something reminiscent of the whistling of Mephistopheles in the opera of the same name by Arrigo Boito, especially as rendered by Chaliapin, in which he mockingly remonstrates against the scorned yet ruling force.

There is probably no other figure in history in which such a magnificent, elemental wit was embodied.

Swift is surrounded by sparkling waves of laughter. Through the power of his wit he made the nobles and ministers respect and admire him. Through the power of his wit he made an entire people, the Irish people, worship him as their great protector. Through the power of his wit he has conquered the centuries and, in his best works, he vies for the title of the most widely read author with the greatest writers of later generations.

Yet, at the same time, this is one of the saddest, most unfortunate and tragic figures of world history. The "tears, unseen by the world", which accompanied his laughter, scorched his soul. And were they really unseen? While "the unseen tears" of Gogol, who ended his life in such bitter despondency, were not at all invisible to the sensitive reader, they were all the more apparent in Swift's works. His boundless joviality, born of his great intellectual superiority over hostile social elements, was organically, chemically a part of his terrible, excessive, torturing grief at the fact that this intellect was, far from being the king of reality, often no more than its helpless moral victor and, as a result of its victorious battles, its stupidly rejected and completely slighted prisoner.

Swift is woe from wit. His great wit worked great woe in him. There is good reason why his name is linked with Gogol and Griboyedov. Those two also had their full share of woe from their great wit.

But neither Griboyedov nor Gogol was our Russian Swift. Our Russian Swift was Saltykov-Shchedrin.

Recall the last and best-known portrait of him. We see a thin, long-bearded old man with a plaid across his ailing knees. There is anguish in his intelligent eyes. Reality had finally done him in. The face of a zealot, a saint, a martyr gazes out at you gloomily. But this was the cleverest writer to have ever graced the Russian land, this is our greatest satirist who had swung his fiery intellectual mace over the lowly skulls of the freaks of reaction and liberalism, but who had become physically exhausted, consumed by the struggle against unshakable stupidity.

Swift was the contemporary of Voltaire, his elder contemporary.

Recall Houdon's statue: Voltaire in his old age, his helpless, wasted hands on his knees, wrapped in a shapeless cloak, looks at you from his emaciated head, so full of cunning, intelligent venom and a magnificently caught combination of the feeling that the battle against stupidity is triumphantly won, and at the same time, a weary confession that stupidity carries on.

III

The bourgeoisie was quickly coming to power in the times of Swift, in the times of Voltaire.

The powerful and wealthy bourgeoisie was fated to win. Its victory was also fated to be the source of new evil and, after gaining its victory, it was not to fulfil the hopes which the masses placed upon it and which it falsely raised.

Since the bourgeoisie in its attack on the old ruling classes appealed also to the masses, it acquired brilliant ideologists from the then developing (and but recently evolved) petty-bourgeois intelligentsia.

The principal political clash between the bourgeoisie and the ruling classes during the reign of Queen Anne took the form of a struggle between the two parties, the Tories and the Whigs.

Swift was neither a Tory nor a Whig. He was a most outstanding individual, carried along on the crest of the liberal-bourgeois wave, and far surpassing its horizons and its tendencies.

Actually, he did not represent the moderate and extremely wealthy bourgeoisie which sought its political expression in the Whig Party, but was a representative of the petty-bourgeois intelligentsia which as yet had not found sufficient support in the masses and which was carrying a peculiar "romance from afar" with the poor.

IV

Swift was born to a poor family, the son of a poverty-stricken widow. Perhaps he never would have survived infancy if not for a nurse who loved him dearly. She kept him for two years, having obtained the permission of his destitute mother.

However, the poor lad had wealthy relatives. It was they who fed and clothed him. They made it possible for him to attend school and, later, university; thus, he was growing into a homeless, indigent proletarian intellectual.

He was known at the university as a nervous, unbalanced and not especially diligent student. Actually, he was being consumed by helpless rage, rage at the contrast between the wonderful gifts he felt he possessed and the hopeless poverty that made life a misery.

The violent clashes between the classes were destroying the old established way of life and awakening a large portion of the population that was striving to steer a way through the confusion and find an outlet in the written word to express their aspirations, indignation and sympathies. Since there was no daily press as yet, semi-legal pamphlets served as the voice of the awakened masses. The names of the authors were kept a secret and the printers were often subjected to terrible punishment for printing them.

In these pamphlets and the first, usually satirical, magazines that followed, and that were echoed in the satirical magazines of the times of Catherine the Great in Russia, Wit tried to take over the reins, it tried to set its clear argumentation and the simplicity of its mockery in opposition to the other social forces.

Gradually, Wit acquired more and more admirers and supporters. The more intelligent men were drawn to the government, while the men in power tried to appear intelligent. The intelligentsia began to exert a definite influence on society, the ministers began to pose as intellectuals.

Upon graduating, Swift found employment with just such a minister who was extremely proud of his intelligence—the well-known diplomat Sir William Temple. Life in his employ was fraught with dire insult for Swift, who was riled by his status of exploited retainer. He left his patron several times only to return. In the end, he chose to become a modest pastor in the village of Laracor, Ireland, where he wrote his first great masterpiece, *A Tale of a Tub*.

Returning to London, he published a witty pamphlet and a number of articles in Steele's *Tattler* under the pen name of Bickerstaff, and soon became one of the leading journalists.

During the early period of his political activity Swift was considered a "peer" of the Whig Party. But when the Whig Party lost power and Queen Anne, influenced by her new favourite, Lady Masham, called upon the Tories, headed by Harley and St. John, Swift deserted his former friends and went over to the side of the new government. He paid dearly for his "treason", for many of his friends violently denounced him. However, Swift considered himself to be far above the miserable quarrels of both parties, he envisioned a power which he could use "for the good of Great Britain".

Swift reached his zenith when the government of Harley and, later, Bolingbroke was in office.

There is a description of how he would appear, a stately and proud figure, his magnificent head high, his deep-set eyes flashing blue fire, dressed in clerical black, at the salons and ministry receptions and there, surrounded by petitioners, friends and flatterers, he would pass judgement upon various matters, convinced that the ministers, captivated by his genius, would never oppose his suggestions.

Swift was the actual head of the Tory government for three consecutive years. They realised full well that without him, the "king of journalists", they would not be able to carry on in office. Nevertheless, Swift remained a poor man. He never knew a desire for riches and later, as Dean of St. Patrick's Cathedral in Dublin, to the end of his days he donated a third of his modest living to the poor.

Although the Tory government had not yet fallen, Swift's satus within it had deteriorated and he left for Ireland. The death of Queen Anne, the ascension of George I and the firm rule of the intelligent but villainous Walpole cut Swift off from the British political arena. Returning to his native Ireland, Swift was struck afresh by the sufferings of his people. Ireland was subjected not only to political oppression, but to unbelievable economic exploitation as well. Ireland was forbidden to export sheep to England, wool abroad, and a currency was being forced upon it that was all but counterfeit. It is difficult to imagine all the infamies the avaricious English nobility and bourgeoisie heaped upon the poverty-stricken people of Ireland. Swift, no longer concerned with power and honours and no longer afraid of danger, became the defender and spokesman of his people. His *Drapier's Letters* were an example of bold, clear-thinking publicism. He became the idol of his people, he awakened their will to live, he threw himself into battle for their defence and forced the all-powerful British Government to retreat, step by step.

However, Swift was dissatisfied by these partial victories. Now, as never before, he felt the great yawning chasm between his intellect and his love for his people and black reality. He became more and more pessimistic. The blackest monument of satirical laughter and tragic grief combined was a pamphlet he wrote at this time, entitled *A Modest Proposal for Preventing the Children of Poor People in Ireland from Being a Burden to Their Parents or Country, and for Making Them Beneficial to the Public.*

Here in a most restrained and sober manner, Swift suggests that surplus children be used as a delicacy for the tables of the rich, as "a most delicious, nourishing, and wholesome food, whether stewed, roasted, baked or boiled".

Swift had reached the bottom of his deepest rage from which he still sent forth glittering sparks of wit. He now began work on a book which was to become world-famous, and the slightly abridged version of which has become a children's classic, one of the most entertaining and jolly in world literature, *Gulliver's Travels,* but which, in all actuality, was a most hopeless, gloomy and despairing satire not only of contemporary mankind but, as Swift believed, of mankind in general. Swift, who was now getting on in years, lost his dearly beloved Esther Johnson, his Stella. Swift's love life was both unusual and mysterious. He had a very close friendship, a gentle and loving friendship with both Stella and Vanessa (Esther Van Homrigh) which was never consummated by marriage but which created a rather peculiar situation, exhausting him mentally by the obscure but most complex of relationships.

Now, alone in his old age, the gloomy Swift began to sink lower and lower. Cursed reality now had its revenge upon his intellect. Not long before his death he became senile and died a wretched madman at the age of 79.

Crowds of poor Irishmen surrounded his deathbed. Someone cut off the grey locks that framed the dead forehead of the great writer and handed them out as remembrances of "our benefactor".

V

In the Introduction to *A Tale of a Tub* Swift clearly reveals its true meaning.

Having in mind the powerfully materialistic *Leviathan* by Hobbes, Swift compares it to a whale which could have overturned a ship, i.e., the nation, if it had not been distracted by a tub—religion, the Church—which Swift believed diverted the revolutionatry forces from directly attacking the government.*

In other words, Swift seems to be saying: The real, important task is to strike out against the government, against class rule, but this cannot be done at present; however, we are permitted a little free-thinking as concerns the Church, so let us make the most of this!

Recall, Voltaire found himself in precisely the same situation. However, this less dangerous battle against the Church was of definite value, even as compared to the struggle against the monarchy.

---

* Actually, Swift's book should have been called *A Tub-Tale*, a tale tossed, as a tub to distract the "whale", i.e., to divert the revolutionary forces from attacking the government.—*Author's note.*

Swift carried it off brilliantly.

The device he uses here, as in so many of his other works, is an outwardly quite serious rendition of the absurdities of life, told with a smile trembling on his lips. A shower, an avalanche of wit pours down upon the reader. In this respect there are few works of world literature that can withstand comparison with *A Tale of a Tub*. Recall the wonderful pages devoted to the philosophy of dressing which later served as the basis of Carlyle's major work, *Sartor Resartus*.

The construction of the *Tale* is such that a brilliant allegory on the history of the Catholic, Anglican and Puritan churches in England alternates with a magnificent attack on contemporary literature.

In the first instance we have an inimitable irony, sparkling with unprecedented, bitter humour, in which the story of Brother Peter adorning his coat and the dinner where the mysteries of Communion are ridiculed so mercilessly, etc., are related. The description of Peter and Jack leaves nothing to be desired in the presentation of the sly and boundless hypocrisy of the Catholic clergy and the stupid, fanatical, ignorant and no less hypocritical teachings of the Puritans. Swift was more moderate in his estimation of Martin, but here, too, there is a magnificent portrayal of opportunism *per se*, while in one of the last chapters, returning to Martin, Swift brings down a torrent of ridicule upon him for his indecisiveness.

This part of the narrative ends in a bold escapade: a plan for creating an original travel bureau for the next world. On the whole, Swift does not conceal his atheism.

Swift's digressions attacking the writers of his time are less clear, but no less brilliant. And the modern reader, and especially the modern writer, will find here a whole arsenal of witticisms and poisoned arrows.

Swift is often obscene. He likes witticisms based on sex and on the natural functions of the human body. Woe to him who would classify Swift among the pornographers for this reason!

The humanist Poggio, one of Swift's predecessors in this field (for Italy was more progressive than England at the time), said that the great and merry writers of antiquity used so-called obscenity to make their readers laugh, while the nasty little pornographers of his time used it to arouse their readers' lust.

Swift's obscenities will certainly never arouse lust. Christianity has debased the animal in man. Swift was influenced by Christianity in this respect, and he gloats whenever he can remind man of his bestiality. Swift's indecent jests always play the part of a burning lash of nettles, a reminder to man that he is practically an ape, a Yahoo.

Swift did not really believe in the longevity of his *Tale*.

In the Introduction he writes:

"Now, it sometimes tenderly affects me to consider, that all the towardly passages I shall deliver in the following treatise, will grow quite out of date and relish with the first shifting of the present scene." He then goes on to deliver a number of magnificent and witty opinions.

Swift was undoubtedly very advanced for his time. But was this not because he reacted to the demands of his time as a man of great intellect who had just awakened and was reaching for a mastery of life? His contemporaneity in the late seventeenth and early eighteenth centuries makes him our contemporary as well. Will this circumstance not reserve a place for him on the library shelves of socialist cities now under construction?

An unidentified Russian translation, formerly confiscated by the tsarist censorship, served as the basis for the present edition. The translation has been edited and supplemented by parts which were simply missing in the few remaining copies. For the reader's convenience the author's *Apology* has been placed at the end, as it was written at a later date as an argument against the enemies of *A Tale of a Tub*.

Thus, *A Tale of a Tub* now first appears in full in Russian translation. (The translation by V. V. Chuiko, which appeared in *Izyashchnaya Literatura* in 1884 has many inaccuracies and is a severely abridged version of *A Tale of a Tub*.)

The present volume has been carefully annotated.

1930

I DO NOT claim, comrades, that in this small paper I shall come to sum up Heine as a thinker—this would be both difficult and not very rewarding. Heine, in fact, never created any system: he presented the world instead with a vast quantity of separate thoughts and sets of ideas, which would be hopeless to try to sum up systematically.

I should like, instead of this, to define the *type of thinker* to which Heine belonged. It seems to me that we shall find the key to all the various facets of his thinking only when we have understood him as a definite type of philosopher, typical of a specific era.

Heine, above all, is an artist, and possesses the three basic features of every artist. The first of these is his unusual sensitivity to his environment, his unusually receptive nature. The second is the rich and complicated method by which he processes internally the material he has received from external sources. And finally, the third feature is his ability to reproduce in his works with the maximum effect, vividness and expressiveness, everything which has been taken from objective reality and then processed and coloured by an artist's subjective temperament. It is the second feature—the internal processing of the material—which, more than anything, the artist and the thinker have in common; it can be observed in the emotional and ideological analysis and synthesis, in the transformation of objective material into images and into a new system of concepts.

The so-called "pure" artist, it appears, creates during an emotional outburst; this only means, in fact, that, for him, thinking in creative images is of decisive significance.

Plekhanov maintains correctly that artistic creation cannot eliminate conceptual thinking. It is, however, possible to imagine someone whose system of logical concepts prevails over his mode of thinking in emotional images.

In the first instance we have the artist-thinker, in the second, the thinker-artist.

If we find a man whose thoughts are completely devoid of imagery (which is as unlikely as the absence of conceptive thinking) then we would be near to the type of "pure thinker".

Heine is an artist-thinker. The thinker and the artist in him are magnificently combined, so that if his works were divided into various categories, their inner integrity would not be weakened; the mind which shines in the artistic works, even the purely lyrical works, and the unusual brilliance of the images, the impassioned feeling in every page of his philosophical works makes them clearly the brain children of one and the same personality.

The element which unites them is one of the basic features of Heine the thinker. It is *wit*.

Wit is Heine's element.

There are a large number of wits, and it is open to doubt whether Heine ranks first among them, but no one would deny that he does occupy a prominent place in their midst.

Wit is the ability to bring together different things, and to distinguish between similar things. Heine expressed it more sharply and simply: "Contrast, the skilful linking of two contradictory elements." In other words, wit is present where dissimilar subjects, ideas and emotions can be united.

If Heine's formula is to be accepted then it will be necessary to separate wit as the dominant element from the wit which plays a subservient role. Thus, for instance, the construction of dialectics is such that it sees unity where superficially there are only contradictions, and sees the disparity in what seems to be elementally whole. But Marx, the great dialectician, concerned himself for the most part with trying to understand, with the help of dialectical analysis, objective reality; for him, wit, in the narrow sense of the word—that is, an effective form intended to incite laughter—was a subsidiary factor. Heine was far less interested in the objective results of an extremely witty approach to a problem; he was interested, above all, in the effect of laughter.

Laughter ensues when a person scores an easy victory over real or imaginary difficulties. So that, for Heine, it is extremely important to create a sudden difficulty which makes you stop for a minute and overcome this difficulty; the victory, even the difficulty itself may be illusionary, but the triumph of a radiant mind is manifested with such grace that you cannot but laugh.

Generally speaking, metaphysics is the antithesis of dialectics and wit. Metaphysics establishes eternal ideas. One can imagine—or rather note—a tendency in art which thinks in complete, indivisible *images*; but it would be difficult for art to express eternal *ideas*. Art, as Hegel brilliantly analysed it, gives us eternal ideas in their concrete expressions. A concrete expression—the reflection, for example, of the ideal of man in Phidias's *Zeus*—is a self-sufficient object which alone and unaugmented aspires to express a certain idea in its entirety. In the great realistic art of antiquity, ideas are presented in their "concrete expression"; eternity does not destroy transitoriness; wholeness is not one-dimensional, nor does it have but one meaning.

The art of ancient Greece and Rome tried to reflect reality objectively. Naturalist artists strove for the same effect in a different way. But if you examine their pictures you will see that the naturalist artists— unconscious mechanical materialists—always look at things as if they are always equal to themselves. A naturalist portrays an object in all its static finiteness, thinking that in this way he attains a more objective and adequate expression. At the same time it is the idea of the object depicted, its real essence, that escapes him.

The impressionists are not like this. Impressionists understand the world not through the essence of an object; they do not try to introduce into their sphere of emotions something which they have discovered in its essence. Impressionists conceive the world by means of a refined subjectivity, by means of that which to them seems essential. Impressionists select the subjectively essential so that it does not coincide with the "vulgarly" essential, thus losing its elegance. In order to present some object or phenomenon, one should not repeat what everyone knows about it. One should not depict that which everyone can see, but only the subtlest phenomena, which only the artist perceives and which should serve as a key to the object itself. For this to be successful, the subject, i.e., the artist, must be comprehensible to a more or less wide audience—otherwise he will simply "select select forms" which no one will understand and he will have no response. The wider the links between the artist-impressionist and his environment, the better it is for him. But at the same time, he should be superior to his audience in his sensitivity to detail, in his ability to work on material and grasp its characteristic features. Treplev, for example, in Chekhov's *Seagull* says:

"Trigorin has already fully developed his literary methods—it is easy for him.... All he needs is a bottleneck to glisten on a dam and the shadow of a water-mill wheel—and there you have a moonlit night."

Impressionism is very close to Heine's formula of wit—"to link contradictory elements"; the incompleteness of such a formula, stressing, as it does, artificially linked contrasts but yet ignoring the actual unity, is characteristic of him.

In this sense, Heine was very much an *impressionist*. In depicting objective reality, he seeks out, with his brilliant wit, the unusual, sometimes also the paradoxical, and with them characterises the given object. With a thinker's wit, he does the same with thoughts: each time he tries to find the original and unexpected aspects of the object he is describing, thereby presenting this object in a completely new light.

In Heine's works the world is depicted to a great extent *subjectively*. He gives what he is describing an emotional colouring, which arises from his mood and which constantly reveals *his ego* in his works— that is, he projects his own internal processes on to his artistic images. The subjective has the upper hand in all Heine's creative activity. One cannot say, it is true, that he considered the world to be "I and my ideas", but he sometimes came close to this position.

In Heine's lifetime Moritz Veit wrote:

"Heine never had any aim other than himself: he was always so preoccupied with the depiction of his own personality that he could never, or only very rarely, rise above himself; he allowed himself every flight of fancy and became so fond of himself in this game that he was unable to subordinate his talent to some higher purpose."

Heine was such a subjective writer that the play of his emotions prevented him from seriously turning to some higher aim.

"He is a long way," his contemporary goes on to declaim, "from a self-sufficient purpose, from a precise awareness of objects and people, because it is only the things which bring him pleasure and which he sees through the tinted spectacles of his own personality, which are valuable to him."

This extreme subjectivism which revealed itself in Heine's impressionism and in his use of wit, which was so characteristic of impressionism, was not, of course, peculiar to him alone. He said that the world was split into two and the crack ran straight through his heart; but it was neither the Universe nor humanity which was split—it was the German society of Heine's time, and the crack ran through the petty-bourgeois intelligentsia. The whole of romanticism was subjective, and the class reasons for this are well known.

When is it possible for one or another class, for one or another representative of a class to sing to the world's objectivity? It is only when he is in agreement with it, when he can say his brilliant "yes" to it. The gigantic representative of the bourgeoisie in Goethe's poetry made a tremendous effort in order to say this "yes" to the world. To do this, he practically disavowed all social factors, transferring his attention to Nature, to the study of Nature and art; and it was on the foundations of Nature, art and, in part, science that he built the radiant temple of his *Weltanschauung*. Goethe's view of the cosmos was closer to ours than the views of any of his contemporaries. But he kept his faith in reality only by reconciling himself with all its imperfections, with all its repugnant aspects even—something which did not come at all easily to him. So that he could say the world was beautiful, that it was necessary to understand it and bow before its laws, Goethe had to refrain from a large number of demands on the world.

Goethe was a bourgeois patrician, and his whole life was an unpleasant, often painful, process of strengthening the link between the German patrician bourgeoisie and the nobility. With such social aspirations, Goethe's eagerness to exclaim: Order above all else; Personality, submit! is understandable.

"You have made a magnificent start, Titans; it is only given to the gods, however, to lead us to that which is eternally good and eternally beautiful; leave them to act ... for no one should try to make themselves equal to the gods." (*Pandora.*)

Proletarian objectivism formulates the task as follows: our vocation is to understand the world, not so that we can interpret it, but so that we can rebuild it. This is the greatest imaginable triumph of objectivism; but a subjective element enters into it, too. This means that the world is as yet incomplete: we accept it, but only as a problem, as material to be moulded, and we consider that we have sufficient strength to rebuild it. Mighty creative processes are involved here: the rebuilding of the world is an architectural task of huge dimensions; at the same time it is an objective task, for it demands exact knowledge of the nature of the world—your material, your own basis, the origin of you yourself.

But in order to approach the world in this way, it is necessary to belong to the creative class which is capable of rebuilding it. This was inaccessible to Heine. He could not follow Goethe's path either, because he lived in another time with a different social destiny.

Let us take the generation of the German pettybourgeois intelligentsia of that time; above all, let us take Heine himself—could he have come to the conclusion that the world was beautiful?

Capitalism, by destroying the foundations of the old economic set-up, had already given birth to its antagonist—the proletariat; but the struggle had only just begun, and both the disposition of the adversaries and the future were still unclear. The bourgeoisie of the period was still too weak to annihilate feudalism, and it compromised, in a really despicable fashion, with the junkers. To Heine, a petty-bourgeois member of the intelligentsia, a person above all of thought and emotion, the situation seemed especially depressing and hopeless.

For this reason, all he could say about the world was that it was evil. What can we do to it when there's nobody with sufficient strength to rebuild it!

Subjectively, there can be three ways out of this position: one can believe that this is an unreal world, that another world exists somewhere which is the real one, and one can try and aspire to this mystic world; or one can maintain that the world generally is not a serious place, that it is best to treat it jokingly and laugh at it; or one can assume that the romantic is familiar with a higher world and can therefore look on reality with irony: I can laugh at the world because I know God. And this higher world does not always mean some mystical, other-wordly existence, but it can be an ideal or a utopia.

Mysticism was alien to Heine; what remained to him, therefore, was mainly irony. His smile was a distorted one, because he could never reconcile himself with reality—he passionately wanted to destroy it.

Heine was unable to accept objectivism, which gave a logical and, therefore, conciliatory picture of reality. In his review of Menzel's book he makes a scathing attack on Goethe:

"The principle underlying Goethe's epoch—the idea of art—is vanishing; in its place, a new epoch with a new principle is rising, and it is beginning with a reaction against Goethe. Goethe himself feels, perhaps, that the glorious objective world which he has created with his own words and example, must inevitably collapse when the idea of art has lost its predominance, and that new energetic spirits, arising out of the new epoch—like Northern barbarians bursting into Southern lands—will raze Goethe's civilised world to the ground, and form, in its place, a kingdom of the most primitive subjectivism."

And Heine *rejoices* that new forces, like Northern barbarians, will burst into the world and on its ruins create a "kingdom of the most primitive subjectivism".

How does the proletariat react to this conception? The proletariat is the keenest, most determined and pitiless critic of capitalism, the force which destroys capitalism. It can never come to terms with capitalist reality. But its struggle is not an expression of despair: it does not seek a way out by unleashing anti-social, destructive forces. To capitalism, it opposes its own positive and *creative world outlook*. It does not bow down in submission before the world, but accepts it as a problem to be tackled, for the working class is a tremendous human force which is superior to anything that has preceded it.

Heine, together with the romanticists, fought against the objectivism of classicism. But romanticism, with its rejection of victory in the world of reality, turned more and more towards the other world until it embraced Catholicism. Heine, on the other hand, especially the young Heine, regarded his subjectivism as something which amounted to social activity. On February 28, 1830, he wrote to Varnhagen von Ense:

"I am however convinced that with the death of 'the era of art' comes the end of the Goethe epoch as well. Only this era of aesthetics and philosophising, which has given pride of place to art, has been favourable for Goethe's ascendency; the era of inspiration and action has no need of him."

He considered that the "era of inspiration and action" had descended upon the German-speaking countries. This was the purest of illusions. The "inspiration" of the German intelligentsia came to the boil and began to cool down precisely because they were unable to give it practical application. The real revolutionary forces grew outside the German national liberation and liberal movement. Was Heine aware of this? Later, in 1842, in a letter to Laube, he repeated the demand for action and emphasised its social significance:

"We must never hide our political sympathies and our social antipathies: we must call evil by its true name, and must unconditionally defend what is good."

Heine met Lassalle in 1845 when he himself hardly felt "inspiration" any longer; and yet he was enchanted by this young man—this man of integrity who radiated active energy. But if this businesslike energy had not infused itself into the proletarian movement, then Lassalle would simply have become a famous lawyer or professor, perhaps a millionaire. Heine, at the end of his life, saw very well the mood of capitalisation among certain "businesslike people", and yet he never realised the social significance behind Lassalle's activity.

In 1843, in Paris, Heine became acquainted with Marx; Heine knew many Communists personally and spoke about them with profound respect:

"The leaders of the German Communist Party, who are all more or less underground, and the strongest of whom have emerged from the school of Hegel, are all great thinkers and without doubt possess the most capable minds and most energetic personalities in Germany. These doctors of revolution and the determined implacable young men who are their followers are the only people in Germany who are masters of their lives; the future belongs to them."

Heine saw the development of revolutionary forces within capitalism. As early as 1833 he had understood the revolutionary significance of Hegel's dialectics. But he was never able to grasp the historical and creative role of the proletariat. Heine had only a very general and vague idea—a premonition rather than knowledge—about something which, for Marx and Engels, was perfectly clear. He never succeeded in grasping the essence of Marxism and in feeling firm ground under his feet. Neither did he ever realise that, when it serves the interests not of a group of exploiters but of the working class, objectivism, which he was fighting against, acquires features linking it with subjectivism on a higher plane, which results in the highest form of freedom of the individual. It seemed to Heine that proletarian collectivism would threaten the freedom of the individuality. In the revolutionary proletariat he still saw the destroyers of machines, and feared the appearance of "sinister fellows who, like rats, will leap from the cellars of the existing regime"; he feared that refined culture would be destroyed, and art and talent everywhere would be dragged down to the same low level. This explains Heine's uncertainty in his approach to revolutionary consciousness.

Again and again in Heine we come across this question: is revolution the right path to take? He spoke about the great exploits of the French revolutionaries, but admitted that he would not have liked to have been alive at that time, or have been one of them. Whenever he recalled his meeting with Weitling—whom, for all his faults, Marx considered a precursor of proletarian thinking—he confessed that he found it difficult to face him and that he was pursued by the sound of chains which seemed to accompany this life-long gaol-bird.

This characteristic feature of Heine should be shown from yet another angle. In his pamphlet *Lüdwig Börne,* he wrote:

"When he discusses Goethe, just as when he discusses other writers, Börne reveals his Nazarene narrow-mindedness. I say 'Nazarene' in order to avoid using the expression 'Judean' or 'Christian', although both mean the same to me, and I use both in the sense not of religious belief but of nature. 'Judean' and 'Christian' are words which are related in meaning and are opposed to 'Hellene', which also signifies not a definite race of people but a specific spiritual way of thought and outlook, which is both instinctive and inculcated. By this I mean that people are divided into Judeans and Hellenes—into people with an ascetic, gloomy and anti-artistic outlook, and people who are essentially happy, flourishing, proud and realistic. Börne was a complete Nazarene; his dislike for Goethe stemmed straight from his Nazarene soul; a direct result, too, is his latest political exaltation which is based on the kind of rigid asceticism and thirst for martyrdom, which are so frequently observed among republicans and are known as republican virtues. . . ."

The "Hellene" is master of the idea, but the idea is master of the "Nazarene".

The "Nazarene" acquires a fanatical, sectarian character since he is limited by the idea which enslaves him. From the point of view of the followers of a definite idea such a person is completely congruous; but you will not find any aesthetic freedom of the individual in him.

With the "Hellene" it is quite different. To be master of an idea is for him the same as being master of a slave girl—he can dismiss it or summon it at will; he is the master and it is his toy; and the more someone is master of ideas, the richer and fuller is his personality and the more varied is his outlook.

As you see, Heine recoils from the thought that it is possible for a person not to be enslaved by an idea and yet not treat it as his plaything, that a *man can be imbued with an idea which makes him free and spiritually rich.* This happens when the idea belongs to the leading class, and the person who is a member of this class, finds, in the fruition of this idea, the fruition of his social significance.

I fully understand that the problems which are linked with the abolition of the contradiction between man as a fully-fledged representative of his class and man as a separate individual, do not, even now, lend themselves easily to solution. But I maintain that the genuine proletarian society will embody to the full this trend of development, which has already established itself to a significant degree here. The petty bourgeois, especially the brilliant and gifted among them, find it difficult to come to terms with this; and since we are witnesses of the conflict between society and the petty-bourgeois individualists even now, then you can imagine with what bitterness Heine—an extraordinarily original, precisely in the petty-bourgeois sense of the word, person—reacted to such a conflict in the ghastly conditions of the Germany of his time.

Had Heine lived in another era, he could have become an aesthete and a gourmand, and could have established for himself the real ideal of his existence: being "master of the idea", to enjoy life and live it out "under a lucky star". But the times in which he lived were terrible, and Heine the "Hellene" *was forced* to take up arms against his environment—he was so possessed by the idea! Although he was lightly armed, he went out again and again to battle—like David going out against Goliath with a sling.

His basic weapons were his wit and his consummate laughter. His laughter won him a moral victory; with it he showed that the vanguard of the new, rising class was already superior, intellectually and socially, to the old society, although it had as yet few forces for a material victory. Such laughter easily becomes laughter through tears, the laughter of bitter irony. It is nonetheless a form of self-defence against an enemy who is superior in physical strength.

In Heine's time the forces of reaction were sufficiently strong to inflict heavy blows; this is why his laughter often becomes "gallows humour"; "the world is a thoroughly disgusting place, particularly in its social aspects; it is impossible to conquer it; stupidity triumphs, and although we cannot reconcile ourselves to it, we have not the strength to vanquish it. So let us then laugh at this repulsive world."

When, in the old days in England, criminals used to be led to the gallows, they considered it especially chic to make salty jokes and mock at the judges and executioners, just to show they were not afraid. This helped to make their final journey more bearable but it still did not prevent them from being hanged by the executioners, rather than hanging the executioners. In social satire such "gallows humour", as I have already said, has greater significance; here it not only shows the moral superiority of the person who is laughing, it not only upholds his courage in a hopeless situation, but it also has the effect of calling on other people to continue the fight. All the same, it leads, not to victory, but only to a substitute for victory; this is why there is always the danger that this laughter will turn into mere guffawing and harm the person who uses it; if one is able to rid oneself of the tragic situation through mockery and carry on living by somehow managing to alleviate life's conflicts, then one will be deprived of the last incentive for a real struggle.

It is possible, from all this, to get some idea of the unusual fluidity of Heine's *Weltanschauung*—a fluidity which is emphasised in the recently published work *Heinrich Heine* by the French critic

Hennequin. I should like to quote the following sentences where the extraordinary way in which Heine is able to pass from one mood to another is defined elegantly and precisely:

"The characteristic feature of his personality is revealed in the extreme variability of his nature which forces him to take all the consecutive steps in passing from one mood to another—from joy to irony, from irony to despair, from melancholy to humour, from gaiety to gravity, from admiration to scorn. Characteristic of Heine were the swift changes, the sudden movements of his soul which contraposed and intermingled both gaiety and gloom. . . .

"It appears that Heine could experience only one feeling which became the prevailing one and which constantly tried to atrophy the rest: every excitement evoked by memory and taken up by feeling can be traced back along a mysterious path to the same spiritual source which leads, in the final analysis, to an unbroken sad thoughtfulness."

Verdruss* came more and more to the fore. And it finally reached the point where, whatever chord of Heine's nature was struck, the note of pensive sadness would ring out above all else.

And so by way of a sparkling humour, by way of easy triumphs in the sphere of wit, by way of playing with images, Heine came to pessimism—to a pessimistic world feeling if not to a pessimistic world outlook.

The brilliant composer Scriabin was, like many artists of this difficult period, also easily carried away by the extraordinary happiness to be found in playing freely with musical images; this romantic playing with images, he would set against depressing reality. At one time Scriabin even wondered whether

---

* Depression (German).—*Tr.*

it was not possible to interpret the world as being created by a god who is an artist.

Heine also wondered about this. In *The Book Le Grand* he wrote:

". . . the world is so nicely confused; it is the dream of a wine-drunken god who has taken French leave of the carousing divine assembly and laid himself down to sleep on a lonely star and does not know that he also creates everything he dreams—and the dream images often take madly checkered forms, and often harmoniously reasonable ones—the Iliad, Plato, the battle of Marathon, Moses, the Medicean Venus, the Cathedral of Strasbourg, the French Revolution, Hegel, the steamboat, etc., are a few good ideas in this creative divine dream. . . ."

Such are the extraordinary contortions this tremendous brain went through—all because he lacked a real social perspective and will. The social will of an individualist is equal to nothing. But in the realm of humour this superb mind was the victor. For him, wit acquired a unique significance, for it was the only oasis where he could still breathe freely. His laughter became unusually profound and socially significant precisely because it was not mere derisive guffawing, but was completely shrouded in black mourning. It was a humour which was fully aware that it stood opposed to the triumph of absurdity.

We know that Marx reacted to Heine very positively; he understood the conditions in which Heine found himself; he understood Heine's weaknesses, which he attributed to his loneliness. I shall remind you only of one episode. When Wilhelm Liebknecht told Marx that he had refused to see Heine in Paris after he had heard that Heine was receiving a pension from Louis Philippe and Guizot, Marx became very angry with him, gave him a good dressing-down, and said that only a petty-bourgeois philistine could reason in such a way, and that Liebknecht was only punishing himself with such moralising by depriving himself of a conversation with one of his wisest contemporaries. Marx was no pedant—he never attacked this poet and individualist with petty reproaches, never denied him completely by saying that many of Heine's features contradicted his basic principles. And Marx, of course, was right. With all his deviations and aberrations, Heine, as a satirist, as a thinker, as a journalist and as a prolific letter-writer, was Marx's brilliant ally—like the cavalry which the Roman legions transferred from the enemy into their own ranks although they did not fully rely on it: it was not very reliable, but very dashing and effective.

This behest of Marx's which he left behind in his talk with Liebknecht helps us to realise the contribution which a genius like Heine could make to the cause of revolution.

Heine gave us a huge arsenal of separate arguments and scattered victorious characteristics; he showed us in virtuoso-like fashion the development of German social thought. He assimilated the element of revolution with great perception, and became, at times, its brilliant representative, despite the fact that sometimes he tottered on the brink of an abyss of pessimism and empty laughter. And although he often talked about himself as though he were a clown, he was nonetheless an outstanding fighter who, from time to time, rendered inestimable service not only to the 1848 revolution but also to our revolution.

Pushkin wrote the following lines about himself:

My name will long be honoured by my people
Whose noble thoughts my lyrics have inflamed;
In this cruel age, to freedom have I sung
And mercy for the fallen have proclaimed.
God's will, O Muse, ordains that you obey—

Offence you must not fear, nor seek reward,
May praise and insult always leave you cold,
And stupid fools should ever be ignored.

M. Gerschenzon has tried to show that this poem
has an ironic meaning and that Pushkin was laughing at the people who imagined that the poet was
fighting for them. But Pushkin was laughing only
at such people as Gerschenzon, whom he called
"fools". As a parallel to Pushkin's *Memorial*, I shall
read you Heine's *Enfant Perdu*; these lines show the
tremendous significance he attributed to the social
aspect of his poetic activity:

Verlorner Posten in dem Freiheitskriege,
Hielt ich seit dreißig Jahren treulich aus.
Ich kämpfe ohne Hoffnung, daß ich siege,
Ich wußte, nie komm' ich gesund nach Haus.

Ich wachte Tag und Nacht—Ich konnt' nich
                         schlafen,
Wie in dem Lagerzelt der Freunde Schar—
(Auch hielt das laute Schnarchen dieser Braven
Mich wach, wenn ich ein bißchen schlummrig war.)

In jenen Nächten hat Langweil' ergriffen
Mich oft, auch Furcht (nur Narren fürchten
                         nichts)—
Sie zu verscheuchen, hab' ich dann gepfiffen
Die frechen Reime eines Spottgedichts.

Ja, wachsam stand ich, das Gewehr im Arme,
Und nahte irgendein verdächt'ger Gauch,
So schoß ich gut und jagt' ihm eine warme,
Brühwarme Kugel in den schnöden Bauch.

Mitunter freilich mocht'es sich ereignen,
Daß solch ein schlechter Gauch gleichfalls sehr gut

Zu schießen wußte—ach, ich kann's nicht leugnen—
Die Wunden klaffen—es verströmt mein Blut.

Ein Posten ist vakant!—Die Wunden klaffen—
Der eine fällt, die andern rücken nach—
Doch fall' ich unbesiegt, und meine Waffen
Sind nicht gebrochen—nur mein Herze brach.

This glorious poem shows how Heine—for all the variety of his lyrics and the tremendous place which a free attitude to his surroundings and his inner world occupied in his work—evaluated his social role; it shows the significance which he attached himself as a political poet. And we have the right to say that, in praising Heine as one of the most outstanding poets of inner freedom, we are introducing him into the pantheon of the great precursors of the genuine revolution—the proletarian revolution which we have the great honour and fortune to be accomplishing.

1931

RICHARD WAGNER

(On the 50th Anniversary of His Death)

IN connection with the 50th anniversary of his death the problem of Richard Wagner arises again and again to confront mankind.

However, it is now quite clear that this problem can by no means be solved from the point of view of "contemporary mankind", for no such integral contemporary mankind exists. The question must be solved anew, since it concerns a re-evaluation of Wagner from the point of view of a victorious proletariat and the new socialist culture it is creating.

We shall try in this brief account to summarise our attitude towards this composer of rare and complex genius.

I

We speak often and justly of the hypnotising, enchanting power of Wagner's music.

No other composer before Wagner had burst upon the listeners' perception with such a cascade of sound, with such a broad river of harmony, with such poignant melodies. Wagner himself called his music an *endless melody*. This may be understood not only in the direct sense, i.e., in the sense of a continuously unrolling musical canvas, but in the sense that Wagner's music seems to create an invisible magnetic field that extends throughout the Universe, and penetrates to the very soul of the listener.

The thunder and clashing of his cymbals, his colossal ensembles, his unisons, which catch one up and carry one off—the entire well-planned whirlwind of sound is staggering. However, Wagner is nearly as powerful when he wants to be winning, when he creeps up to our subconscious unawares. Then he uses the most delicate of skeleton keys to make his way into the very depths of the human heart.

When they say that Wagner was, first and foremost, a man of iron will, that he craved for power above all, one cannot but agree. Indeed, music to him is like an assembly of spirits which he marshals and sends marching forward, to win millions of human souls for him.

However, Wagner's music is not simply organised sound. It is not even emotions translated into sound. Nietzsche reproached Wagner for being, in all actuality, not a musician, but a mime, a man of the theatre. This desire to conquer his audience, to impress his own ideas upon it, to be its teacher, its leader, its prophet, was expressed through his active use of histrionics.

Wagner's histrionic talent was truly magical. Indeed, a Wagnerian symphony is magnificent in itself in a concert performance, but it acquires its true significance only on the stage. I would like to note, however, that the stage perhaps cannot yet meet the demands Wagner placed upon it.

Thus, Tolstoi, when he wanted to ridicule the various conventions of the opera, speaks seemingly good-naturedly of the brightly painted men in cardboard armour who, instead of speaking, open their mouths wide and sing, of the make-believe dragons and suchlike attributes of the cheap puppet comedy.

Tolstoi is obviously wrong, since he is attempting to attack the conventionality of the theatre in general. It is still an open question as to what is more normal for a person experiencing great exultation, for an outstanding person caught up in great events—to speak, and perhaps lisp and stammer to boot, or to sing, to limp and stumble, as the majority of the petty bourgeois do in real life, or to dance. But Tolstoi is undoubtedly right when he points out the artistic squalor of the contemporary operatic stage as compared to Wagner's grandiose ideas and the grandiose nature of his music.

However, the fact remains that Wagner's music is unimaginable without action and words, which are at one with it.

It was under Wagner's influence that Nietzsche wrote of the two sources of theatrics: its Dionysian origin and its Apollonian origin. The music itself, the churning forces and passions, the dynamics and pathos is Dionysius. Then blue mists seem to rise from this churning; they condense into clouds and, finally, into human images that are essentially Apollonian. The musical idea is expressed in human shapes, emotions, thoughts, actions, words, relationships, fates, victories and defeats. Thus, tragedy and the theatre is born. Perhaps the most ideal listener and viewer of Wagner's works is one who is quite familiar with the libretto and had perhaps caught two or three hints of Wagner's vision in the mediocre production and can, by closing his eyes, truly see all the refined Wagnerian images, which arise in orderly processions to the sound of an orchestra, magnificent in its abundance and diverse in its flow, including the human voice as well.

II

Wagner's images are generalities, they are myth-images. Tannhäuser in Venus's sparkling cave, tearing himself away in anguish from the sweet embraces of the goddess; a young girl accused of a terrible crime is rescued at the last moment by a saintly knight who comes sailing up on a giant swan; the Rhine maidens who dart about, singing, like golden fish in the glittering depths of a metaphysical river; the winged Valkyries who appear amidst thunder and lightning with their wild cry of "Ho-yo-to-ho" as they fly on their aerial steeds; the dimming light of the world and the mournful one-eyed giant god who cannot avert death from himself and his own; love that rends the human heart with such force that it slips unobtrusively into death and makes death like unto itself; the dying, whose eyes are full of grief and mystical joy; wounded Amfortas, whose festering wound does not heal, and the shining Holy Grail which cures all ills, etc., etc. Hundreds of paintings have been based on Wagner's themes and hundreds more may be so.

But Wagner is not only a musician and an actor (which is cause enough to produce the necessary prerequisites for creating a true musical theatre). Wagner is a great thinker besides. He is not concerned with a given situation, or with a given personage as such. He wants to reveal the true essence of life through his various personages and their relationships. In his desire to be a prophet he could not confine himself to merely exciting the audience by depicting various events. He wants to use these events to capture a person's mind, to wrench him from the mundane and cast him upwards to a great height from which the true meaning of existence will reveal itself to him.

That is why words play such a great, though subordinate, part in Wagner's works. The words define and clarify the music. Wagner the poet, and a great poet at that, is the indispensable colleague and helper of Wagner the composer.

Such, in general outline, is Wagner the artist. He is uncommonly interesting and versatile, integral for all his versatility, and powerful.

He is difficult to understand. He demands concentration and work. There is good reason why

Nietzsche said he was bathed in sweat after listening to a Wagnerian opera. Listening to Wagner for light entertainment before supper is in the worst possible taste, it is barbarous, the very thought of it used to throw Wagner into a rage.

At the same time, Nietzsche's reproaches still hold true to a great extent. He said that the overall structure of Wagner's works is overloaded and baroque-heavy, that the music is over-wrought, extremely ecstatic, it violates our consciousness and turns our soul inside-out, as it were.

III

Every genius is always the result and the reflection of some deep social change. What social phenomenon produced such a giant as Richard Wagner?

Richard Wagner began his career in the 1830s. He created his music during a time immediately preceding the events of 1848 which could not have but influenced it. Later, we see a change in Wagner's outlook, a change in his convictions. He became a different man entirely.

The great social phenomena which were reflected in Wagner's works were, first, the rise and development of democracy in Germany and subsequently, the downfall of the democratic movement. He dreamed of complete and perfect democracy, a democracy which would develop into a classless society, into socialism. His outlook was roughly similar to Chernyshevsky's in Russia 10 or 20 years later.

Lenin once said that people of different social groups and strata advance towards a proletarian revolution along different roads.

Wagner's theoretical works, especially his book *Art and Revolution*, cast a comprehensive light on the "first" Wagner of yore. Wagner did not proceed from revolution to art, but from art to revolution. That was good. That meant he advanced towards the revolution, driven on by the demands of his talent and his craft.

Wagner looked with horror upon what the bourgeoisie was doing to the theatre. The theatre was becoming a place of light entertainment, the theatre was becoming a commercial enterprise. This aroused a feeling of repulsion in Wagner. Recall that from the very start he was a man of iron will, that he dreamed of becoming a prophet and, by prophesying through art, of ruling his century. He wanted to be the teacher of his time, he believed that the great artist could be a teacher of his time. He believed that the hour had struck for such a teacher to realise his mission, for the artist to become a teacher not by chance, but consciously. Thus, the theatre, too, must become the new temple. It was here, in the theatre, that the people were to create their new myths, i.e., to embody their convictions and their goals in living images, to steel themselves for battle, celebrate their victories and learn to bear any temporary defeats courageously. According to Wagner, the creative artist was the chief element in the theatre. However, all the performers had to be inspired with profound realisation of the serious nature of art. The theatre was not a symbol of frivolity, thoughtlessness and a good time. The theatre is, in the fullest sense, the focus of the people's conscious life, the place in which all that is best that they possess turns into the pure metal of imagery and inversely influences them, organising their forces.

Such was Wagner's unusually high conception of the theatre.

The opera *Rienzi* was written under the strong influence of these ideas. Wagner was still quite abstract and sought to express his ideas in a rather generalised way. *Tannhäuser* and *Lohengrin* do not immediately reveal their progressive essence. Nevertheless, despite the marked obscurity of these operas, they have a powerful effect upon us to this day.

Wagner then envisaged a gigantic work. He took as his theme the basic Ancient Germanic myth, the Nibelungs. However, his approach contradicted the meaning imparted to it by the intellectuals of yore who had created the myth. The myth apparently has its roots in the very depth of man's primitive beliefs. It has as its basis the fate of the Sun, with its constant eclipses and resurrection. If you describe this fate, beginning with the birth of the Sun and ending with its death (from morning to night, or from spring to winter), you will achieve the prototype of a pessimistic world. However, if you do the opposite, i.e., begin with a description of the Sun's demise and end with its resurrection (the appearance of a victorious son, of a shining hero, victory over death), then you will have an optimistic concept of life in general, of the philosophy of existence.

Originally, Wagner planned his tetralogy in an optimistic vein. The main concepts which were set in opposition to each other, were a fatal myth, a myth in which all depended on fate, even the gods themselves, and the gradual development of a free individual, born of free love, beyond the pale of legalised matrimony (Siegmund and Sieglinde), developing under special conditions that forge his independent will. This independent individual, governed only by his conscience, becomes the screw with which the fate of the world can be turned. It is he who will finally break the iron chain of fate, who will return youth, joy and freedom to life.

But Wagner lived in a capitalist world and, at that revolutionary time, he hated the bourgeoisie which was beginning to appropriate the world at an ever-increasing pace. He believed gold was poison. In this respect his views coincided with those Marx noted and praised in several poets of antiquity, in Shakespeare and others. Fate, first and foremost, is a common craving for gold, enslavement by greed. Siegfried's freedom, first and foremost, is the fact that he rises above gold, above greed. That is why he acquires not only the features of an individual, free in the sense of anarchy, but the features of a hero throwing off the yoke of capital.

IV

In criticising Stirner, Engels notes in passing that the fact that Raphael was able to fully develop his talents depended on the social conditions of his epoch. This observation holds true in the case of any artistic genius, including Wagner as well. Wagner was not fated to develop his talent along the course he originally embarked on. He carried within him from the very beginning the soul of a petty bourgeois, but as a result of the fiery breath of revolution he rose to a great height, and if this favourable revolutionary summer had continued, most probably all the fruit that had begun to grow on the branches of this mighty tree would have fully ripened. Under the influence of the revolution, Wagner would probably have written mainly songs of struggle and victory, songs glorifying life in this struggle, blessing Nature and man, for a revolutionary is an optimist: a revolutionary is in love with Nature, man and life; a revolutionary is he who wishes and is able to change the world, i.e., to complete it in a humane way, to transform this would-be arena of happiness into a true arena of happiness. But this was not to be done by Wagner. Wagner went over to the side of reaction.

For thirteen years he lived in exile. For thirteen years he vacillated, becoming, however, ever more gloomy. The revolution lay on the ground with broken wings. The titans, who were spiritually so far above Wagner, did not despair; they had realised that it was not the petty bourgeoisie, but the proletariat that would one day triumph. They had already sensed wherein Siegfried had been born. They had already heard him forging the sword of his future vengeance in the growing factories; they knew that he had discovered the key to the "birds' songs", the prophetic songs of the laws of social order and the means of reviving life.

Such were Marx and Engels, but Wagner was not of their kind.

However, Wagner was, at the same time, a man of action; he was a man with an unquenchable thirst for glory, power, influence and, finally, the wealth and honour that went with them. Exonerating himself in every possible way, growing old and changing inwardly, going through a deep molecular process of degeneration, as it were, Wagner advanced along his new, false way. There was much disgrace in store for him along this false way. The triumphant big bourgeoisie was creating a mighty Prussia with its capital and army. It was advancing towards victory over France, towards the years of capitalisation, towards the efflorescence of militaristic imperialism, towards all the pompous triumphs of Wilhelm's reign. And Wagner became a nationalist. He began writing brassy marches in honour of the conquerors, and the heavy form his music took had its beginnings in the very same pompousness of triumphant capital which left its heavy stamp on many Berlin streets and squares as well.

Proceeding along this course, Wagner came to a full conciliation with the most reactionary cultural pole—orthodox Catholicism. If this plunged Nietzsche into despair and he returned again to his criticism of Wagner, trying to explain the reasons for his former idol's fall, Marx, if I am not mistaken, merely expressed a single casual phrase in regard to the Bayreuth Festival plays. "A stupid celebration in honour of a court musician."

V

Wagner became a renegade. This reneging was the turning point in his development, and was caused by the crisis in social development. Wagner could not fully develop his talents under the existing social conditions. The Wagner of the second period, this man who gave the world such great masterpieces, was now crippled—a poisoned Siegfried.

But there are different kinds of renegades. There are happy-go-lucky, merry renegades. They gleefully don the gilded livery of their new master.

No, Wagner, was not one of them. Having gone over into the service of the bourgeoisie, having had a good look at the new world from his new standpoint, he shuddered inwardly.

Yes, the bourgeoisie had won. But why then was its favourite philosopher, Arthur Schopenhauer, a pessimist? Why then did Hegel, who stood on the threshold of the bourgeois epoch, put so much effort into proving that Prussian bourgeois reality was quite in keeping with reason, while Schopenhauer, who had cursed Hegel most scornfully, tried to prove that the world in general was a thing most absolute in its unreasonableness? This can be explained by the fact that the most alert members of the bourgeoisie sensed the worm that was eating at its heart.

Greed was the bourgeoisie's guiding principle, greed of commerce, greed of accumulation. Its principle was universal competition and a trampling of rivals, expansion and stockpiling billions upon billions.

Schopenhauer's metaphysical "will" is but a scale model of the capitalist spirit. According to Schopenhauer, this will can never be satisfied. It knows neither happiness nor respite. It is either tormented by greed or tormented by boredom. It needs soul-searing action, it craves tense, painful striving to keep it from falling into an apathetic state, so alien to its nature, from languishing in a stupor.

But, according to Schopenhauer, there is a way out of this horror. One can wrench free by destroying any and all human feelings one may have, by the Hindu striving for Nirvana, and in this, art, and especially music, is man's best helpmate. Music is an accurate reflection of the very essence of the world. When we fully perceive this reflection, we free ourselves of the essence itself. Art breaks the magic spell of the world. As we sink sweetly into art, we sink into death, into peace, released from existence, which is hell. Art is the redeemer.

Perhaps Wagner would have approached these conclusions himself, but Schopenhauer was there, and Wagner joined him.

What then did the world become to him? The world was undoubtedly doomed. This was undeniably a funeral procession heading to blackness. It was a procession full of mutual struggle, treachery, greed and crime. There were outstanding individuals, but they, too, were doomed. They could do nothing to avert the fatal events. However, only one who is enlightened by the wisdom of art could prepare for a solemn death, overcome existence and in majestic, though sorrowful reverie, dissolve into nothingness.

Wagner strives for such redemption. His tetralogy would no longer proceed from winter to spring. It would end with an eclipse, it would end with the death of the world. Free man had been unable to conquer. The forces of evil had triumphed. But they triumphed merely in fact, while only an awareness of fate, submission to it and the desire to escape it, thus escaping from life as well, triumphed in a moral, musical sense.

The opera *Tristan and Isolde* proclaims this still more mournfully and venomously. The poison is very sweet. Wagner offers us a phial of love and death, the focus of the entire opera. We have drained the cup of life and we are alive. Life is sweet. Love is the meaning of all life. It is full of the charm that only an artist can reveal to us. Only an artist can teach us how great the temptation of life is, how excessive and fascinating is the deceit which, like the Sun, shines in the ghostly world of existence. But the honest artist must also reveal that love is death, that all existence, like the vortex of a whirlpool, rushes towards destruction. The artist must not terrify us by such a prospect, but must make us bless it as a true deliverance.

Such is Wagner's Hindu, Christian, Asiatic artistic and musical moral sermon. Such is the black, destructive "prophecy" of the new Wagner. Moreover, he dots his "i's" when, in his old age, he descends, according to Nietzsche, to the foot of the Cross, and creates a variation on the Catholic mass in *Parcifal*.

The circle is complete. The revolutionary has become a reactionary. The rebellious petty bourgeois now kisses the slipper of the Pope, the keeper of order.

VI

What should our attitude be towards Wagner? Perhaps we should cast him aside, since he is a reactionary? Perhaps we should say: Only from here to here? And accept the first Wagner uncritically, forgetting how immature he was, how many admixtures there were? Or should we discard the second Wagner completely, forgetting the powerful music, the passionate emotions, the shining artistry of this genius, a prisoner of reaction?

None of this is right. We would never be forgiven if we did not know how to analyse, if we would have cast away the rich gold ore simply because, at first glance, it contained very few grains of gold. We would never have been forgiven if we had accepted at face value a piece of impure metal, corroded from within. Our analysis cannot manipulate masters and opuses as a whole. We must delve deeper. An understanding of Wagner from a socialist point of view is a very intricate affair. Woe to him who impoverishes the world by crossing out Wagner's name with a censor's pencil. Woe to him who would let this cunning magician, this talent tainted by an evil disease, into our camp and, as in Heine's famous poem, would let the plague-stricken titan press his lips against the face of young proletarian culture.

Beware! Quarantine! All baggage must be checked! We must see what is what! Not a shade of mechanicism! Chemical decomposition! The ability to point out how the contradictory has been interwoven: the ability of healthy organism to differentiate between the nourishing and the indifferent and harmful!

In this respect, and sometimes taking advantage of anniversaries, we must judge by the stern and piercing insight of the proletarian court the past and all the great creators of the treasures we have inherited.

Here we shall discover the most diverse relationships. We shall meet our great predecessors and teachers of the past whom the immaturity of their epoch sometimes prevented from rising to complete understanding and who, with some minor changes, could be wholly and gloriously permitted to work with the living.

Here we can come upon imaginary giants whose greatness is either empty and puffed-up, or dependent upon their servitude to classes whose successes and interests were completely hostile to the development of mankind. The imaginary glory of such celebrities will be torn away by the stern and just analysis of history.

But more often than not we come upon mixed-up giants such as Wagner, where the positive and the negative are closely intertwined and seem to have entered into a chemical combination.

In this instance the task is most difficult. It is quite easy to make a mistake one way or another. The task calls for a knowledge of the subject, it calls for a knowledge of history and culture and the specific nature of the field in which a given master worked.

I have no intention of attempting such an analysis here. This calls for the efforts of a specialist. I simply want to note some of the more obvious pros and cons of the great German musician.

First of all, there is the sound of Wagner's music, the intensity, the depth, courage, variety, passion, psychological and acoustical charm of his musical texture. Here one can learn much from Wagner. We will rarely find such intensity and generosity, such depth and density of the musical stream in pre-Wagnerian music. And we will rarely find such integrity, such unity, encompassing vast musical worlds, we will rarely find musical phrases and chords that have been so fully thought out and emotionally tested in post-Wagnerian music. Richard Strauss, for instance, produces a greater festive virtuosity than Wagner; Gustav Mahler, for instance, produces more intricate chords and orchestral colours. But one has the impression that the peak of *pathétique* music has been passed. It is as if these musicians are merely imitating reality.

Wagner's music is shrouded in a magnificent cloak. The cloaks of the outstanding composers of *pathétique* music after Wagner are more majestic still, but no longer does the goddess who found shelter beneath Wagner's cloak abide with them. Wagner has bequeathed this wealth, this seriousness, and, in the sense of musical ideas, this meaningfulness to future centuries.

Likewise, the combination of a philosopher-musician and a philosopher-poet, and a dramatist at that, has apparently made him the greatest proponent of the true union of music and literature. And we need this, too. We *will* need this very, very much.

Wagner could at times channel his exalted musical and dramatic force to serve ideas that were wrong and even harmful, thus making this great power poisonous, but he never demeaned it to become a reflection of the petty, he never debased it to the level of the trivial or the casual.

No matter if he depicted love or vicious hate, greed, power-madness, or a flight towards freedom, etc.—he portrayed them all in great, commanding images and raised them to such generalisations as to make the emotions he described all-meaningful. This ability to raise art, to raise the theatre to such great heights and artistic abstraction—but abstraction that is not emaciated, that encompasses the concrete, summing it up and making it understandable and significant—this is an ability that we, too, need, and we possess it in a very small measure, which can be proved, firstly, by the fact that our poets and composers have not yet been able to produce a major opera about our revolutionary passions, our world struggle.

1933

MARCEL PROUST

TOWARDS the end of the 19th century, the concept of the "French novel" became extraordinarily well defined. The French novel might, of course, treat of various subjects and might vary in quality, but, nevertheless, it had become a most precisely defined commodity. Whatever its quality, it retained a constant value on the literary market. The smallest editions ran to one thousand copies, the largest—into millions. All this was written by a whole series of talents, sometimes highly original, and published and sold by a whole series of merchants, sometimes quite remarkably unsuccessful. However, in the overwhelming majority of cases, the net result was the same little straw-coloured volume of about three hundred well-printed pages costing $3^1/_2$ pre-war francs—the so-called type Charpentier.

Publishers considered thinner or thicker volumes with evident repulsion. Two volumes they looked on as a personal insult. Selected and complete works were, naturally, broken up into volume-units of this same size.

* * *

When the young Romain Rolland, a revolutionary in every sense of the word, began, on the one hand, to publish his novels in the form of *cahiers* and, on the other, to drag out his *Jean-Christophe* over a dozen or more volumes, this was considered a freakish trick, evidence of the author's weakness in matters of composition and a sure sign that his work would not be a success.

It cannot be said that this revival of the long novel (*A la recherche du temps perdus*) was an immediate success. Nevertheless, there can be no denying that this novel, so incredibly serious in content, so colossally significant ("Not French at all," the critics exclaimed; "surely it can't be seriously regarded as literature?"), enjoyed sufficient popularity to demonstrate quite unmistakably to all and sundry that it established a dangerous literary precedent.

The well-known critic Paul Souday remarking on a long series of novels from the pen of a hitherto unknown writer, Marcel Proust, pointed out that, in this, Proust was following in the footsteps of Rolland. Let us hope Monsieur Souday will not be offended but, on the first appearance of Romain Rolland's work, he quite failed to grasp all its gigantic literary and cultural significance. On the other hand, it must be admitted that, even after reading only the first volume, he did have some kind of premonition of the significance of Proust's vast project.

French literary criticism had not yet anything like grasped the importance of Proust's colossal reminiscences, had not yet understood that their very "prolixity" was their essential characteristic and a condition of their appeal. However, through Monsieur Souday, it had already put the question: might not this be a new kind of literature? And is not this terrible fault, this "prolixity", in this particular case, something in the nature of a virtue? And might not Proust be a new kind of writer in the style of Rolland? And do not these two write for some new type of reader? The very fact that this kind of question was put at all is to Souday's credit, even if it was still all rather vague.

*   *   *

It is impossible to understand Proust's socio-literary character without going into certain aspects of his personality.

Proust was a member—let us say a passive member—of an extremely wealthy Jewish bourgeois family, closely connected with the Rothschilds.

Having become a chronic invalid at an early age he was constrained to lead a strange, almost entirely nocturnal existence. All his life he kept up with his social and literary acquaintances but, of course, in his own eccentric way. Literary and cultural pursuits occupied a great place in the sick man's life, but to no greater extent than the snobbish pursuits of the polite world.

Although Proust always remained a man of incredible, morbid sensitivity and more or less paralysed activity, the first part of his life is nevertheless by far the most fresh and immediate—above all because of his astonishingly strong reaction to "all the impressions of his earliest days", and to every note in the scales of feeling and of thought. As he approached forty, Proust felt that new impressions became less and less vivid. The present paled before his memories. These memories were distinguished by an extraordinary vitality: it was as though, after the abundant incoming wave of life which once, long ago, had come foaming inshore from the boundless sea of opportunity, there had followed another wave, this time an imaginary one, an exact repetition of the first wave of impressions, but, this time, already familiar to the senses, analysed through and through down to the last nuance, totally and exhaustively relived. This astonishing wave of memories which, of course, plays a great part in all creative writing is, in Proust's books, both overwhelming and tragic. Not only does he love his *Temps perdus*, he knows that for him they are not *"perdus"* at all, that he can roll them out at will again and again like great carpets, like shawls, that again and again he can finger over these torments and delights, these flights and falls.

Like the Covetous Knight he sits among the treasure-chests of his memories, and a pleasure very similar in type to that experienced by Pushkin's hero takes possession of his whole being. The treasure-house of his memories is in fact his *oeuvre*. Here, he is all-powerful. This is a world which he can bring to a stop, shuffle, dissect, so as to get to the bottom of its every detail, grossly magnify, put under a microscope, refashion as it seems good to him. Here he is a god, limited only by the very richness of this enchanted stream of memory.

This monstrous reworking of the first half of his life becomes the second half. Proust the writer is no longer living, he is writing. The music and light of the true wave of life have no importance for Proust in his later years. The important thing is this astonishing chewing the cud of the past which is going on in all his 77 stomachs and which constantly renews this past and seems to deepen its implications.

How could such an epopee be anything but rambling? It is as though Proust had suddenly said to his contemporaries: "I shall lie back—artistically, comfortably, freely, in a vast brocade dressing gown on a vast velvet sofa—and remember my life in the gently rotating convolutions of a mild sedative; I shall not drink off my life as a man tosses off a glass of water, I shall savour it with the concentrated attention one accords the complex bouquet of a uniquely rich wine."

Such was the character of Proust the author from the point of view of form. Such was the basic determinant of his famous lyrical epic.

* * *

Gradually, the incomparable refinement of Proust's gift became evident. A respectful and, as it were, ecstatically compassionate veneration replaced the original bewilderment of the critics.

Let us then take a closer look at Proust's literary, philosophical, social and moral message; at what he teaches and whither he is going.

Convinced Proustians will, of course, shrug their shoulders over such questions: "He teaches nothing, leads nowhere and nothing like that is of the least interest to him. Really, these Marxists!"

To which we reply: "He both leads and teaches, to some extent even deliberately. Really, these foxy formalists!"

* * *

What we have just been trying to put into words—what constitutes the charm, the power, the essence and the principle of the Proustian school—is the culture of memory. More than once the most gifted representatives of various literatures have asserted the immensely close relationship between art and memory (particularly interesting in this respect are Hoffmann and Kleist), and have found support among the theoreticians. Here, it is possible to distinguish two features. The first is the artist's urge to conquer time, to command the moment: "Abide, you are so fair!" Or, more broadly speaking: "You are meaningful, you are worthy of a life outside Heraclitus's river where nothing remains equal to itself for so much as one moment, you are worthy to be fished out of this river by the divine hand of art and to be set apart in another world—the world of immutable aesthetic values." The second feature is the desire to refashion reality with the aid of art, or, as the saying goes, to create a new world.

To be gifted with excellent taste, to select those events from the general stream which are worthy of immortality and to have the ability to transform the particular and temporal into the general and eternal

—such is the essence of art (a definition close to that offered by Hegel). Art is not only the perpetuation of the object found in reality and afterwards, perhaps, stylised; it is also an act of creation. This is not the place to go into the complicated interrelationship of artistic realism and artistic imagination. We will simply say that, in our opinion, artistic imagination is a derivative of the artist's experience of reality, and is indeed the key factor to that refashioning to which reality must be subjected if it is to achieve immortality in the eyes of the author.

Naturally, there is more than one type of artist. In the correspondence between Goethe and Schiller it became clear how important is the division between those who go from the reality to the generalisation, and those who begin with generalisations and seek to breathe real life into them.

Of course, in Proust's work, imagination, stylisation and, occasionally, pure invention do play a large part. Nevertheless he is, on the whole, a realist.

As we have already said, the charm and the very essence of his creative act is memory.

Like every other element of man's psychological make-up, memory is a live and slippery business. Even in the sphere of scholarship, particularly in history, this brings us face to face with a great number of most interesting problems. Leaving these aside for the moment, let us take something more or less objective as our point of departure: the evidence of an eyewitness, a life history compiled from memory for a court deposition.

Everybody knows that the evidence of an eyewitness, a life history compiled for a court deposition, or any other kind of document are misleading and inclined to be subjective. For any work of history with pretensions to the "establishment of definitive truth", dependable reminiscences are an essential foundation; for instance, certain historical memoirs are only of value from this point of view if they are written by an unbiassed witness while the events are still fresh in his memory. In this field, scholarship demands that a comparison should be made with other eyewitness accounts and, from time to time, we are afflicted by the diabolically sceptical assumption that, even by comparing evidence and even on the basis of documentary material, it is still not possible to reconstruct what really happened, but only to give an approximate portrayal of it.

Literary reminiscences are something quite different. They can afford to brush aside the scholarly sediment of the memorial genre and to associate themselves with that wide stratum of writing which Goethe so felicitously defined as *Dichtung und Wahrheit.*

The title of this, the greatest book of organised reminiscences which, thanks to Goethe, humanity possesses, has been the subject of some argument. It has been maintained that the word *Dichtung* in the title meant all that part of the book in which the author was writing about his work, whereas *Wahrheit* covered that devoted to a straightforward account of events. But this is not altogether so. Goethe does not deny that in his memoirs his creative life has been given a specific interpretation or that he is always accurate in his handling of facts because, very often, the inner logic and the meaning behind his reminiscences were more important to him than the effort to reconstruct the exact truth through the misty patches of memory. That was how that great work which might also have borne the title *A la recherche du temps perdus* come into being.

It is hardly necessary to say that the lengthy literary reminiscences of Marcel Proust which really were published under that title cannot compare with Goethe's classic edifice, either in content or in method and technique.

Proust is an impressionist, Proust loves his "living ego" which is not particularly whole and well constructed in itself but, on the contrary, shifting, capricious and occasionally morbid. This is why, for Proust, the whole, finished structure only has meaning in so far as it brings order to a series of isolated moments, or, occasionally, to whole systems of moments, but it has no aim in itself.

Proust is dead. His reminiscences were finished but have not all been printed. We are still not in a position to survey the whole structure of which we have been speaking. However, it is already possible to forecast with the utmost confidence that Proust's memoirs will astonish by the palpitating richness of their content rather than by any general conclusion to which they may lead.

This is not to say that Proust's memoirs are formless, are nothing but a great, gleaming heap of exceptionally beautiful things. No! In the first place, this remarkable artist sought to give the whole thing a certain unity of style, to make us feel that the whole enormous work is nevertheless a portrayal of "live personalities". In the second, he introduced a certain system of subdividing the whole into large parts—true, not altogether successfully from the artistic point of view. This point, however, is the last calculated to retain our attention here.

* * *

For Proust, in his life as in his philosophy, the most important thing is the human personality and, above all, his own personality.

Life is, first and foremost, *my* life.

In just the same way, objective social life, any objective life, the life of the whole world—is a kind of interweaving of "my lives". As a disciple of Bergson, an allegiance which he has never finally thought out in his own mind (Proust, although possessed of a formidable philosophic talent, is not a philosopher), the author sees life as a splendid rapestry woven from subjective lives combining to form an eternal and, taken by and large, harmonious whole. For him, existence has a somewhat Leibnitzian flavour. Of course, Proust's connection with Leibnitz is by way of Descartes and Pascal, but this makes little or no difference. What we have here is the exquisite, highly rationalist and extremely sensual, realistic subjectivism of the 17th century, a refined version of which we find in Frenchmen of a later age—particularly in Henri Bergson. From the very outset, Marcel Proust approaches his quest for lost time not in order to recreate an epoch (that is a secondary aim for him) but in order to relive his life once again on a particularly profound and savourous level and, at the same time, so to speak, to take the reader along with him; therefore, if we are to grasp the whole meaning of this work, the question of the basic bearer of the whole process, of the personality and, in particular, of "my personality", becomes one of the first importance.

Let it be noted here and now that Proust, although, as an intellectualist, he was far from foreign to problems of cognition, did not make such problems the object of his work and, on the whole, they remain in the background. The foreground is given over to the *pleasure* afforded by the creative act of art, that is to the pleasure of this new, artistically reworked, second experience of life, and to the pleasure of the work itself which, in its turn, is undertaken so as to resurrect the past in all its freshness and fullness, so as to make sense of it aesthetically—a process of tasting and trying by the mind and the senses.

This is why Proust's favourite aspect of his own wonderful books is a kind of cinematograph of his own memories. Here, Proust is without equal. Lying in bed, pen in hand, he really does surrender himself to a kind of creative cinematographic process which appeals equally powerfully to the eye, the ear, the intellect and the emotions. He plays the part of himself and this film, *My Life*, is produced with unheard-of lavishness, profundity and love. Such reproaches as are levelled at him even by benevolently disposed critics—the leisurely tempo, the wealth of detail, the sometimes un-Gallic length of sentence, extended so as to include everything he needs to tell us, etc.—all these flow naturally from this cinematographic aspect of his work.

Proust really did spoil the French language a little. His followers set less store by laconism, brilliance, logic. But his object as a writer was different and so, therefore, was his style. Proust's style—with its cloudy, colloidal, honeyed consistency and extra-ordinarily aromatic sweetness—is the only medium fitted to induce tens of thousands of readers to join you enthusiastically in reliving your not particularly significant life, recognising therein some peculiar significance and surrendering themselves to this long drawn out pleasure with undisguised delight.

1934

THE MAN WHO PAINTED HAPPINESS

(*In Viewing the Canvases of Renoir*)

NOT long ago I had occasion to spend a few days in Paris. My visit happened to coincide with an exhibition of paintings by one of the greatest—perhaps the greatest—French impressionist, Renoir.

Renoir lived to be very old. When he was nearing seventy he began to develop terrible rheumatism of his hands, which were gradually transformed into something like hooks or bird's claws.

Every day, almost until the very day of his death, the famous artist would sit down at his easel, get himself into a position in which he could use his left hand to guide his right, and say:

"E-eh ... no, mustn't let a day go by without work!"

"Why are you so persistent?" a visiting admirer once asked him.

Renoir, completely absorbed in his canvas, replied:

"But there is no greater pleasure!"

And added:

"And then, it's a duty, in a way."

At this point the eighty-year-old master glanced up at his interrogator with a smile and went on:

"And if a man has neither pleasures nor duties, then what's the good of his going on living?"

It is not, of course, our intention here to give a list of all Renoir's masterpieces or to go into the part played by his school in the history of art, or by him—in his school. It is another question which claims our attention here: what exactly was Renoir looking for in his art and what was he trying to achieve?

Here, however, we must make a brief diversion.

Not long ago, the extremely interesting letters of another French genius, Nicolas Poussin, the leader of 17th-century classic school of painting, appeared in print.

Poussin, as might have been expected from a great artist whose art is dominated by the mind, was not only himself a man of powerful intellect, but shared the general conviction of his age that intellect was the primal factor in cultural life.

"Painting," Poussin maintains, "is, for the artist, a constant exercise in 'seeing' in order thereafter to teach others to see the world aright with the help of his drawings and pictures."

"But," Poussin adds hastily, "it would be quite wrong to think of 'seeing' as of an act involving the eyes alone. It is not just a matter of distinguishing colours and, thanks to that, the outlines of things, or of the fine arrangement of distances, or in general, of reproducing nature as exactly as possible. 'To see' should mean to assimilate a given object into one's own inner world, as a good or as an evil, as something lofty which is as it should be, or, on the contrary, as something imperfect which is striving towards greater perfection, and so on. Living beings and, particularly, people reveal their general character and what they are feeling at that particular moment when you see them.

"But, for the true 'seer', even buildings or a grouping of water and plants, can express distinct values: a sublime order, austerity, tenderness and so forth."

Modern psychology has long since found an expression to indicate "superficial vision" and "deep vision". The first it calls "perception", the act of noticing something, and the second apperception, a word for which the Russian language offers several splendid alternatives, the beauty of which will become clear to the reader if he will pause to think about them: expressions such as understanding, assimilation, mastery of the subject, and so forth.

All these expressions mean that a given object or system of objects is absorbed, by means of a certain complex effort, to become a part of the artist's philosophy of life.

If certain elements of the outside world observed by a real artist appear in his work, then this means that he has assimilated them; in the picture or in the story they appear as a part of the author's own "world".

Three elements are essential if this process of assimilation is to take place: the subject, his "world", that is, the determinant of whatever feeling for and understanding of the world go to make up his personal philosophy, and the object, existing in its own right before assimilation. Here, we have a particularly obvious example of the principle of class self-determination at work in the artist, for, in the last analysis, apperception is quite simply the assimilation of an object by a class or social group through the medium of the artist.

Now that the austere and, at the same time, clever Poussin, has helped us to find the answer to our general question, let us try to find Renoir's personal answer to the question: What am I looking for—for myself and others—in my painting?

II

After the great bourgeois revolution in France it was the bourgeoisie, upper and middle, who became the ruling class. The petty bourgeoisie, although it had played a very active part during the revolution, was relegated to the background.

The ruling section of the bourgeoisie, which had collectively made itself the champion of the principle of the "golden mean", adhered to this principle in art as well. Their art was academic, often deriving from the antique, often from the Renaissance. It was, on the whole, an honest, conscientious art, sometimes even more (Ingres), but it was profoundly stable and profoundly conservative.

The petty bourgeoisie, as in other spheres of art, opposed to this stability the principle of romanticism under the leadership of several distinguished exponents of this school, the greatest of whom was Delacroix.

The whole manner of the romantic school of painting, particularly their use of colour, was distinguished by nervosity and brilliance and was more inclined, by virtue of its very intensity, to contrast with reality than to learn from it. In the ideological sense, the romantics seldom went further than opposing various aspects of exoticism to the mundane.

In the meantime, capitalism marched forward with iron tread. It steadily increased the importance of science in everyday life. It created a wide group comprising the bearers of scientific knowledge—the technical intelligentsia. This technical intelligentsia considered itself in part to be the bourgeoisie's apprentice and, as always happens in such cases, split off into groups ranging from the servilely submissive to the indignant and explicitly discontent, although the latter could see no way of ridding themselves of their "hard taskmaster".

All these moods found expression in realistic art as a whole, including painting, the greatest repre-sentative of which was the "non-party communard" Courbet.

Here we bring our lightning survey of the develop-ment of petty-bourgeois 19th-century art in France up to the moment which is of particular interest to us, the moment concerned with Renoir.

K. S. Stanislavsky, A. V. Lunacharsky and George Bernard Shaw, 1931

The very term "realism" acquired a dual interpretation.

The first definition was: "Reality is an object which I observe."

This definition is correct, materialist; yet the so-called realist art of the last decades of the 19th century (even Courbet) had their own, conventionalised understanding of this reality. They saw it as they had long been used to see it, and portrayed it as they were accustomed to portray it, so that the result was a kind of "naive realism" on the basis of studio conventions.

Under the influence of the greatly increased numbers of the technical intelligentsia, artists began to introduce elements of "scientific experiment" in their methods of observation. The second definition of reality began to take pride of place: "Reality is the result of my observation."

This definition—not materialist this time, but positivist—could only be reconciled with materialism given the following interpretation: a true, socially valid portrayal of reality (like that which, as we have seen, Poussin was searching for in the 17th century) is a result of the attentive and conscientious observation of reality.

However, the French intelligentsia of the end of the 19th century—in the persons of the leaders of its artistic avant garde (Manet and Monet)—was not particularly interested either in material reality or in the possibility of organising social forces through their pictures. These artists considered themselves sons of science whose mission it was to free art from the tyranny of the studio and who desired to show things exactly as they saw them: in the fresh air, by various lights, and so on and so forth. This is why their movement received such a subjective-sounding name as "impressionism".

So now we have, once again, arrived at Renoir.

Renoir was an impressionist. He owed a great deal to impressionism. It chased him out of the dark studio. Impressionism opened his eyes to the immediate, picturesque and sensual beauty of the sunlight. It taught him all the hidden luxury of colour in shadows which had formerly appeared merely brown or grey. It revealed to his talented and sensitive eye all the vibrations of light and colour on the surfaces of objects and in the space between them. It gave him the possibility of admiring, and of helping others to admire, the rich, generous, enchanting, joyful play of colours.

The impressionist Renoir was above all an artist enamoured of a myriad shades of colour, of tone, for which the world of objects served, so to speak, as a mere scaffolding.

The world of objects itself was of less interest to our artist. Space, structure, beauty and purity of line and, together with these, all attempts to interpret what was going on in time and space, seemed to be left out of account. These were not considered to be the artist's business. The business of the artist was blissfully to drink in the dance of colours, the songs of light and the profound accompaniment of shadow.

Of course, this was no mere kaleidoscope: it was a whole world. Renoir's pictures show landscapes, flowers, children, women, small and large groups of people. But they are all shown as fireworks of remarkable elegance and variety of colour.

Renoir is too great to be contained by impressionism: he is one of the great masters of humanist painting. He himself was not averse to emphasising this, and it was not by chance that he liked to hear his name mentioned in one breath with the great, triumphant name of Tiziano Vecellio di Cadorna, one of the titans of the Renaissance.

This is not the place to enter into a detailed comparison of Renoir and Titian. Goethe once said in a similar context: "To put my young contemporaries in the sphere of drama (he was referring to Tieck and Kleist) on a par with me is as ridiculous as to put me on a par with Shakespeare." Yet there is something in common between one, very important aspect of Titian's almost superhuman art and the radiant, warm, caressing art of Renoir.

Claude Monet, as we know, made countless studies of one particular object, a haystack for instance, taking it in the morning, at noon, in the evening, in the moonlight, in the rain, etc. It would be a fair enough assumption to suppose that these Japanese-type exercises of Monet's would produce a kind of scientific catalogue in colour on the subject of the famous haystack. What they in fact produced were little poems. The haystack rears up in majestic pride, is plunged in sentimental reverie, in melancholy, and so forth.

It was at this time that the Germans, in their attempts to describe the ever-increasing numbers of impressionist landscapes, began to show a special fondness for the term *Stimmungslandschaft*, that is "a landscape of mood".

But what, exactly, is "mood"?

It is that psychological music which seems to come wafting from the landscape, but which in fact the artist himself has put into it from the abundance of his own lyricism, his own experience.

Here, the landscape painter slips naturally into the role of the poet.

Renoir was a craftsman of immense power. In drawing, there were few to equal him during his lifetime. The keenness of his vision, the wealth and elegance of his portraits, the inexhaustible animation of the eyes, lips and faces in his pictures, his unfailing good taste, his lightness of touch—all these put him in the very first rank of artists of the last century. Yet it is precisely in his ability to evoke a "mood" that we feel him at his most significant, his most irresistible, his most enchanting.

The best impressionists were not, as I have already said, representatives of the ruling section of the bourgeoisie. Most of them held this ruling class in intense aversion: they hated and despised its tastes and the artists who pandered to it.

Their talent and their way of living had been formed at a time when they lived in garrets, argued like men possessed in dirty little restaurants and cafés, dreamt and worked like the devil and sold nothing. Many died. Some were rewarded by posthumous fame. Others won through to success and fame but, in their art, remained faithful to principles they had worked out in their hungry youth.

Such a one was Renoir.

Whereas the other impressionists, particularly those who were closest to him, set almost more store by "mood" (by the "poetry" of painting) than by the actual craft, Renoir was characterised by an exceptional constancy of mood; in fact, his mood was always the same, though exceptionally rich and varied in itself. This mood was—happiness.

Once upon a time a young man, often burdened by the awkward tools of the painter's trade, could have been seen wandering about Paris: strolling about its green and lovely suburbs, around its buildings and alongside its stretches of water, mixing with the crowd, with every conceivable type of Parisian who can be met with as you walk the streets, down to the very poorest. Reddish-haired with big, grey-blue eyes, almost always a little hungry and, for many long years, thoroughly down-at-heel, he walked like a man who had been invited to some fantastic fair. The sun played such unexpected tricks on him that he would laugh at it, now quietly and conspiratorially, now triumphantly, out loud. The sky was hardly ever the same.

Yet, when one came to think of it, it was always beautiful, and the great, eternal blessing for which there is no sufficient thanksgiving—light!—filtered through the mysterious exhalations of the air down over the earth, illumining living creatures and inanimate objects.

And here the new carnival began.

What a fair! What a market of wonders!

Renoir's persistent, penetrating eyes would work like clever fingers to disentangle the huge, hot, blazing knots of chiaroscuro. Then, suddenly, as if turned to stone, he would stand and gape after a passing girl. Yes, yes, everything about her amazed him—the walk, the young breasts, the kindly, catlike face. He is young, *parbleu!* Would it not be a delight to entice her to his unfurnished bachelor's garret? But what he would have done first of all would have been to open the window and to sit her down beside it, and then he would have found out how the light of the great world had got into her great, bright eyes and how it had been transformed into a promise of happiness, and why a promise of happiness invested those soft, moist, crimson lips and the silvery down on her cheeks.

As he walked on he said reflectively out loud: "What festive gleams I would set dancing round your kind, kitten's face." As, at that very moment, he happened to catch some fat lady a painful blow on the knee with his paint-box, it was not altogether without justification that she shouted after him: "*Les paintres sont toujours fous!*" ("Painters are always balmy!").

Nowhere did the happiness of the world strike Renoir in so pure and triumphant a form as in children. He is one of the greatest painters—or poets —of childhood.

Why yes, there is much happiness scattered about

in nature. But the unhappiness? The injustices? And what is to be done to combat all this?

But here—Renoir passes! It is no use expecting anything from him here.

No, he is not a bourgeois artist. But neither is he a revolutionary. He is a man with an appetite for happiness who found it in abundance. He is a man who painted it in abundance. He is a man who gave it to others in abundance, scattering it about in a special airy coinage which could only appear false to the most coarse of boors.

Titian, in his almost superhuman art, also reflected and created a great deal of happiness. But he can also show the truly terrible Cain murdering Abel, and portraits of men and women with predatory eyes, wise and ruthless as black panthers.

Renoir, too, was the creator of a whole world; but his world is much narrower. His women are uncommonly sweet, warm and friendly beings—but seldom, for all their enchanting freshness and irresistible appeal, do they have any pretensions to intellect. His world contains a whole collection of children; they are unforgettable and it is possible to find comfort in them in moments of sadness. His crowd is free, joyous and festive. His earth is a beauty rejoicing under a smiling heaven. For that, great thanks are due to him. We should not forget how many good things fate has granted us or—at the very least—how happy we might be.

If that is what you ask of Renoir—he will give it. If you ask great craftsmanship—he will give it. If you ask the clarity of soul of an almost holy man—he will give it.

Is that not enough?

1933

GEORGE BERNARD SHAW

WE may hail in George Bernard Shaw one of the most brilliant master wit in the history of art.

When you read Shaw you are amused, you find yourself constantly smiling or laughing. But, at the same time, you are horrified. A reader who is the target of Shaw's arrows of mirth may well be horrified, a sympathetic reader will also be awe-struck when Shaw unmasks the gloomy essence of capitalist reality.

Shaw had a wonderful predecessor, a powerful and gloomy genius, whose humour reached the same virtuoso heights but was of a darker cast. He was a master wit like Shaw, though circumstances and the time in which he lived made him more morbid. This was the great satirist Jonathan Swift.

Swift knew how to laugh in a merry, graceful, tinkling way. His *Gulliver's Travels* has long been a favourite of bourgeois and proletarian children alike, yet the very same Jonathan Swift proposed with frightening humour that the English bourgeoisie should consume the infants born in such great numbers into the families of the Irish poor, and suggested ways of salting and curing their flesh and of preparing dainty dishes so as to turn the misfortune of overpopulation into a source of food.

If we compare the laughter of Swift with the laughter of Shaw we will arrive at some very interesting conclusions. In general, a man laughs when he is victorious. Physiological laughter is the release of psychological and physiological tensions which we let go when we find that a seemingly insurmountable problem can be easily dealt with. When we laugh we are reflecting the nervous activity of the brain; we are converting it into movements of our face and muscles, thus relaxing our control.

Laughter is a magnificent instance of the body demobilising; when mobilisation is suddenly proved unnecessary, we burst into joyous laughter. Laughter is victory.

But we know that laughter does not always come from above, from the heights of victory, crashing down upon the heads of a vanquished enemy. It can come from below, aimed at the ruling countries, the ruling class, the ruling power.

But if laughter is a banner of victory, how can it emanate from classes and groups that are still oppressed?

Russian literature has a great satirist who can justly take his place beside Swift and Shaw—Saltykov-Shchedrin. Saltykov-Shchedrin is an unusually gay writer. You will laugh unceasingly as you read his works, but, as in Swift, there will be dark clouds threatening the bright sunshine of his laughter. You will find a terrible combination of laughter and wrath, hatred, loathing, cries to action, you will see him close to tears and sense the lump in his throat when he is laughing. How is such a mixture possible? You will hear such laughter when the oppressed individual has long since vanquished his oppressors morally and intellectually, when he regards them as fools, when he despises their principles, when the morality of the ruling class is no more than a conglomeration of absurdities to him, when he considers his own class a generation of giants compared with the Lilliputians (when he knows that lightning will strike the doomed), but when he is still politically weak, when he is not mature enough to bring the imminent economic upheaval to a head. At such moments he will experience this terrible churning.

If we compare Shaw with our own gloomy-jolly Saltykov-Shchedrin or with the eighteenth-century satirist, Swift, we shall find Shaw to be much gayer than they. Shaw senses the closeness of victory, he is confident that the absurdity of the bourgeois system cannot last long. He can even laugh lightly. He spends more time laughing graciously, teasing his enemies while his predecessors Swift and Saltykov-Shchedrin launched out at their enemies with a contempt that was nearly a torture.

A very talented American journalist who visited Lenin later wrote an interesting account of the interview. Part of it reads: "When I spoke to Lenin I was most amazed to see him laughing continuously, laughing ironically and merrily. It made me wonder. Why was this man, whose country was stricken by famine (as was the case at the time), who was surrounded by enemies and was in a position that might very well have seemed hopeless, why was he smiling and joking? I realised that this was Marxist laughter, the laughter of a man who was convinced that the social laws of nature would bring him victory, this was laughter peculiar to people who are gently tolerant of children that have not yet perceived the significance of phenomena which are quite clear to adults."

We find something akin to Lenin's victorious laughter in Shaw's works. However, we must not overlook Shaw's poison. He laughs, but he knows full well that far from everything is funny: he laughs to burn out human failings with his laughter. He laughs venomously, cunningly, ironically, sarcastically. These are not innocent buds of humour. He is using a subtle and magnificent weapon of the new world aimed at the old.

During his stay here, George Bernard Shaw called himself an old revolutionary. It was he who wrote *A Rebel's Catechism*, which is full of pointed, unusually sharp and direct attacks on our enemies. Some of these aphorisms were recently published in *Literaturnaya Gazeta* and anyone can see how truly revolutionary they are in spirit. However, Shaw's chief satirical and revolutionary work is to be found in his plays.

Shaw has written an extensive series of plays, a great number of articles and many aphorisms, all of which give him the right to the attention of our contemporaries and to a long life in the literature of the future.

George Bernard Shaw is seventy-five years old, he is entering the later period of his life at a time when capitalism, which he has so abhorred and censured, is entering its final stage. Never before have the very foundations of capitalist society been shaken as they are being shaken today. Its walls are shaking, they are crooked and cracked.

At a time when the adherents of the old world must tremble, for Judgement Day has come for the sins and crimes of capitalism, George Bernard Shaw believes it is only natural for an intelligent, educated person to be a socialist, and that he who is not a socialist, no matter how intelligent and educated he be, is an odd being.

However, it is one thing to be a socialist by conviction, it is quite another thing to contribute actively to the advent of socialism. The destruction of the capitalist world is not in itself socialism. The capitalist world might have crumbled and not left an heir. In a speech in honour of Lenin, which Shaw delivered for a sound film in Leningrad, he said that quite a number of civilisations had crumbled with no one to save them, but now Lenin's way promises salvation and a transition to higher forms.

Why is it that a seventy-five-year-old writer who has noticed dangerous ruts on the road he is following asks himself: Is there not something positive